MW00719083

A TIME FOR HEROES

ALSO BY
ROBERT L. DILENSCHNEIDER

POWER AND INFLUENCE: MASTERING THE ART OF PERSUASION

A BRIEFING FOR LEADERS:
COMMUNICATION AS THE ULTIMATE EXERCISE OF POWER

ON POWER

DARTNELL'S PUBLIC RELATIONS HANDBOOK

THE CORPORATE COMMUNICATIONS BIBLE

MOSES: C.E.O.
LESSONS IN LEADERSHIP

THE CRITICAL 14 YEARS OF YOUR PROFESSIONAL LIFE

THE CRITICAL 2ND PHASE OF YOUR PROFESSIONAL LIFE:
KEYS TO SUCCESS FOR AGE 40 AND BEYOND

50 PLUS! CRITICAL CAREER DECISIONS FOR THE REST OF YOUR LIFE

BUSINESS LEADERS, POLITICIANS,

A TIME

AND OTHER NOTABLES

FOR

EXPLORE THE NATURE OF HEROISM

HEROES

ROBERT L. DILENSCHNEIDER

Copyright © 2005 by Phoenix Press
9663 Santa Monica Blvd., #789
Beverly Hills, CA 90210

All rights reserved. Written permission must be secured from the publisher to use or reproduce any part of this book, except brief quotations in critical reviews and articles.

ISBN: 1-59777-000-0

Library of Congress Cataloging-in-Publication Data Available

10 9 8 7 6 5 4 3 2 1

DEDICATION

To a real hero who stood for all the principles
reflected in this book: my dad.

ACKNOWLEDGMENTS

How individual our heroes are! Almost everyone I spoke with while writing this book chose heroes who surprised me. Orrin Hatch, known for his conservative views, picked an AIDS activist; Steve Forbes, whose life has been nothing if not privileged, named a World War II journalist who extolled the virtues of ordinary G.I.s; Glenn Schaeffer, a Las Vegas businessman, selected a Nigerian writer known as a political activist.

These unexpected answers and others like them helped shape this project in a way that was quite different from what I had imagined it would be. So let me begin by extending sincere thanks to everyone who shared thoughts about heroism with me, whether it was in a formal interview or a dinner party conversation.

In particular, I want to acknowledge Lamar Alexander, Marty Baron, John Brademas, Dominic Cavello, Steve Forbes, John Hamre, Orrin Hatch, Karen A. Holbrook, Phil Holland, Joel Kurtzman, Marty Lipton, Monk Malloy, Mel Manishen, Robert F. McDermott, Marilyn Carlson Nelson, John O'Keefe, Glenn Schaeffer, Arthur Schneier, and Jim Wieghart. They gave generously of their time and their ideas, and I am most grateful.

My extraordinary assistant, Joan Avagliano, reliably goes to the core of every matter and knows precisely what to do. This book would not have been possible without her. Supporting Joan is the able team of Laura Garrison, Anne Ruemanapp, and Jennifer Westcott, each of whom also deserves recognition. Joel Pomerantz, who has forgotten more than most people know about history and editing, deserves special thanks.

This book would not exist without the support and assistance of my publisher, Michael Viner. I am grateful to Mary Aarons, Carol Buckley, Kerry DeAngelis, Julie McCarron, and Carolyn Wendt.

I also want to thank Nancy Hathaway, whose heroic efforts made this book a reality.

Finally, all hail to my wife, Jan, and my intrepid sons, Geoffrey and Peter. All three are heroic, and not just because they put up with me. They approach life with courage and conviction, and the world is better for it. I only hope I can live up to their examples.

CONTENTS

CONTENTS

INTRODUCTION

After September 11, 2001, two concepts gained new heft. One of them was international terrorism, which for the first time in American history became a tangible reality and a certain threat. The other was heroism.

Prior to that day, heroism had become so devalued that the term "hero" was primarily applied to athletes, to comic book and video-game characters, and to the Arnold Schwarzenegger–like protagonists of Hollywood blockbusters made back in the days when Arnold himself was merely a movie star. Instead of real heroes, we had super-heroes and action heroes. As a concept, heroism had come to seem outmoded and naive.

September 11 changed that. In the wake of that catastrophe, a few public figures—a very few—ascended to heroic heights, along with hundreds of firefighters, police officers, emergency medical technicians, and ordinary men and women, their names unknown. "Times of heroism are generally times of terror," Ralph Waldo Emerson wrote. September 11 proved it.

Since that day, heroism no longer sounds like an old-fashioned idea. On the contrary, it seems fresh. With the world in peril, we need heroes to provide leadership, to inspire us, and to invigorate the spirit that sustains tolerance, abets human freedoms, and promotes progress.

My concern is that we have too few heroes in life today.

Many heroic acts are small and unseen, performed virtually every day by ordinary people who do the right thing. We need those acts of heroism, however minor they may seem. But we need something more. We need heroism projected at a higher level. We need the kinds of heroes who become symbols for other people to emulate. We need heroes so that we might become heroes.

But what does it mean to be a hero? And who should our heroes be? Those are two of the questions I set out to explore in this book.

WHAT IS HEROISM?

Some people define heroes as those who are willing to forfeit their lives for others. Like legal scholars who interpret the Constitution in a narrow way, these people might be considered strict constructionists: no sacrifice, no heroism.

Myself, I'm a loose constructionist, if I may use that term. I believe in all manner of heroes.

There are those who spend a lifetime in pursuit of a grand vision. Think of Nelson Mandela, imprisoned for twenty-seven years before he triumphed over apartheid and became president of South Africa.

There are those who rise to Olympian heights for a single, luminous moment, like many of the heroes of September 11.

Some heroes are intellectual pioneers whose ideas open up new territories of thought. Charles Darwin, Isaiah Berlin, and Sigmund Freud are examples.

Others alert us to problems in our midst, like Rachel Carson, whose book *Silent Spring* warned of the dangers of pesticides.

Some heroes motivate people to aim higher, perhaps to create a more equitable society or to actualize their own abilities.

All of them have courage—the courage to dare, the courage to fail, the courage to persist.

But courage is a highly subjective term. Ernest Hemingway defined it as "grace under pressure." Karen A. Holbrook, the president of Ohio State University, defines it as "the capacity to make things happen." I think there's something to both statements.

I am reminded of Sidney Hook, a twentieth-century thinker who described two varieties of heroes. The first kind are "eventful" individuals who find themselves in a situation that requires them to make difficult, sometimes life-or-death choices. Many of the heroes of September 11 fall into that category.

The second kind are "event-making" individuals who, for good or ill, create the pivotal moments that define their times. Hook considers them the most significant figures in history. "Such individuals are not made by events so much as events are made by them," he writes. These people can be humanity's most despicable tyrants. But they can also be our most commendable heroes, regardless of whether their names are shouted from the rooftops. Think of Bayard Rustin, the civil rights strategist and organizer of the 1963 March on Washington. Martin Luther King, Jr., a hero of the first rank, galvanized the country that day with his "I Have a Dream" speech. Bayard Rustin, the hero behind the hero, made it happen. And yet few know Rustin.

Not everyone has the ability to be an event-making hero. But all of us regularly stumble into situations where we could, if we so chose, act heroically. Heroes do what Yogi Berra recommended: When they come to the fork in the road, they take it. The rest of us pull out our cell phones and call a friend.

WHERE ARE THE HEROES?
(*Not necessarily on the cover of* People)

When I started to think about heroism, I had to grapple with an old shibboleth: the notion that there are no heroes anymore. I've heard people say it, and I don't want to believe it. But I also remember that, when I was growing up, it seemed as if heroes walked the earth. In those post–World War II days, giants like Winston Churchill and General Dwight D. Eisenhower dominated the headlines. There were fantasy heroes like Superman, scientific heroes like Dr. Jonas Salk, athletes like Joe DiMaggio and Willie Mays. And there were G.I.s—seemingly ordinary men who lived in my neighborhood—who had risked their lives to defeat Hitler. There were plenty of people for a boy to admire.

I don't want to romanticize the 1940s and 1950s. Those were also the days of segregation, Senator Joe McCarthy, and the glorification of conformity. Nonetheless, when I started thinking about this book, I could not shake the perception that yesterday's heroes are long gone, and today's heroes are missing in action. I've seen several explanations for their absence. One writer even blamed feminism—though I would argue that feminism has increased the number of heroes many times over.

To me, the dearth of heroes is a by-product of the culture of celebrity, which shines a brilliant spotlight on those who would be heroes, giving them their allotted fifteen minutes—and illuminating their all-too-human flaws for all to see.

When I was young, we weren't barraged with inside information about the personal lives of heroes. Take President John F. Kennedy. His glamour, intelligence, and wit were apparent to everyone, detractors included. His numerous extramarital dalliances, on the other hand, were a state secret—whereas Bill Clinton's low-life love life was embarrassingly public in all its particulars. It's hard to be a hero when your weaknesses are on display.

And yet even the greatest heroes are inevitably and touchingly ordinary. That's the meaning of the expression: "Even Napoleon puts his pants on one leg at a time."

HEROES AND CELEBRITIES

It's also hard to find a hero when we are entertained with a never-ending stream of instant celebrities who may be worthy, but whose deeds simply aren't consequential enough to justify wearing a hero's laurels.

Private Jessica Lynch, for example, appeared on the cover of *People* magazine. Is she truly a hero? In many ways, yes. She volunteered to join the armed forces, went to war to protect our country, was injured in the line of duty, and ended up in an Iraqi hospital. She acquitted herself well, no doubt. Nonetheless, I suspect that five years from now, few people will remember this brave young woman who was rescued by a cadre of her fellow soldiers.

But the honor roll of women, who will, or should, be remembered as authentic heroes is long and impressive. It includes towering political figures like Eleanor Roosevelt, Golda Meir, and Indira Gandhi as well as lesser known, but equally extraordinary, women like Rosalind Franklin, the brilliant micro-biologist whose groundbreaking research laid the foundation for the discovery of DNA's structure—the double helix—and the genetic revolution. Sadly, she was totally overlooked when James Watson and Francis Crick shared the 1962 Nobel Prize in Medicine.

Fourteen years later, in 1976, the Stockholm jury compensated somewhat for that lapse by awarding the coveted Nobel Peace Prize to two genuinely heroic Irish women, Mairead Corrigan and Betty Williams. Organizers of the Community of Peace People, these valiant women, defying powerful men on both sides, earned the admiration of peace-loving people around the world as they mobilized Catholic and Protestant women seeking to end the terrible communal violence in Northern Ireland.

And, of course, there was Katharine Graham, CEO of the *Washington Post*. Kay Graham's courage made a major statement about the way the world, at least in America, is shaped today.

All too often, we apply the word "hero" to victims. By doing so we devalue the term. The actor Christopher Reeve, injured in a horse riding accident in 1995, was a hero not only because he struggled to overcome paralysis but also because he became a leading advocate for others with similar disabilities. Despite devastating limitations, he made things happen.

We also need to distinguish between icons and heroes. Michael Jordan, the most spectacular athlete of our time, is an icon. So was Jim Brown in football. But Jackie Robinson, who broke the color barrier on the baseball diamond, is a hero. The most inspiring heroes are more than admirable; by their actions, they enlarge the world of possibility for us all.

As Daniel Boorstin, the Pulitzer Prize–winning historian and former Librarian of Congress, writes, "We can fabricate fame, we can at will (though usually with considerable expense) make a man or woman well known; but we cannot make him great. We can make a celebrity, but we can never make a hero."

A cover story in *People* magazine may be—okay, is—a publicist's dream. But the kind of heroism that operates over the long term cannot be created by a publicity machine. After more than three decades in the public relations business, I should know. Heroism requires grit, wisdom, selflessness, commitment, and, in the case of the most inspiring heroes, a breadth of vision that enables them to transcend their flaws. The heroes of the moment, their faces splashed across the tabloids, may soon be forgotten, despite their praiseworthy qualities. The most influential heroes are the ones who have passed the test of time. In the majority of cases, those heroes, by definition, are figures from the past.

NO HERO LIKE A DEAD HERO

The ancient Greeks understood this. The heroes they admired—the offspring of gods and mortals—were bigger and braver and stronger than human beings. They dated from the earliest days of creation because, even then, the age of heroes was long, long ago.

There's a good reason for that: Living heroes, no matter how admirable, are in constant danger of tarnishing their image. Take Salman Rushdie, an influential writer who had to spend years in hiding after Islamic clerics, offended by one of his novels, issued a fatwa calling for his death. Rushdie became a hero who represented, among other democratic values, artistic freedom and freedom of speech.

Since the fatwa was issued in the 1980s, Rushdie has continued to express precisely those values. He has written other books and spoken out on other causes. He has moved on. Not surprisingly, his image has changed—which is why I recently read a short piece in the New York Times that gently mocked his celebrity and described his girlfriend in salacious terms. Stick around long enough, and, if you have sufficient renown, your image will be besmirched—and that's true no matter what you do. Heroes who are busy leading their lives are in danger of tumbling off the pedestal, if only because sooner or later they become old news.

But if you're truly old—or, better yet, dead—your heroism may become iconic. John Lennon, gunned down in the entranceway of the Dakota, seems infinitely more heroic than his fellow Beatle, the aging, recently remarried Paul McCartney. That's just the way it is.

SHIFTING REPUTATIONS

Of course, even dead heroes are occasionally stripped of their laurels. When I was a boy, Thomas Jefferson, principal author of the Declaration of Independence, was as much admired for his political values as for his intellectual and architectural brilliance. Today, to many, he's a hero no longer, his image tarred by his relationship with Sally Hemings and by the perception that he somehow made his peace with slavery.

Harry Truman, on the other hand, has been elevated into the heroic ranks. When I was growing up, he was perceived as a plain-spoken guy who could never hope to equal his predecessor, Franklin D. Roosevelt. Today, his reputation has been upgraded. Several people I interviewed even named him as a personal hero (see page 87). The passage of time changes the way we view our heroes.

And one more thing . . .

ONE MAN'S HERO IS ANOTHER MAN'S SCOUNDREL

I don't know who coined that aphorism, but it's true. Even Mother Teresa turns out to be a controversial figure. Virtually a saint in the eyes of most, she has been disparaged by a few for, among other less-than-saintly accusations, faking miracles and maintaining a financial tie to Haiti's Papa Doc Duvalier.

Or consider President George W. Bush. Is he a hero for standing up to Saddam Hussein, as many people I spoke with maintained? Or is he a misguided lightweight who decimated the economy, fueled the fires of anti-Americanism, and increased the global threat of terrorism? It depends on whom you ask.

We choose our heroes on the basis of our values and experiences. In talking with dozens of people, I noticed that some names—Martin Luther King, Jr., Franklin D. Roosevelt, Abraham Lincoln—came up repeatedly, but only in passing. The heroes people talked about most enthusiastically, the ones who captured their imagination in a deeply personal way, were more idiosyncratic choices. Believe me, when I started this book, I didn't think I'd be writing about Lenny Skutnik or King Juan Carlos I of Spain or I. F. Stone. Those people weren't on my personal list of heroes.

They are now.

AND SPEAKING OF SCOUNDRELS...

I want to say a few words about CEOs. Most of these men and women do plenty of good in the world. They make a useful product, employ hundreds or thousands of workers, and give to charity. They're not bad people, despite the bottom-line system in which they must operate.

But they aren't heroes either. I find that many CEOs have risen to their level of incompetence. I'm talking about people who are pulling down seven- and eight-figure salaries, enjoying a huge package of stock options, flying in private jets, and surrounding themselves with what in effect are battalions of servants who do their bidding. These high-level executives talk a great game, thanks in no small measure to their public relations people. But their fine words about, say, diversity, are not reflected in their payrolls. Their so-called family values often don't extend to decent medical insurance for their employees. And as for their shocked disavowal of ageism—well, let's just say that these are smart people with clever lawyers, and most of the time, discrimination against the over-fifty set is not traceable.

These privileged, talented people have the resources to change the world. They don't because the system mitigates against it—and because they have been bought. They shy away from heroic acts because they don't want to put their reputations or their compensation at risk. It's that simple. Once you've lived in a mansion, you can't go back to renting a walk-up.

A CEO who did the right thing might decide to make an environmentally friendly product, even though the profit margin might be lower . . . or to sell medications at a price that the average person could afford . . . or to insist that chickens be raised humanely, even if it is their fate to be fried.

A CEO who did the right thing might provide day care, health care, educational benefits, generous salaries, decent pensions, and a host of other benefits that don't seem unreasonable to the average person. Such a CEO might encourage employees to volunteer for community organizations that serve the less fortunate. He or she might even use company resources to provide services that government is too strapped to offer.

What would happen? From the CEO's point of view, nothing good. Because by performing a heroic act, CEOs become subject to speculation. And God forbid that the company stock should take a dip. It's a risk most CEOs cannot afford to take. They may start out as mavericks, but they become conformists. Breaking the mold is not something that is done easily in the executive suite.

At the end of the day most CEOs do the pragmatic thing. They do it for the shareholder—and they do it for themselves. They are captives of Wall Street. From their point of view, they have no choice: They are surrounded by accountants and lawyers and advisors, and they don't want to rock the boat. If they don't operate within the boundaries of convention, they'll become so controversial that they won't be able to remain in the job. So they content themselves with incremental progress at best. They don't make the sweeping, dramatic changes that heroes make. And yet these are the people with the ability to direct the resources.

Are there heroic CEOs out there? Sure—I discuss a few of them on pages 115 and 117. Those individuals are the poignant exceptions.

As for politicians, they have the greatest opportunity of all to be heroic. But the forces lined up against them are formidable. They face many obstacles and must pick their way among constituencies with contradictory needs. Yet they are expected to cling to principle and, if necessary, to go down fighting. In addition, as John F. Kennedy pointed out in *Profiles in Courage,* they have to do it all in public. "In no other occupation but politics is it expected that a man will sacrifice honors, prestige and his chosen career on a single issue," he wrote. "Lawyers, businessmen, teachers, doctors, all face difficult personal decisions involving their integrity—but few, if any, face them in the glare of the spotlight as do those in public office."

Fortunately, heroism is an equal opportunity virtue. Anyone can sign on. In my imaginary pantheon of heroes, I see leaders like Vaclav Havel hobnobbing with Peace Corps volunteers and organ donors and firemen. I see Rosa Parks and the Burmese pro-democracy activist Aung San Suu Kyi and the Iranian lawyer Shirin Ebadi, winner of the 2003 Nobel Peace Prize. I see politicians who have taken brave stances, sometimes to their own detriment, along with artists and writers who have expressed ideas that enable us to see the world in new ways. If I'm not mistaken, I see a dentist I know in there and a young writer who hacked her way through Soviet-style bureaucracy to rescue a tiny child languishing in a Siberian orphanage. My pantheon of heroes is a big place. I hope you'll come on in.

HEROISM AS A GOAL

What makes a hero? Whether on a large scale or a small one, heroes provide a service to society. They may be leaders like Winston Churchill who hearten us in troubled times. They may solve a difficulty of the ages, the way Thomas Edison did, or illuminate a serious social problem, as John Steinbeck did in *The Grapes of Wrath.*

Or they may perform a single extraordinary deed, like the courageous passengers of Flight 93 who, armed only with plastic butter knives, died in a field in rural Pennsylvania on September 11 rather than allow their plane to hit its intended target. Which of us, hearing that inspiring story, did not wonder: Would I have cowered in the back of business class? Or would I have been brave enough to join that fight, a fight which—surely they knew—was bound to be to the death? Would I have acted heroically?

I believe that the capacity for heroism exists within us all. Heroes are not saints. They are filled with self-doubt. They may not even be role models. (Look at Rudy Giuliani, widely acknowledged as a true hero of September 11, despite his messy divorce and aggressive personality.) What distinguishes heroes is that they rise above their fears, if only for a moment; they put something—a cause, a principle, a value, the welfare of another person, the good of the community— ahead of their own well-being; and they take action when it's hard. Especially when it's hard. Because, sooner or later, heroes are assured of getting knocked to their knees. The game is to get up and keep on going. Heroes have that kind of determination. They are willing to fail. They are willing to sacrifice their time, their money, their peace of mind, their reputations or their careers or even their lives—but not their integrity, their humility, their humor, or their hope for the future. Those qualities are essential elements of heroism.

And those qualities, among others, are precisely the ones most needed today. We are living in terrifying times. As I write, the war in Iraq is sputtering on, there are serious problems elsewhere in the Middle East, our economy is on the decline, and a new disease called SARS is scaring the hell out of people. We need heroes, and we need them now.

When I began this book, I knew who my own heroes were. They included members of my family; historical figures who were alive when I was a child; professors and colleagues who mentored me; various figures out of American history; several world leaders I have had the privilege to know; a few CEOs; and a clutch of writers and journalists including Edward R. Murrow and the legendary Nellie Bly, who went undercover in 1887 to reveal what really went on in the nation's insane asylums. More recently, I would add the name of the *Wall Street Journal*'s courageous foreign correspondent Daniel Pearl, whose brutal murder in Pakistan only a few months after September 11 shocked the civilized world.

My heroes also include John Klink and Bob Charlebois, who, on their backs, carried children out of the Cambodian jungle; Bishop William Lori, who tackles every big problem the Catholic Church faces and addresses the most vicious critics with courtesy and humility; Joel Klein, who gave up high-paying job opportunities to bring New York City schools to a higher level; David Brennan, the multimillionaire who researched and found ways to dramatically increase the graduation rate in inner-city schools that most others had abandoned; Glenn Schaeffer, a CEO who uses his own money to sponsor writers of conscience who speak out against oppression; and Rabbi Arthur Schneier who, while very public on international issues, always finds time for a private moment with a person in need.

I also wondered what other people—and influential people in particular—considered heroic. Did they too find sustenance in the deeds of others? And if so, whose? The conversations that resulted form the basis for this book.

To my surprise, the people I interviewed often suggested the names of individuals I may have been familiar with, but who did not, at first blush, fit into that rarefied circle we hail as heroic. My investigation also became an invaluable learning experience for me about some truly remarkable human beings.

It is my hope that readers of this book will be stimulated to find their own heroes and to nurture within themselves the qualities of heroism.

The times demand it.

CHAPTER 1

A Conversation With
LAMAR ALEXANDER

On Alex Haley and Others

W hat do heroes have to do with history? Thomas Carlyle, the nineteenth-century philosopher, held that history was the creation of great, not necessarily good, men whom he called heroes. He called history "the Biography of Great Men."

Other thinkers see the relationship between heroes and history in exactly the opposite way. They believe that heroes are extraordinary individuals who embody the spirit of their times by responding to historical forces that are already in play.

Either way, we can hardly conceive of our history without imagining the remarkable men and women who lived there. Stories about those individuals make the study of the past come alive. They also illuminate the possibilities of the present by teaching us, through example, what we might do and what might happen as a result. Without Gandhi, there can be no Martin Luther King, Jr.

Stories about heroes from the past also contribute to a sense of national identity. Lamar Alexander, onetime Republican presidential hopeful and now the junior senator from Tennessee, made that point in a recent conversation:

LA: Our understanding of American history is always focused on key events and key individuals and key stories, as well as on key documents. For example, we celebrate the endurance of the Pilgrims, most of whom died the first winter. We celebrate the heroism of the soldiers in Valley Forge, who walked across the Delaware River barefooted

> on the ice to remind us of sacrifice. We celebrate John
> Adams' defense of the British soldiers, who killed patriots,
> as an example of independence and reliance on a rule of
> law. We celebrate the ingenuity of Benjamin Franklin and
> Eli Whitney and other inventors. All of these qualities,
> which are expressed through a collection of stories,
> become aspects of the American character.

As a society, we are increasingly and disturbingly ignorant about history and government. Which is why Senator Alexander introduced the American History and Civics Act. It aims to elevate the importance of those subjects and to motivate teachers and students through a series of summer academies focused on aspects of our past. To no one's surprise, the bill gained overwhelming support and passed in the Senate by a vote of 90 to 0.

I only hope we also pay attention to world history, another subject about which most Americans are woefully uninformed.

LAMAR ALEXANDER

Lamar Alexander grew up with an awareness of government in action, thanks to his father, a grade school principal who was elected to the local board of education and served for twenty-five years. As a boy, Alexander met his congressman. As a teenager, he was elected governor of Boys State. He first ran for public office in 1974, when he won the nomination for governor of Tennessee but lost the election. It wasn't a good year for Republicans. As he told an interviewer, "I learned it's better not to run in a year when the president of your party is nearly impeached and resigns. . . ."

But looking back, he also realized that he could have run a more effective campaign. "I flew around in a blue suit from one Rotary meeting to the next, preaching to the converted," he said.

Four years later, he donned a red plaid shirt and literally walked a thousand miles around the state, talking to all kinds of people along the way. This time he won. He served as governor from 1979 to 1987, then took off with his wife, Honey, and their four children for a six-month stay in Australia. Afterward, he became president of the University of Tennessee. In 1991, during the administration of the first President Bush, he was appointed secretary of education.

In 1995 and again in 1999, he sought unsuccessfully his party's nomination for the presidency. He was ready to get out of politics completely when Senator Fred Thompson of Tennessee unexpectedly announced that he would not seek reelection. Alexander campaigned for the seat and won. In his maiden address ("We still call it that in the United States Senate," he observes) he introduced the American History and Civics Act.

...AND HIS VIEW OF HEROISM

What makes a hero in Lamar Alexander's world? Here's part of our conversation:

RD: Let's talk about the qualities you consider essential to heroism.
LA: Courage would be the first word that comes to my mind, but not necessarily in the sense of charging a battlefield. I don't think that all heroes are courageous in the way of Charles Lindbergh or John McCain. They have the courage to be true to themselves rather than the courage to do a particular thing. I admire people who have the courage to do things their way. An example would be Gandhi and his long pilgrimage in India.
But heroism encompasses a great many qualities. The dictionary tells us that heroes are celebrated for their courage, nobility, or exploits.
RD: What do you mean by nobility? It's not a word we often use.
LA: Nobility can be a matter of character. It can be a matter of honesty or kindliness or civility. When we think of specific men and women, we admire many qualities about them.

RD: For example?

LA: I admire Sam Houston. He was a rowdy visionary who had a great vision—first, of Tennessee where he grew up and was elected governor in 1827, and then of the Cherokee Indian nation where he lived until 1832, and finally of Texas, where he became the first president of the Republic of Texas and, in 1859, governor of the State of Texas. He saw well beyond other people.

I admire Will Steger for his courage. He lives in Elie, Minnesota and was the first person to take a dogsled unassisted to the North Pole and to cross Antarctica. He's a modern hero.

I was law clerk to a man named John Minor Wisdom who was a federal judge in New Orleans in the 1960s. In the face of threats and tremendous local opposition, he ordered Ole Miss [the University of Mississippi] to integrate by admitting James Meredith in 1965. He had the courage of his convictions.

I admire John McCain for enduring five years in a Vietcong prison. I admire Howard Baker for his unfailing civility.

I worked for a man named Bryce Harlow who was President Nixon's first assistant in charge of congressional relations. I remember him for his ethical standards. Once he needed a vacation and an old friend invited him and his wife to go to Mexico for a week. Bryce thought there would be nothing wrong with that since his friend had never asked him for anything. But about a week before they were to leave the friend called up and said, "Oh, by the way, Bryce, I have a small favor I'd like to ask." And I remember overhearing him say that he had to find a way to cancel the trip without embarrassing his friend. A day later, he called his friend back and said, "The President has asked me to do something. I won't be able to go to Mexico." I may have been the only person in the world

> who knew that. It wasn't a famous incident, but it taught me a lesson. He was scrupulously ethical.
>
> I also admire Alex Haley, the author of *Roots*. He was a Tennessean, a friend for about ten years, and I respected him a lot. I admired his perseverance in researching his family's history and then writing a book about it. But what impressed me most was his consideration of other people.

I was pleased to hear Senator Alexander talk about Alex Haley. I'll never forget watching *Roots* on television in the 1970s. It opened up my understanding of our history in a profound and startling way. I think a lot of Americans felt that way.

ALEX HALEY
A Heroic Storyteller

Although Alex Haley (1921–1992) was born in Ithaca, New York, he grew up all over, wherever his father, a professor of agriculture, could get a teaching job. His mother, an elementary school teacher, died when he was ten years old. But every summer throughout his childhood, Haley and his two younger brothers went to Henning, Tennessee, where his grandmother told the family legends—stories that dated all the way back to a man known as "the African."

On the cusp of World War II, the seventeen-year-old Haley dropped out of college and enlisted in the United States Coast Guard. He began as a mess boy on a ship in the South Pacific and retired twenty years later as chief journalist, the first to receive that rating. It was in the Coast Guard that he taught himself how to write.

On ship, he ghosted love letters for his less eloquent fellow sailors. He also read and reread every book he could find. But there weren't many. Finally, he decided to write one of his own—an adventure story, a genre he especially enjoyed. He wrote "every single night, seven nights a week—mailing off my efforts to magazines and collecting literally hundreds of their rejection slips." After eight years of steadfast effort, he sold a story.

"The characteristic of heroism is its persistency," Ralph Waldo Emerson wrote. Those eight years of apprenticeship were not the only time Haley proved his ability to persevere.

When Haley retired from the Coast Guard in 1959 after twenty years of service, he turned to freelancing. One assignment was to interview Malcolm X for *Playboy* magazine. After a publisher requested a full-length memoir, Haley spent a year interviewing his subject and another year shaping the material into a book. In February 1965, shortly after the manuscript was finished, but prior to the actual publication, Malcolm X was assassinated. *The Autobiography of Malcolm X* became wildly successful.

The Roots of Roots

After its publication, Haley took a trip to London and became fascinated by one of the treasures of the British Museum: the Rosetta Stone. A twenty-two-hundred-year-old piece of basalt inscribed in Greek, Egyptian script, and Egyptian hieroglyphics, it enabled nineteenth-century scholars to decipher hieroglyphics for the first time. For some reason, the Rosetta Stone reminded Haley of three or four mysterious words he had heard his relatives speak on the front porch in Henning, Tennessee. Family legend held that those words were originally spoken by "the African," who insisted that his name was Kin-tay and that he was chopping wood one day when he was abducted by slave traders and taken to Annapolis. Haley wondered if it might be possible to identify the original language and thus to know where his people came from.

And so his quest began. He interviewed professors and hung around the United Nations stopping anyone who looked African. When he discovered that the words were probably from the Mandinka language and that his ancestors had probably lived in Gambia, he flew to Africa. There he found a griot, an elderly man who had memorized the oral history of the Kinte (pronounced Kin-tay) clan going back hundreds of years. The griot recited the ancient chronicle for two hours before he reached the part about a man named Kunta Kinte, who went to chop wood "around the time the King's soldiers came" and was never seen again.

Haley discovered that in 1767, English soldiers had arrived in Gambia to guard a fort on the river. He decided to track down anything he could find about slave ships that might have come to the area. At Lloyds of London, Haley got permission to look through stacks of English maritime records. For weeks, he diligently examined one carton after another of eighteenth-century shipping logs. In the seventh week, he picked up the 1,023rd piece of paper and found what he was seeking: a boat that arrived in Gambia in 1767 and left with a full cargo of slaves bound for Annapolis.

Ultimately, Haley was able to trace the genealogy of his family for seven generations, from Kunta Kinte to himself. Can anyone in the era of the Internet ever understand what doing this kind of laborious research used to mean? Haley visited over fifty libraries and archives on three continents. He pored over census records and other legal documents both on paper and on microfilm (a hellish torture all its own). Researching and writing his story took twelve years.

The book, published in 1976, sold 1.6 million copies during the first six months. The 1977 miniseries was broadcast over eight consecutive nights in January. A riveting show about a horrifying topic, it personalized slavery in a way that had never been done before and gave shape to a cultural heritage of which Americans have been ashamed and ignorant. It gave witness. It also turned people most of us had primarily thought of only as victims—the slaves—into indomitable heroes.

Roots made an enormous impact. Fully 85 percent of the viewing public tuned in. It was like a World Series; everyone was talking about it. But the conversation about *Roots* continued for months and years afterward. It inspired African Americans (and plenty of others) to research their family trees. It also brought Haley the National Book Award and the Pulitzer Prize. And it made him an American hero—so much so that his grandparents' home in Tennessee was restored and listed in the National Register of Historic Places.

"Find the Good and Praise It"

Lamar Alexander admires Haley not only as a writer but also as a man who extended himself to others. He was curious about people. He was also kind. "He lived his life by the words 'find the good and praise it,'" Senator Alexander recalled. "In every encounter and with every individual, he was looking for something good. To me that is a quality worth emulating."

CHAPTER 2

A Conversation With

JOHN BRADEMAS

On Reinhold Niebuhr, Adlai Stevenson, and King Juan Carlos I of Spain

One of my heroes is John Brademas, an Indiana Democrat who served for twenty-two years in the House of Representatives, the last four as majority whip. Like a lot of heroes, he has energy and brains to spare, and his values are bone-deep. One of them is an ardent belief in democracy.

Born in Mishawaka, Indiana, in 1927, Brademas imbibed his politics early. He remembers sitting on a porch swing with his grandfather, a Hoosier school superintendent who corresponded with U.S. senators, visited the White House, and was a delegate to Indiana state Democratic conventions. Inspired, Brademas studied government at Harvard and at Oxford, where he was a Rhodes Scholar.

When he returned to Indiana in 1953, his father, a Greek immigrant, encouraged him further. "John, we Greeks invented democracy," he said. "Some of us should practice it." Brademas decided to enter politics. He ran for Congress in 1954 and lost by one half of one percent of the vote. Planning to run again, he worked in 1955 and 1956 on Adlai Stevenson's presidential campaign staff. In 1956 both Stevenson and Brademas lost for the second time. In 1958 Brademas ran for a third time and was elected to the House of Representatives. He was reelected ten times.

During his years in Congress, Brademas helped pass some of the most socially conscious legislation of the day, including most of the federal legislation concerning education; the arts and the humanities; and services provided to children, the elderly, and the disabled.

Among other accomplishments, he was a major coauthor of Head Start and of the Comprehensive Child Development Act, which President Nixon vetoed.

He was principal House sponsor of the 1974 statute that assured ownership by the federal government of the tapes and papers of the Nixon presidency.

Recalling that the Ku Klux Klan, once important in Indiana, had boycotted his father's restaurant because he was not a WASP, Brademas was also a champion of civil rights legislation.

With the retirement of House Speaker Thomas P. "Tip" O'Neill and the resignation of Majority Leader Jim Wright, Brademas was next in line to become Speaker. But in 1980, he and a lot of other Democrats were swept out of office in Ronald Reagan's landslide victory over President Jimmy Carter.

A few months later, Brademas landed a new job: president of New York University in Greenwich Village. During his tenure, he led the transformation of NYU from a regional commuter school into a national and international research university. Not only did he bring fund-raising to new and exalted heights by initiating a campaign that produced $1 billion in ten years, he also raised the level of scholarship.

Moreover, he made NYU an international institution. During his presidency, he established the Center for Japan-U.S. Business and Economic Studies, the Onassis Hellenic Studies Program, Casa Italiana Zerilli-Marimo, the Skirball Department of Hebrew and Judaic Studies, and the King Juan Carlos I of Spain Center.

By the time he stepped down in 1992, he had turned what is now the largest private university in the world into the first-rate university it always should have been. Said scholars Jonathan Van Antwerpen and David L. Kirp in a 2003 study, "NYU is *the* success story in contemporary American higher education."

While NYU president, Brademas was chairman of, among other organizations, the Federal Reserve Bank of New York. Since "retiring," he has chaired, by appointment of President Clinton, the President's Committee on the Arts and the Humanities as well as the National

Endowment for Democracy, an organization "that encourages democracy where it does not exist."

But democracy is not his only value. Brademas is also a man of faith. His father was Greek Orthodox, his mother was a member of the Disciples of Christ, and John is a Methodist. For a while he even considered becoming a minister. He's interested in both God and Caesar. I wasn't surprised, then, that the first person he named in response to my query about heroes was a man for whom religion and politics were linked on the most profound level: Protestant theologian Reinhold Niebuhr—"an intellectual and moral, indeed, religious hero of mine."

REINHOLD NIEBUHR
A Man of Faith and Politics

Niebuhr was one of the great thinkers of the twentieth century, although most young people have no idea who he was. (To be fair, even people my age who recognize the name generally can't tell you much about the man.) In his time, he had virtually a cult following— and I mean among the best and the brightest. He straddled the worlds of theology and politics, and his influence, according to his friend Arthur M. Schlesinger, Jr., was penetrating, fortunate, and enduring.

A rigorous thinker and exciting speaker, Niebuhr was a pessimist who rejected the sentimental, utopian views of the day in favor of what he called "Christian Realism." He thought, for instance, that freedom creates anxiety, which in turn leads to sin. (The original sin, in his opinion, was pride. He noted that ministers, whether fundamentalist or liberal, were often guilty of encouraging it.) Sin affects us both as individuals and as members of society. ("The moral and social dimension of sin," he asserted, "is injustice.") It even creeps into business, which he didn't hesitate to criticize.

Nor did he hesitate to criticize the church, committed though he was to it. He pondered the implications of love and justice, morality and power, Christianity and Marxism, social problems and social policy. He thought about the relationship between faith and politics, and he was aware of the dangers of dogma. Yet he believed that faith had an important part to play in politics, especially in a democracy. He even ran for office several times.

In addition, he had an extravagant personality. I never saw him speak, but Brademas met him several times and heard him preach in Harvard Yard. He can attest to the fact that Niebuhr could be incandescent and explosive—two words that have been used over and over to describe his speaking style. The force of Niebuhr's intellect—his ability to toss off brilliant ideas, his relentless challenging of his own arguments, his wicked sense of humor—was irresistible. Gesturing wildly, he would examine issues from every angle, never hesitating to refine his previous conclusions or to cast them out completely. His thinking evolved over time because his mind was constantly engaged and always honest.

To my mind, that honesty is the heart of his heroism. Most people stop growing intellectually at a very young age. Their minds stiffen long before their joints do. In a world of constant change, their ideas rapidly become irrelevant. Niebuhr wasn't like that. He never ceased to contemplate the implications of his own ideas, to wrestle with paradox, or to confront his doubts, both religious and political.

The son of German immigrants, Niebuhr was born in 1892 in Wright City, Missouri. When he was ten years old, his father, an Evangelical pastor, asked him what he would like to be when he grew up. Niebuhr answered that he wanted to become a minister because his father was the most interesting man in town.

He followed through on that childhood ambition and attended the local church-sponsored colleges. He was still enrolled in April 1913, when his father went into a diabetic coma and died. For a few months, he took over his father's Sunday services. But he longed to pursue his education, and when he was admitted—on probation—to the Yale Divinity School, he seized the opportunity. He reveled in the intellectual atmosphere he found in New Haven. Nevertheless, after he got his master's degree in 1915, he left school, in part due to his self-confessed "boredom with epistemology" and in part due to family financial pressures. He was ordained as a pastor and assigned to Bethel Church in Detroit.

For the next thirteen years, Niebuhr lived with his mother and ministered to his tiny congregation, which grew ten times over. As he got to know his flock, which included a couple of millionaires and a great many autoworkers, he also came to understand the impact of racial prejudice, unemployment, and other social woes in a city dominated by a single industry.

He supplemented his meager salary by speaking and writing. In that manner, he came to the attention of Union Theological Seminary, which hired him as associate professor. He moved to New York, married, and entered politics.

In 1930, he ran for the New York State Senate, and two years later, for Congress, both times on the Socialist ticket. Like Brademas, he lost both times; unlike Brademas, he never gave it a third go. But Niebuhr's involvement in politics did not cease.

In the late 1920s, Niebuhr was both a Socialist and a pacifist, a political and moral position he reached after learning about the horrors of World War I and visiting Germany. In the 1930s, the growing threat of Hitler convinced him to change his thinking. Resolutely denouncing the Nazi leader, he rejected the soft anti-Semitism of many Christian groups and persuaded many Christian pacifists that it was essential to fight against the Third Reich.

His political affiliations were also in flux. When he received a letter from the Socialist Party urging him to support its policy of nonintervention, he resigned. After leaving the party, he became chairman of Americans for Democratic Action, a liberal, anti-Communist group and helped found New York's Liberal Party. He also assisted German refugees and resisters. After the war, he helped the State Department bring about a compassionate peace settlement in Germany.

Niebuhr also continued preaching, teaching (he was always surrounded by students), and writing, even after he was felled by a series of small strokes in 1952. He died in 1971. Throughout his life, his spiritual beliefs and his political activities built upon each other, not in a self-righteous or zealous way, as is so often the case today, but in the spirit of intellectual exploration and moral passion.

An Unexpected Legacy

Because Niebuhr was a profound intellectual, you might think that his words would live on primarily within the walls of cloistered seminaries and graduate schools. Actually, millions of people repeat his words—or in any case, something akin to them—every day. One Sunday in 1943, in the Union Church of Heath, Massachusetts, Niebuhr gave a sermon that included a new prayer he had composed. Since then, that prayer has become world famous, thanks to the founders of Alcoholics Anonymous, who revised it (a little) and made it a central element of their program. The original version, penned by Niebuhr during World War II, goes like this:

> God, give us grace to accept with serenity the things that cannot be changed, courage to change the things that should be changed, and the wisdom to distinguish the one from the other.

Several sources I have read claim that Niebuhr adapted this prayer from a traditional German devotion. Niebuhr's daughter, Elisabeth Sifton, disagrees. "People usually presume that it's very old . . . It's surely rabbinical in origin, or Stoic, derived or translated from Latin or Hebrew, maybe Scottish. . . ." she writes in her fascinating book *The Serenity Prayer.* "In Germany false confidence about the prayer's venerable antiquity has gone further. And it is superbly centered on the presumption that of course the prayer is German."

But the Serenity Prayer, as it is known, is American, written by a great American hero. And although it is probably Niebuhr's best known creation, it is not the work that most excites John Brademas. That honor goes to a book Niebuhr published in World War II: *The Children of Light and The Children of Darkness,* subtitled *A Vindication of Democracy and a Critique of Its Traditional Defense.* In it, Niebuhr makes a statement that Brademas finds meaningful and inspiring: "Man's capacity for justice makes democracy possible; but man's inclination to injustice makes democracy necessary."

"That quote," Brademas told me, "was a lodestone for me when I entered the arena of politics. So I found Niebuhr a very compelling figure, intellectually, morally, and theologically."

Then he added, "I also had great respect for Adlai Stevenson."

ADLAI STEVENSON
The Politics of Integrity

Do young people have a clue about Adlai Stevenson? I doubt it. Losing presidential candidates are soon forgotten.

But a select few live on in cultural memory. Eugene McCarthy, who failed even to win his party's nomination in 1968, is one. Thomas Dewey is another, if only for that memorable *Chicago Tribune* headline, "Dewey Defeats Truman," printed in advance of Truman's 1948 victory. Adlai Stevenson is a third. As recently as April 2003, he was in the news.

A Democrat, Stevenson came from a patrician family with a long political heritage. His grandfather, the first Adlai Stevenson, was vice president under Grover Cleveland. Stevenson followed the pre-ordained route for a young man of his class, attending Princeton and Harvard, receiving a law degree from Northwestern, and entering the legal profession in 1927. In the 1930s, he worked for the administration of Franklin D. Roosevelt. After the war, he helped in the formation of the United Nations and was a delegate to the General Assembly in 1946 and 1947.

In 1948, for the first and only time, he ran for political office and won, becoming governor of the state of Illinois in a landslide. He performed spectacularly, cleaning up corruption and improving the educational system, the welfare system, the roads, and so on. As one of the few Democratic governors, he was in a strong position to run for president. But because the Republican candidate, General Dwight D. Eisenhower, looked invincible, Stevenson was hesitant.

When he was asked to campaign for the nomination, he took the compliment and demurred. As he often said, "Flattery is all right—if you don't inhale."

He seemed above politics. "In America, anyone can become president," he once said. "That's one of the risks you take."

Nonetheless, when he was drafted in 1952, he accepted the nomination. His two speeches at the convention were so promising that, according to one observer, "Politically speaking, it was the Christmas morning of our lives."

Stevenson was witty, urbane, eloquent, honest, and high-minded, with campaign advisors who included some of the most influential intellectuals in the country. He promised to "talk sense to the American people," and he did so without pandering. When accused of being too cerebral and talking over people's heads, he accepted the charge with equanimity. "Eggheads, unite!" he cracked. "You have nothing to lose but your yolks." His supporters adored him.

Along with his devoted followers, Stevenson had powerful enemies. Among them were Joseph McCarthy and J. Edgar Hoover, who accused him of being a Communist and a homosexual. Another enemy was Richard Nixon, the Republican candidate for vice president, who called Stevenson "Adlai the Appeaser . . . a Ph.D. from Dean Acheson's cowardly college of Communist containment." Adlai refused to take the bait. "If the Republicans will stop telling lies about us," he said, "we will stop telling the truth about them."

The main issues in the campaign, according to one of his biographers, were foreign policy, with Stevenson favoring containment of the Soviets and Eisenhower taking a more hawkish line; ownership of offshore oil, with Stevenson favoring federal control and Eisenhower wanting to cede ownership to the states; and humor. The Republicans—whom Adlai dubbed the "Grouchy Old Pessimists"—did not employ it. Stevenson used it frequently and was adept at off-the-cuff, self-deprecating remarks. Once when he was giving a speech, the sound system created a distracting echo. "I think what I am saying is worth listening to," he quipped. "But it's certainly not worth listening to twice."

Stevenson lost the election in a landslide, 449 electoral votes to 89 in Eisenhower's favor. But then something amazing happened. Instead of tumbling into the famous dustbin of history, he gained new stature in the public's estimation. He came to symbolize something noble—the best of American values. He emerged from his electoral defeat unsullied and unbowed, a classic hero.

In 1956, Stevenson ran for president a second time. One of his assistants was John Brademas, who had come to Stevenson's attention four years earlier with an essay entitled "Why I'm Voting Democratic in November," which he published in a student newspaper at Oxford and distributed back home in Indiana. Brademas served as liaison to Stevenson's brain trust advisors such as John Kenneth Galbraith, Paul Samuelson, and Arthur Schlesinger, Jr.

The 1956 campaign was vigorous, idealistic, and bound to fail. Running against a popular World War II general in the middle of the Cold War, Stevenson campaigned against the draft and in favor of a nuclear test ban treaty, an idea Nixon called "the height of irresponsibility and absurdity." It didn't help Stevenson's case when Soviet premier Nikolai Bulganin endorsed the concept.

But then, Stevenson was not afraid of pursuing issues he thought were important, even if it cost him votes. On the contrary, he seemed to embrace them, a phenomenon Brademas observed firsthand. "What impressed me about Stevenson was his courage in taking positions that were not politically attractive," Brademas told me. "I might say to him, Governor, on this issue, this is what we think the right thing to do is. But I have to warn you: If you say this, it's going to hurt you. Stevenson would say, 'Tell me more!'"

In 1956 as in 1952, Stevenson's supporters were wildly enthusiastic— "madly for Adlai," as the button said. When he was photographed preparing for a speech with a hole in his shoe, they took to wearing small lapel pins in the shape of the worn-out sole. In their eyes, he was simultaneously an intellect and a man of the people. At one campaign stop, a woman called out, "Governor, you have the vote of every thinking person!"

"That's not enough, madame," Stevenson shot back. "We need a majority."

He lost the election. Four years later, the nomination went to John Fitzgerald Kennedy who, to Stevenson's dismay, did not appoint him secretary of state. Instead, he became U.S. ambassador to the United Nations. It was there that he had a dramatic confrontation with the Russian ambassador—a confrontation that, over forty years later, was recalled in the headlines as . . .

The Adlai Stevenson Moment

In his public life, Adlai never wanted to vilify the Soviets. He believed that peace required working with them—containing them, just as Nixon said. And yet, when it was time to confront the Russians, he did it with aplomb.

The year: 1962. The place: the United Nations Security Council. The issue: Soviet buildup in Cuba. Valerian Zorin, the Soviet envoy, had equivocated about whether there were Soviet missiles in Cuba. In a televised speech, Stevenson called him on it. "Do you, Ambassador Zorin, deny that the USSR has placed and is placing medium and intermediate range missiles and sites in Cuba? Yes or no? Don't wait for the translation. Yes or no?"

Stonewalling, Zorin replied that he was not in an American courtroom.

Adlai responded, "You are in the court of world opinion."

Zorin wouldn't budge. "You will receive my answer in due course," he said.

"I am prepared to wait for my answer until Hell freezes over," Adlai said, whereupon he presented the incontrovertible evidence: twenty-six large photographs clearly showing the missiles.

As Arthur Schlesinger, Jr. later wrote, this demonstration "dealt a final blow to the Soviet case." Within days, Russian ships heading for Cuba turned around and Zorin was replaced as UN ambassador.

Stevenson's performance became a standard against which subsequent politicians were measured, as Colin Powell discovered in 2003 when he presented his case for war against Iraq to the Security Council. Was it an Adlai Stevenson moment? commentators asked. The consensus was clear: No.

A Hero of Diplomacy and Democracy

Less than three years after that dramatic confrontation, Stevenson died. He was sixty-five. At the United Nations, Secretary of State Dean Rusk said, "Three presidents of the United States sent Adlai Stevenson to the United Nations. They sent you our best."

But perhaps the best commendation came from a Latin American diplomat who several years before had suggested a simple epitaph for Stevenson: "Once upon a time there was an American diplomat."

Brademas asserts that Stevenson's importance goes beyond what he accomplished in his lifetime. "He helped make John Kennedy possible because of the way in which he articulated the nexus among values, ideas, and action in the political order."

Despite losing elections, a painful divorce, and great disappointment at the way he was treated during the Kennedy administration, Adlai Stevenson remained true to the democratic ideal. He was a great American hero.

Adlai Stevenson's Heroes

In a conversation with a journalist shortly before he died, Adlai Stevenson named a few of his heroes. First on his list was Abraham Lincoln, who "has always been my hero, as he is the hero of most Americans." He added that his great-grandfather was a close friend of Lincoln's "so I was naturally saturated with Lincoln from infancy."

Next came Woodrow Wilson. Stevenson met him as a child and was charmed and inspired.

Stevenson's third hero was Franklin D. Roosevelt, for whom he worked in the 1930s.

Adlai's heroes suggest something I've often noticed: Heroes you read about in books can be inspiring. But there is nothing more impressive than a hero to whom you feel a personal connection.

As John Brademas would be the first to tell you, not every hero of democracy is an American. Consider, for example, King Juan Carlos I of Spain.

KING JUAN CARLOS I OF SPAIN

Juan Carlos de Borbón, the king of Spain, is an unlikely hero. Born in Rome in 1938 during the Spanish Civil War, he was the grandson of King Alfonso XIII, who went into exile in 1931. Juan Carlos attended school in Switzerland and did not even visit Spain until he was ten years old. There was little reason to believe that he would ever sit on the Spanish throne.

Nor was there any reason to think that, if he did rise to a position of power, it would necessarily be a good thing. After all, in 1969, Juan Carlos was the protégé and designated successor of General Francisco Franco. For six years, he was photographed at the Generalissimo's side, quietly absorbing—presumably—lessons in fascism. When Juan Carlos was crowned in 1975, two days after Franco died, no one expected him to become an avatar of democracy. In fact, no one expected much at all. He was perceived as lacking both brains and leadership ability. A Communist functionary named Santiago Carillo expressed a widespread sentiment when he called the new king "Juan Carlos the Brief."

But people can surprise you.

In his first speech, Juan Carlos announced his intention to restore democracy. And he did exactly that. He oversaw the transformation of Spain from a Fascist dictatorship to a constitutional democracy. He didn't do it quickly. He didn't do it dramatically. And he hit a few bumps along the way. He appointed many men who had been powerful under Franco, and the Spaniards distrusted him. The first several years of his reign were marred by strikes, riots, a disastrous economy, and political terrorism in the Basque country.

Nonetheless, under Juan Carlos, Spain had democratic elections for the first time in over forty years. There was a new, democratic constitution and a new parliament.

These reforms were not universally welcomed. A few elements of society wanted Juan Carlos to continue Franco's policies. Six years after he became king, there was an attempted coup d'état. That was when Juan Carlos had his Adlai Stevenson moment.

The Coup Deferred

The date: February 23, 1981. The place: Madrid. Lieutenant Colonel Antonio Tejero and two hundred armed guardsmen burst into the parliamentary chamber and took control. Meanwhile, Tejero's compatriot, Captain-General Jaime Milans del Bosch, declared martial law and began to contact high-level military men, seeking support "in the name of the king." At first, Juan Carlos simply called these same men one by one to insist that they ignore Milans. Several hours later, he realized that there was a better way. After inviting a television crew to come to his palace, he launched a counterattack.

In it, he stood his ground. He had already told Milans privately that he would rather be shot than acquiesce to the wishes of the conspiracy. Addressing the people, King Juan Carlos I declared that he would resist all efforts to disrupt the democratic process. Wearing his military uniform, he faced down the coup. And it fell apart.

The king's valor saved the Spanish democracy and earned him the love of his people. Those who had been lukewarm or negative in their evaluation became his enthusiastic supporters. Even Carillo, the Communist who had predicted a short, unhappy reign for the new monarch, appeared on television saying, "God save the king."

As John Brademas has said, "At a critical moment in the life of the new Spain, it was the brave and farsighted stance of His Majesty, King Juan Carlos I, that protected the institutions of the new Spanish democracy."

Since then, King Juan Carlos has acted on the world stage, working with Latin American countries, emphasizing the importance of education and language, and acting to spread Spanish culture. One way in which that happens is through John Brademas.

The King Juan Carlos I of Spain Center

Even as a child, Brademas was interested in Hispanic culture. As a schoolboy, he read a book about the Mayans, decided he wanted to become an archaeologist, began learning Spanish, and, at seventeen, hitchhiked to Mexico with a classmate. As a Harvard undergraduate, he spent a summer in working in Aztec villages in the mountains of rural Mexico, and he wrote his honors essay on a right-wing Mexican peasant movement.

As a Rhodes scholar at Oxford, he became fascinated by the anarchist movement in Spain and wrote his doctoral dissertation on the Catalonian anarcho-syndicalists of the 1920s and 1930s. His study was published in Barcelona in 1974.

Nine years later, as president of NYU, Brademas conferred an honorary degree on the king and established a chair in his name. In 1997, in the presence of King Juan Carlos, Queen Sofia, and Hillary Clinton, then First Lady of the United States, he dedicated the King Juan Carlos I of Spain Center at NYU to promote research and teaching about the Spanish-speaking world.

OTHER HEROES

In our conversation on the subject, Brademas named many other heroes, including Franklin D. Roosevelt, Father Theodore Hesburgh of Notre Dame, Elie Wiesel, Tip O'Neill, and John W. Gardner, founder of the Urban Coalition.

But I do believe that he has a special place in his heart for the three heroes discussed here: Reinhold Niebuhr, the philosopher who melded religion with democracy; Adlai Stevenson, the politician who put the values of democracy above personal ambition; and King Juan Carlos I, who faced down the military and stood up for democracy when it mattered the most.

DEMOCRACY'S DILEMMA

Still, democracy presents certain problems for heroes. On the battlefield or in a totalitarian regime, things are black-and-white and the hero's way is generally clear. In a democracy, where the loser allows the winner to take office, even in a squeaker, and the majority agrees to protect the rights of the minority, even when it's inconvenient, it's not always heroic to insist on your point of view. It may be simply bullheaded and self-defeating. Brademas and I touched on that in our discussion:

RD: I think you'd agree that taking a stand when it isn't to your personal advantage can be one of the qualities of heroism.

JB: Yes. Stevenson was willing to take an unpopular position, and I admired that. But it's also true that to get anything done in a democratic political system like ours, with 1 president, 100 senators, and 435 representatives, you cannot always be out on the battlements shouting, "Follow me, follow my flag into battle." You negotiate, you bargain, you trade. That's the nature of the legislative process in a democratic society. And in a sense that does not make for heroes.

RD: You have to pick your battles.

JB: If you're a member of the House of Representatives, you run for re-election every two years. So you do not go out of your way seeking opportunities to say, "Look how brave and how heroic I am." That's a path to defeat.

RD: The philosopher Sidney Hook says that in a democracy a hero must be ready for failure because "he cannot use any means to achieve his ends no matter how worthy those ends are. Whoever makes success the be-all and end-all of his policy, like the person who literally will do anything in order to survive, is building an epitaph of infamy for himself, since he will betray every principle, every value, every human being that stands in his way."

JB: I agree with that statement. If winning above all is your target, you may do things you shouldn't do. In politics you have to be prepared to lose. As I used to tell my freshmen colleagues in the House of Representatives, "You'd better know what your values are before you get here because this is not the place to learn them." While there is something to be said for classes in business ethics if you're going for an MBA, it's a little late to be learning your ethics by that stage of the game.

The question then is this: What should a human being, especially in a highly civilized, well-educated society, strive for? It shouldn't be solely materialistic. I took a look at what the *Encyclopedia Britannica* had to say about heroes and hero worship. One line that struck me was this: "The hero ... symbolizes man's urge and struggle to transcend the limitations of his existence and to conquer a fuller and more total life."

RD: I like that. Heroes don't do what they do for personal gain. Heroes do what they do because they think something bigger, better, and more fulfilling is going to happen as a result. To me, heroism is about pursuing that vision, even if the pursuit ends in failure. The effort is everything.

CHAPTER 3

A Conversation With

DOMINIC CAVELLO

On Edmund G. Ross and Others

Hero worship is a funny term, one that makes me a little nervous. I admire my heroes. I try to emulate them. But worshipping them is another story. History is filled with ugly episodes of hero worship. Especially when it is focused on a single individual, hero worship can destroy a society. That's one reason I believe in having many heroes.

Another reason is that, as we age, some heroes grow stronger and more vivid in our estimation while others fade. This was brought home to me when I spoke with Dominic Cavello, principal of St. Charles Preparatory School, a Catholic boys' school in Columbus, Ohio. According to Mr. Cavello, St. Charles prides itself on its high standards. I can attest to that: I went there myself.

A veteran of the war in Vietnam, Dominic Cavello has been at St. Charles for over thirty years. He began as a classics teacher and became principal in 1985, although he still teaches Latin. I looked at his syllabus, and I can tell you, the academic standards have not dropped. Nor have the standards of civility, as I learned when I received an award from my old alma mater. When I walked into that auditorium, everyone in the room stood. I was incredibly touched at this show of old-fashioned gallantry. To this day, St. Charles teaches manners.

Dominic Cavello is a hero to me because he is the motivating force behind that institution. Every year, nearly a hundred well-trained, well-educated young men graduate from St. Charles and go out into the world. In no small measure, their success is a tribute to their principal. Naturally, I wanted to know who his heroes were. I discovered that his heroes, like mine, have evolved over time.

ON CLASSICAL AND HISTORICAL HEROES

We began our conversation by talking about ancient Greece. Their heroes were the offspring of gods and mortals. Like gods, they had extraordinary abilities. Like human beings, they made mistakes and knew what it was to suffer. The Greeks worshipped them as demigods. They even had their own shrines, although the shrines of the heroes were nearer to the ground than those of the gods, as befit their lower status. People prayed to them in times of crisis, much as they pray to Christian saints today.

But as Dominic Cavello pointed out to me, the heroes of the ancient Greeks were often, by our standards, completely amoral. Here's part of our conversation:

RD: When you think about heroes, who comes to your mind?

DC: When I'm in the classroom teaching Homer's *Iliad* or Virgil's *Aeneid,* I'm talking about heroes in the classical sense. In that world, a hero was defined as someone with great courage or physical abilities. His main concern was his reputation, and his aim was to obtain honor for himself or his family—generally on the battlefield or in another violent situation. Honor meant that you were held in high esteem by your peers. That concept is fundamentally at odds with what we believe now.

RD: How would you define a hero in today's world?

DC: A hero is someone who overcomes adversity. That hasn't changed. But today's hero overcomes great adversity in order to do the right thing. There's a moral component to being a hero today, whereas you could be a hero in a classical sense and be amoral.

RD: That's a big change. I wonder if there's a similar shift in our personal lives. Have your ideas of heroism changed since you were a boy? And did you look up to mythological heroes?

DC: When I was in grade school I hadn't read *The Iliad* or *The Odyssey* or Virgil's *Aeneid* or any of the other great classics. A hero to me was a highly decorated soldier or an athlete who set records in a sport.

As I grew older, the moral dimension became important. When I read about people who were doing the right thing for the good of humanity, those people became my new heroes—especially if they were going against the grain. For instance, I remember in high school reading John Kennedy's book, *Profiles in Courage*. The people he wrote about chose to do the right thing, even though in many cases doing the right thing hurt them politically.

I also remember studying figures in the abolitionist movement who had their lives destroyed because of the stance that they took. The same thing happened in the twentieth century with people like Martin Luther King, Jr. These people were heroic.

RD: Are there other historical figures you consider heroes?

DC: Sure. In my time, I've done a fair amount of reading about the founding of this country and I hold George Washington in great esteem. I think he was a genuine hero. I feel differently about Thomas Jefferson. Jefferson, in my view, was too partisan. Washington kept his eye on the prize more. And Abraham Lincoln is a genuine hero.

In many respects, I like Franklin Roosevelt because of what he tried to do to turn the country around from the Depression. I don't like all of his policies, but I like what he tried to do for mankind in general. I admire the input he had into the Marshall Plan and what went on in Europe after the war. We didn't just defeat our foe. We tried to help people when the fighting was over.

RD: That was the right thing to do. And it's more important now than ever.

ON PROFILES IN COURAGE

I was glad that Dominic Cavello mentioned *Profiles in Courage*. It presented a standard of conduct in public life that is worth remembering.

Long before he was elected to public office, John F. Kennedy was a hero. He was so designated in World War II, when his torpedo boat, PT-109, was hit by a Japanese destroyer and sunk. Kennedy, whose physical ailments could easily have kept him from having to serve in the armed forces, kept his crew alive and saved one badly burned man by hauling him through shark-infested water for several hours. Later, as president, he faced down the Russians; introduced civil rights legislation (passed under Johnson); and brought youth, culture, and ideas to the White House. Dashing and well-spoken, he was the youngest president ever elected, as well as the first Roman Catholic. And, of course, he had a beautiful, stylish wife. When he was assassinated on November 22, 1963, his heroism reached epic proportions. For many years, it seemed as if every butcher shop and candy store in the country had a portrait of JFK—and later on, Martin Luther King, Jr., and Robert F. Kennedy—hung prominently on the wall.

But gradually, as his policies were questioned and his reckless personal behavior revealed, his heroism began to dim. Only one person I spoke with during the course of writing this book named JFK as a hero.

Yet ever since 2002, when historian Robert Dallek, author of *An Unfinished Life: John F. Kennedy, 1917–1963*, revealed the extent and seriousness of Kennedy's medical ailments, I have sensed a shift. Perhaps we have finally gotten over the shock of his obsessive infidelities. Or maybe it is hard not to admire Kennedy's lifelong stoicism in the face of what we now know to have been intense physical pain.

Profiles in Courage is a legacy of his terrible health. In 1954 and 1955, he underwent surgery for back problems. While convalescing, he wrote the Pulitzer Prize–winning book. It examines the influence of courage, the virtue Kennedy admired most, in the lives of eight senators who obeyed the dictates of their consciences even though it meant putting their careers on the line. Although some of these men are in our eyes fatally flawed (several, for instance, were slave owners), they were all denounced by their contemporaries because they stood up for something that was right.

Of the heroes Kennedy discussed, one of the most obscure was the renegade Republican who single-handedly stopped the impeachment of Andrew Johnson—and sacrificed his political career for a man he did not even like.

EDMUND G. ROSS
Capitol Hill Hero

In 1866, the Civil War was over, Abraham Lincoln had been assassinated, and the federal government was in turmoil. Andrew Johnson, the new president, was intent on following Lincoln's agenda and bringing the Southern states back into the Union in an expeditious and charitable manner. The Congress had other ideas. So the president would veto a bill because it treated the South too harshly, and Congress would override the veto, and back and forth it went.

But every so often, a senator would support the president. One such man was Jim Lane, a conservative Republican from Kansas. When his "radical" Republican constituents back home learned how active he was in Johnson's defense, they got together at a public meeting and attacked him. Distraught over the public humiliation, Lane shot himself.

His replacement in the Senate was a former newspaperman and Union soldier named Edmund G. Ross (1826–1907). Ross had been emphatically antislavery in the years before the Civil War, and he was no fan of Andrew Johnson. The radical Republicans figured they had an ally. And for the most part, they were right. Ross voted with them in almost every case.

But by the time Ross got to Washington, late in 1866, the friction between the two branches of government was throwing off serious sparks. The issue at hand was not policy; it was power. The president and the Congress were engaged in a tug-of-war about who would run the government. (Does this sound familiar?) When Johnson asked Secretary of War Edwin M. Stanton to resign, the man refused to step down until Congress was in session. A week later, Johnson appointed Ulysses S. Grant to take Stanton's place. The Senate announced its collective support for Stanton; Grant walked away from the whole mess; and Stanton, to underline the fact that he wasn't going to step down, barricaded himself in his office.

The radical Republicans thought that their moment had arrived. Knowing that there was rising public anger against Johnson for resisting Congress, the Republicans in the House of Representatives unanimously voted to impeach him. The measure easily passed.

The trial moved to the Senate, where thirty-six votes were needed. Of the forty-two Republicans, thirty-five favored impeachment and six opposed it. Only one was undecided: Senator Ross. Although not a supporter of Johnson, he was disturbed by the implications of the trial. He saw that what was happening was little more than a partisan coup. It seemed to him that the independence of the executive branch, and hence the sanctity of the entire system, was at stake. So he voted for acquittal, knowing that his vote of conscience would end his political career. "I almost literally looked down into my open grave," he later wrote. "Friendships, position, fortune, everything that makes life desirable to an ambitious man were about to be swept away by the breath of my mouth, perhaps forever." And he was right; like the other six Republicans who voted against impeachment, he was never elected to political office again. Afterward, he was ostracized both in Congress and in Kansas, denounced as "a miserable poltroon and traitor" (in the *New York Tribune*), and even physically attacked. Finally, he moved to New Mexico and, after many years, was appointed territorial governor. Almost four decades after the attempted impeachment, public opinion swung his way and his magnificent act began to be recognized. He died in 1907, his life largely defined by a single act of conscience.

Kennedy's Other Heroes

Other heroes discussed in Profiles in Courage *included:*
- *John Quincy Adams (1767-1848)*
- *Daniel Webster (1782-1852)*
- *Thomas Hart Benton (1782-1858)*
- *Sam Houston (1793-1863), who gave up his position as governor of Texas rather than secede*
- *Robert A. Taft (1889-1953), a man who had been groomed to follow in his father's footsteps and become president. It never happened, in part because he always spoke his mind, even when it was not politic. For instance, he objected to the Nuremberg Trials after World War II because he thought the trial was unfair, not a worthy demonstration of democratic justice in action. "The trial of the vanquished by the victors cannot be impartial no matter how it is hedged about with the forms of justice," he said. No one, except for a Nazi leader who'd been acquitted, agreed.*

ON THE YOUNG

You don't need to be famous to be somebody's hero. You don't even need to be accomplished in the usual sense of the word. And age has nothing to do with it. Heroism springs from action and from attitude, and some of the most heroic people are some of the youngest. Dominic Cavello, who began our conversation by talking about mythological heroes, ended by talking about several students who number among the most heroic people he knows. Here's what he had to say:

DC: After thirty-one years in education, a number of my heroes are present and former students. I have taught young men who have had to overcome great adversity. They were inspirational to me. For instance, I remember a boy who had always wanted to go to St. Charles. His grandfather had gone to school here and they had a close relationship. He came here as an eighth grader. But when he had his required physical examination, he found out that he had leukemia. He was all right his freshman year. But then he had a couple of bouts of illness and had to be hospitalized. He ended up needing a bone marrow transplant. We did a lot of private tutoring with him.

I got to know this young man pretty well because I would go to his house to tutor him. He did everything we asked of him. At the end of his junior year, he went off for one more bone marrow transplant and just didn't make it. He had never complained about his workload or his illness. He always did the best he could.

I also had a student who attempted to escape from Vietnam four times before he finally got out. I'm talking about a fifteen-year-old kid who got on a boat by himself, sailed to Hong Kong, and waited for a placement service to get placed in the United States. He came to Columbus along with a boy from Laos. We took them in here at St. Charles, which is probably one of the toughest high schools in Ohio, in terms of standards, and they didn't speak a lot of English. They each graduated with nearly a four-point accumulated average. That's overcoming adversity.

The last example of heroism is a young man who has severe juvenile rheumatoid arthritis. It has severely stunted his growth. He's in a wheelchair most of the day and he is in constant pain. There's never a minute without pain. Once every two weeks, he spends a day in the hospital receiving transfusions. Yet you see this boy with a smile on his face—and he too has almost a four-point average. That's overcoming adversity.

My whole perspective on heroes has changed over the years and it's because I've been brought into contact with young men such as these. I'm sure there are great sports heroes and political heroes today. But it's interesting that as an adult, I can look at a fourteen-year-old or a fifteen-year-old and say, "You're my hero."

I feel the same way about some youngsters I know, including my sons. Dominic Cavello, one of the few people I spoke with who mentioned young people, told me that he was overwhelmed by what kids are exposed to today. I feel the same way. Kids are disturbingly sophisticated today. They face problems that I couldn't have dreamed of when I was their age, and they live in an era that is frightening. Yet they soldier on, overcoming their fears, doing the hard work required of them, and reaching out to others. I have profound regard for them.

I wish they could look to more heroes in the public arena. Heroes offer hope and leadership. That's why the ancient Greeks prayed to them. That's why we need them ourselves. But frankly, I don't see a lot of heroic behavior out there.

My son Geoffrey has expressed a similar concern. "What leaders?" he wrote in a poem entitled "Why Don't the Heroes Lead the World?"

I'm hoping that this book might inspire a few people to act heroically and, in so doing, to become the leaders we need.

CHAPTER 4

A Conversation With

STEVE FORBES

On Theodore Vail, Winston Churchill, Ernie Pyle, and Others

Certain people can't get a break in the public imagination. Malcolm Stevenson Forbes, otherwise known as Steve, is probably one of them. Yet in many ways, he and his family epitomize the American dream.

His grandfather, B. C. Forbes, was a Scottish immigrant with a grade-school education. The sixth of ten children, he taught himself shorthand and by sixteen was working as a newspaper reporter in Aberdeen, Scotland. After coming to this country, he became a financial columnist for the Hearst newspapers. In 1917, he founded his own magazine, *Forbes*. A dynasty—and an institution—was born.

When B. C. died in 1954, his flamboyant son Malcolm became publisher of the magazine, which prospered under his command. Malcolm's son Steve began to work for the magazine in 1970, a year after graduating from Princeton with a degree in American history. "It's true that I came to the attention of the top management of Forbes magazine at a fairly young age," he said in 1996. "As my father liked to say, there's nothing wrong with nepotism, as long as you keep it in the family." When Malcolm died in 1990, Steve took over as president and CEO of Forbes, Inc. and editor-in-chief of the magazine. Like his father and grandfather before him, he writes the editorials.

He also shares with his forebears an interest in politics. The father of five daughters, Steve Forbes ran for president as a Republican in 1996 and 2000. Despite being, in his own words, "charismatically challenged," he did surprisingly well. True, he had the means to keep himself in the race, despite the media's relative indifference to him. But it's also true that, unlike many candidates, he had an actual idea, and an astounding one at that: the flat tax. Not that he didn't also have other propositions. But the flat tax caught people's attention. And although it did not, ultimately, prove to be popular, it addressed a serious issue in this country and made a real contribution to the national dialogue.

In his own understated way, so opposite that of his headline-grabbing, motorcycle-riding father (who famously threw a five-million-dollar birthday party for himself in Morocco), Steve Forbes has chutzpah. He put a controversial idea on the table and ran a campaign of ideas, not personality. I admire that.

A few months after the war in Iraq started in 2003, Steve Forbes and I talked about heroism. Here's part of what he had to say:

SF: Heroes are people who perform extraordinary deeds or provide extraordinary, selfless examples. They go beyond what is expected and they have the character and stamina to stick with something. We live in an age that does not want to acknowledge the hero. Rather, we want to look for people's flaws. These "tearer-downers" can't seem to grasp that we all have flaws; we all have shortcomings. But that is precisely why when people do extraordinary, positive things, we should applaud them. Heroes also respond well under crisis. An example along those lines would be the POWs in Vietnam who survived the prison camp known as the Hanoi Hilton—most notably, John McCain.

Heroes also possess great vision. In the political sphere there are people in modern times, such as Margaret Thatcher or Ronald Reagan, who changed the course of events when many told them it couldn't be done. George W. Bush is moving into that category. In our history, Lincoln and Washington are prime examples. Lincoln never tired in his pursuit of preserving the Union. He recognized when many others were willing to throw in the towel that if we didn't preserve this country, we'd lose the freedom we cherish. He was an extraordinary, humane man, but absolutely relentless in his pursuit of this goal.

Franklin Delano Roosevelt is another. In his late thirties, he gets a debilitating disease and his mother—she was a formidable person—wanted him to spend the rest of his life as a gentleman of leisure. He would have none of it.

RD: I wouldn't have expected you to mention FDR.

SF: It's not a matter of policies. It's a question of character.

RD: That's absolutely right. Who are some of your personal heroes?

SF: My father was an inspiration. I admired his energy, his sense of innovation and imagination, his ability to come back quickly from very real setbacks. My siblings and I learned from him that you try to heal those wounds as quickly as possible and move on. Life is too short to nurse grievances. From our mother, we learned that the small and unpublicized things are also important in the book of life.

RD: What about people who are more known to the general public?

SF: Growing up, I admired John Glenn. I admired certain sports heroes. This is way back, before they became subject to the tearer-downers, who focus on the warts and moles. I liked Sandy Koufax, who showed extraordinary physical courage. He had severe arthritis in his arm and still pitched. After he retired, he was in one of these celebrity golf tournaments. A pro told him, "If you straighten out your left arm, Mr. Koufax, you'll hit that golf ball much better."

Koufax said, "If I could straighten out my arm, I'd still be pitching." You had to admire that.

RD: What about business figures?

SF: I admired Alfred P. Sloan who took over a bankrupt company, General Motors, in the early 1920s and made it into a mighty corporation. He pioneered annual model changes, different colors for cars, installment buying, all kinds of things we think of as normal. And I certainly admire Theodore Vail who created the old AT&T.

RD: In what way was he heroic?

SF: He had a vision of service. He believed you could serve the public first. And Vail was an innovator. When he faced a crisis, he didn't just cut costs to make the company efficient. He pursued his own vision. A contemporary example is [Louis] Gerstner, the turn-around artist who saved IBM when it nearly went under twelve years ago. He pulled it out, gave it a new purpose. And there are people in the news like [Bill] Gates or [Larry] Ellison or [Steve] Jobs. They created something that most would have thought impossible.

RD: I don't think most people see business as fertile ground for heroism. But you obviously do.

SF: Yes. The whole nature of commerce is based on looking to the future. When you start a business, you may think it's going to work, but there's no guarantee it will. Business forces you to pay attention to the needs and wants of other people. Success depends on meeting those needs and wants. Successful businessmen are oftentimes also successful philanthropists because philanthropy is the opposite side of the same coin as commerce. In both cases, you're serving the needs and wants of other people.

It's easy to disparage business, and I personally have known more than a few slimy businessmen. But Steve Forbes makes a point that is too often overlooked. Although business may make some people inordinately rich (check the Forbes 400 to find out exactly who they are), successful businesspeople can also make life better for the rest of us. A case in point . . .

THEODORE N. VAIL
Father of Universal Service

The nineteenth century was a time of expansion. It saw the growth of the railroads, the opening of the West, the closing of the frontier, and the fulfillment of Manifest Destiny, the idea that this nation would span a continent. A great idea. But how were residents of the East Coast ever going to communicate with their restless progeny in California? The Pony Express was not a long-term solution. Alexander Graham Bell had a better idea, but he was an inventor. It took a businessman to make it happen.

Born in Ohio, Theodore Newton Vail (1845–1920) came from a distinguished family with an established interest in communications. Among his relatives were several backers of Samuel F. B. Morse, whose invention of the telegraph changed the world. In 1844, when Morse sent his famous message over the Washington-Baltimore telegraph line ("What hath God wrought!"), the recipient on the other end was Vail's cousin, Alfred Lewis Vail, who also claimed to be the inventor of Morse code.

Born the following year, Vail grew up in New Jersey, where his father worked for The Speedwell Iron Works, which had been founded by another entrepreneurial relative. Vail thought about becoming a doctor or a minister. He pursued neither course (although he did maintain a lifelong habit of moralizing) and seemed to lack ambition. His father was sure that his son would never be able to support himself.

After high school, Vail worked in a drugstore that included a telegraph office. Knowing the family legend, he became fascinated with the process. But he was restless. With the Civil War raging, he wanted to enlist in the Union army. His father would not allow it. So Vail found a job in New York with the United States Telegraph Company. He was not enthusiastic about it. When his father moved to Iowa in 1866, Vail followed. He worked on the farm, taught school for a while, and drifted farther west. He ended up in Pine Bluff, Wyoming, working as a mail clerk for the Union Pacific Railroad.

That was when his prospects began to look up. By 1876, he was in Washington, D.C., working for the federal government as general superintendent of the Railway Mail Service.

Two years later, he was offered a job as general manager of the American Bell Telephone Company. He was hesitant to take it. Some people were still resistant to the new invention, which they saw as a "talking toy." And the company was suffering from financial and management problems. Vail's cronies advised against it. "Listen to the prophecy of an old fool to a friend," one wrote. "One or two years hence there will be more telephone companies than there are sewing machine companies today. . . ."

When Vail decided to take the job, it had less to do with the future of the telephone than with the U.S. Congress, which determined his salary at the Railway Mail Service. The Senate met for an entire day to consider whether to allow him an additional five dollars a day. Vail was so disgusted with the waste of time and the pettiness of the matter that he decided to leave government service and throw his lot in with the telephone company.

When Vail took over, Alexander Graham Bell had yet to profit from his invention and the company was in chaos. Vail turned it around. Over the next nine years, he merged various local companies, purchased other companies to provide electricity and equipment, and saw licensed telephone exchanges open throughout the nation. He also inaugurated something we now consider an inalienable right: long-distance service. When the first long-distance line opened in 1884, the *Boston Journal* put the news on page one. Vail was on his way. He became a wealthy man as well as a socialite and a patron of the arts. But by the time he was forty-four, in 1889, he was so thoroughly exhausted that he retired to his farm in Vermont.

For the next few years, he invested in all kinds of business. Among them were a company that made a flawed heating system that almost wiped him out, an ostrich farm that produced a single egg, and a Colorado mine that made him rich again. He spent several years in Argentina setting up a railway system in Buenos Aires and a power plant in Córdoba. His business ventures also took him to England.

He was there in 1905 when his wife caught a chill and died. And he was there two years later, when his son died of typhoid.

Vail was at loose ends. Five years earlier, a fortune-teller in Paris and another in London had told him that he would make his most important contribution after age sixty. It seemed unlikely, especially after he rejected the suggestion that he run for governor or senator.

But in 1907, eighteen years after his retirement, his old company came calling and Vail became president. Now known as AT&T, the company was facing intense competition. Its patents had expired and independent companies were springing up everywhere. Vail knew precisely how to deal with it. He acquired some competitors, including Western Union, and leased AT&T lines to other independents. He also accepted a set of government regulations that essentially turned the company into a state-sanctioned monopoly. In this way, he turned the ailing company into a monolith. Vail's slogan— "one policy, one system, universal service"—became a reality.

In 1915, almost thirty years after the first long-distance call, transcontinental service became available. The first coast-to-coast telephone call was a ceremonial conference call. The participants were Alexander Graham Bell in New York; his long-ago assistant, Thomas A. Watson, in San Francisco; and an ailing Theodore Vail, speaking from an island off the coast of Georgia.

"Away back in the old days I dreamed of wires extending all over the country and of people in one part of America talking to people in another part of America," Alexander Graham Bell later said. "It was the dream of a dreamer, but Mr. Vail has made it come true."

Was Theodore Vail a hero? Absolutely. He had vision and organizational ability. He had a knack for invention, with a dozen patents to his credit. He believed in transparency, even when he was under the gun. ("My idea of a lawsuit is to get out the facts, all the facts, then see where the rights are," he said. "I am opposed to all forms of concealment in litigation.") He looked to the future. And he possessed one of the cardinal heroic virtues: hope.

A Hero for the Ages

Vail is not someone I would have thought to name. I discovered, however, that Steve Forbes and I do share a hero: Winston Churchill. Steve collects his books and letters. Unless you count the porcelain figurine I keep in my office, I am not a collector of Churchill memorabilia. I understand the impulse, though. Winston Churchill (1874–1965) is the kind of hero we need.

SIR WINSTON CHURCHILL
"We are all worms.
But I do believe I am a glow-worm."

Like all heroes, Churchill had his flaws. He was egotistical, unabashedly ambitious, bullheaded, short-tempered, intimidating, and prone to "Black Dog" depressions. His judgment was sometimes spectacularly bad. He was also magnanimous, indomitable, a man of enormous vitality and eloquence. And in the worst of times, he aroused in the English people the willingness to sacrifice and the determination to seek victory, whatever the cost. Say what you will about the man; he saved Western Civilization.

A Miserable Childhood

Churchill's glamorous American mother, Jennie, was attentive to him throughout her life, despite her many lovers. ("In my interest," Churchill said, "she left no wire unpulled, no stone unturned, no cutlet uncooked.") But his adored father, the failed politician Lord Randolph Churchill, was unapproachable and dismissive. He was also increasingly deranged, due to the inexorable progression of syphilis. Winston's was not a happy home life.

Far worse were his experiences at school, "a sombre grey patch upon the chart of my journey." Befuddled by Latin, mystified by mathematics, no good at cricket, frequently beaten, he developed a stammer and was rated dead last in his class.

But he was fond of playing with toy soldiers. His father, certain that his talentless son couldn't get into Oxford or Cambridge, therefore slated him for a military career on the grounds that he might gain admission to a military academy. He was right, but just barely. Churchill took the entrance examination three times before he made the grade—and even then, it was a low pass. Yet once he was enrolled, he blossomed. Fascinated by war both as a subject worthy of study and as an experience he longed to acquire, he graduated 20th out of 130 students. Shortly thereafter, his father died. Two months later, Churchill went to war—one war after another.

A Hero with Promise

When he couldn't go as a soldier, he wangled newspaper assignments and went as a journalist. In that manner, he traveled to Cuba, where a rebellion against Spain was in progress; to India, where he was nearly killed in the bloody Frontier War; and to the Sudan and Egypt, where he rode with British and Egyptian troops against the dervishes. Upon returning from Egypt, he ran unsuccessfully for Parliament as a Conservative.

Afterward, he traveled to South Africa to write about the Boer War. In a dramatic series of events, he was captured in a train wreck and imprisoned in Pretoria. One moonless night, he escaped. After hiding in a mine shaft and traveling under a tarpaulin on a freight train, he arrived in Durban and was hailed as a national hero for the first time. Back in England, throngs of flag-waving, drumbeating citizens cheered him in the streets.

Throughout this period, he was a prolific writer. He even wrote a novel, which a reviewer described as "rapid and thrilling, and crammed with fighting." Yet he hankered after the political life and decided to run for Parliament once more. This time he won. Afterward he went on a lecture tour in the United States and was introduced by Mark Twain as "the hero of five wars, the author of six books, and the future Prime Minister of Great Britain." He was 26 years old.

Gallipoli and Other Disasters

Over the next six decades, Churchill would learn what it meant to be both beloved and reviled. Throughout his life, he was in and out of office. He held many posts and switched parties many times. But with his vast self-assurance and rhetorical flair, he was never entirely forgotten.

In 1911, as first lord of the admiralty, he built up his country's navy. But in World War I, Churchill made a tactical error. After Turkey entered the war on the side of Germany, he became convinced that a British assault on the Turkish port of Gallipoli would convince other countries to align with Great Britain. The attack was launched. But for reasons that were not entirely his fault, it was a fiasco. In 1915, Churchill resigned in disgrace.

Six months later, he rejoined the army, although he was still a member of Parliament. He spent time in the trenches and was given command of the Sixth Royal Scots Fusiliers. By 1917, his political career was back on track. In fairly quick succession, he was appointed minister of munitions, minister of war, and secretary for the colonies. He had bounced back.

But in June 1921, Churchill's sixty-seven-year-old mother died, leaving behind a husband twenty-three years her junior. Two months later, his two-year-old daughter, Marigold, died of meningitis. When he ran for election in 1922, the political tide had turned—and just when he should have been campaigning, he needed an emergency appendectomy. After he lost the election, he said, "I am without an office, without a seat [in Parliament] . . . and without an appendix."

Forcibly retired, Churchill bought enviable real estate; painted (a lifelong hobby); gardened; collected exotic butterflies; learned to lay bricks (and joined the bricklayer's union); began writing *The World Crisis,* a six-volume history of the war; and ran for public office. He lost repeatedly.

On the fourth try, he was elected to the House of Commons. On the ascendancy again, he was appointed chancellor of the exchequer. In addition to reducing income taxes and introducing pensions for widows and orphans, he returned England to the gold standard. That disastrous mistake led to a general strike, which he helped break. His pattern of great successes and terrible failures was set.

In 1929, he lost his cabinet post. Although still a member of Parliament, he was effectively marginalized for ten years. Jeered at and shouted down in Parliament for even the mildest of statements, he was convinced that, as a politician, he was finished.

Winston Is Back!

With the hindsight of history, we can see it coming: a wartime performance so exceptional that he would be hailed as "the greatest Englishman of our time" and even the "Man of the Century."

That's not how it seemed at the time. In 1938, Churchill was on the verge of bankruptcy. His constituents tried to throw him out of the House of Commons. And his warnings about Germany went unheeded. Prime Minister Neville Chamberlain, a proponent of appeasement, rejected Churchill's suggestion that Great Britain band together with other nations to confront the Nazi threat. Instead, in September 1938, Chamberlain signed the infamous Munich agreement, handing Czechoslovakia to the Nazis. "The whole equilibrium of Europe has been deranged," Churchill said in an address to the House of Commons. ". . . And do not suppose that this is the end. This is only the beginning of the reckoning. This is only the first sip, the first foretaste of a bitter cup that will be preferred to us year by year unless, by a supreme recovery of moral health and martial vigor, we arise again and take our stand for freedom as in the olden time."

Hitler invaded Poland on September 1, 1939. Two days later, Britain declared war and Chamberlain returned Churchill to his old post, First Lord of the Admiralty. The Board of Admiralty signaled the news to its ships around the world with a simple message: "Winston is back!"

In May 1940, Hitler invaded France and the Low Countries. Chamberlain resigned and Churchill finally gained the job he had wanted most of his life: prime minister. Three days after being appointed, Churchill addressed the House of Commons. "I have nothing to offer but blood, toil, tears and sweat." The members of Parliament rose to their feet and cheered.

After years in political exile, Churchill felt "a profound sense of relief . . . as if I were walking with Destiny, and that all my past life had been but a preparation for this hour and for this trial. . . ."

His Finest Hour

Although there was reason for pessimism in 1940, Churchill's magnificent oratory braced the people to accept nothing less than victory. In his first broadcast as prime minister, he warned them that ". . . the long night of barbarism will descend, unbroken by even a star of hope, unless we conquer, as conquer we must, as conquer we shall."

The German threat was formidable. Belgium surrendered, then France. When the Nazis started to bomb London, Churchill prophesied more hardship to come. Yet his immutable presence fortified the spirit of soldiers and civilians alike. Throughout the Battle of Britain, he was visible, flashing the V sign and visiting bomb sites and fires, often with a crowd of journalists and even his wife, Clementine, in tow. He was adored. A general who accompanied Churchill one day recounted this scene in a letter to him: "At one of the rest centres at which you called, there was a poor old woman who had lost all her belongings sobbing her heart out. But as you entered, she took her handkerchief from her eyes and waved it madly, shouting, 'Hooray, hooray.'"

His unwavering message was clear: "We shall never turn from our purpose, however somber the road, however grievous the cost, because we know that out of this time of trial and tribulation will be born a new freedom and glory for all mankind."

Politically and militarily, Churchill made plenty of miscalculations. But unlike Chamberlain, who thought that Hitler could be reasoned with, Churchill understood that Hitler was a madman who was to be resisted in every way. He demanded unconditional surrender. His intransigence was restorative. And his language dazzled. As the newscaster Edward R. Murrow said, he "mobilized the English language and sent it into battle."

After the attack on Pearl Harbor in December 1941, the United States joined the war, to Churchill's joy. "So we had won after all! . . ." he later wrote, remembering his reaction. "Hitler's fate was sealed. Mussolini's fate was sealed. . . ." In thought if not in deed, the crisis was over, the victory assured.

And so, imperceptibly, Churchill's heroic moment passed. In 1943, he met with Roosevelt and Stalin, who suggested that once victory was achieved, it would be smart to shoot fifty thousand Germans. Churchill explained that mass executions would not fly in Britain and would "sully my own and my country's honor."

As 1943 faded into 1944, Churchill contracted a bad case of pneumonia and had a heart attack. Forced to rest, he was back in shape by June 1944, when the Normandy invasion began. By war's end in Europe, eleven months later, he was riding high.

Anticlimax and Reversal

Still, in July 1945, the Labour Party handily defeated the Conservatives and Churchill was thrown out of office. For six years, he was leader of the Opposition as well as a world leader. He argued in favor of European unity and, in a speech in Missouri, coined the phrase "Iron Curtain." Then in 1951, he again became prime minister. In 1953, he was knighted and he won the Nobel Prize for Literature. (Among his multivolume works are histories of both world wars, a biography of his father, and *A History of the English-Speaking Peoples,* completed in 1954.) He also had a serious stroke.

In 1955, he was forced to retire as prime minister. During the last ten years of his life, he painted, bred racehorses, socialized with his wealthy friend Aristotle Onassis, and worried about his legacy. He died on January 24, 1965, at age ninety. Charles de Gaulle, when he heard the news, is said to have lamented, "Now Britain is no longer a great power."

"A hero cannot be a hero unless in a heroic world," wrote Nathaniel Hawthorne. With his actions and even more, with his words, Churchill helped create such a world, for those who listened to him found wellsprings of fortitude they didn't know they had—and so became heroic.

And that, my friends, is one reason why we won the war.

HEROISM IN JOURNALISM

In the spring of 2003, when journalists were volunteering to travel with military troops in Iraq in order to report from the front lines, I asked the editor of a major urban daily if he thought there were any heroic journalists out there. "Not that I know of," he said. "It's our job to go into those kinds of situations. Simply performing one's duty and performing one's job to me doesn't qualify as heroism."

I disagree, as does Steve Forbes. He spoke about two heroic reporters who volunteered to travel with the army's Third Infantry Division in the latest Iraq war: David Bloom of NBC television and Michael Kelly, an editor and columnist who covered the Persian Gulf War in the 1991. Deciding to go to war was a fatal decision for both. "David Bloom could have easily stayed behind or followed at a safe distance," Forbes told me. "Instead, not only was he embedded, he went with a division that was potentially going to be in the thick of it."

The same was true of Kelly. "He was a superb journalist and a successful editor," Forbes said. "He knew full well what the nature of the enemy was. It wasn't a matter of youthful ignorance. And yet he didn't hesitate to go right over there."

After their deaths, Bloom and Kelly were praised. But not every journalist who went to Iraq was lionized. Take Peter Arnett. His fearless reports from Baghdad during the first Bush administration made the Persian Gulf War real to many Americans. Twelve years later, he announced on Iraqi television that "the American war planners misjudged the determination of Iraqi forces." Not only did NBC fire him, he was unfairly denounced by a senator for "aiding and abetting the Iraqi government during a war." Yesterday's hero; today's traitor. Lest anyone forget, heroism can be a fleeting thing—especially for those who do not die.

For those who do, their heroism becomes their legacy. That is certainly the case with Steve Forbes's World War II hero Ernie Pyle, the most famous war correspondent of his day. The original embedded journalist, he championed the American G.I. but never glorified war. He was so famous that in the midst of the war, Hollywood made a movie about him. *The Story of G.I. Joe,* starring Burgess Meredith as Ernie Pyle and Robert Mitchum as a hard-boiled captain with a heart of gold, was nominated for four Oscars in 1945. I'm sorry to report that the film does not hold up. The reporting does. Here's why:

ERNIE PYLE
The Worm's-Eye View

Beloved journalist: To a contemporary ear, that phrase sounds oxymoronic. But Ernie Pyle was beloved. When he was killed by Japanese machine-gun fire six days after Franklin Roosevelt's death, headlines blared forth the news. "The nation is quickly saddened again, by the death of Ernie Pyle," said President Harry S. Truman. "No man in this war has so well told the story of the American fighting man as American fighting men wanted it told."

But let's not commit the sin of hagiography (or, in any case, let's not commit it too frequently). Ernie Pyle was far from perfect. He was a complainer and a hypochondriac who suffered from a slew of ailments that included stomach spasms, low blood pressure, anemia, blurry vision, and impotence—not to mention self-pity and depression. He drank too much and once posed for a cigarette advertisement, a misstep he came to regret. He was an unfaithful husband who divorced his suicidal wife, he claimed, in an effort to shock her out of depression. (In his defense, he missed her terribly and soon remarried her, albeit by proxy from Africa.) Despite all his flaws, World War II brought out the best in him.

Born in 1900, he was a shy farm boy, "puny" and "no good at games" by his own admission. Afflicted with a lifelong case of wanderlust, he studied journalism at Indiana University but dropped out a semester short of a degree when he landed a job at a local paper. His first editor found him "bashful and unimpressive" and noted that he "didn't look like a newspaper man." Ernie turned his opinion around by infiltrating a Ku Klux Klan rally and, despite threats, publishing his accurate report. Four months later, he was offered a job at a Scripps-Howard tabloid in Washington, D.C. He worked there for the next few years.

He also wrote an aviation column, an idea he proposed in 1928, less than a year after Lindbergh's celebrated flight over the Atlantic. The column, a great success, presaged his later achievements. In it, he expressed his admiration for ordinary pilots, such as the ones who delivered the mail, in preference to celebrities like Lindbergh. The ordinary pilots reciprocated by funneling the news to him. It wasn't long before he knew everything and everybody. "Not to know Ernie Pyle," said Amelia Earhart, "is to admit that you yourself are unknown in aviation."

In 1932, he reluctantly accepted a position as managing editor of the paper, a job at which he was skilled but miserable. "For Christ's sake, don't ever let 'em make you editor of a newspaper," he wrote a friend. "It's a short-cut to insanity."

Worn out after three years, he and his witty, bohemian wife, Jerry, took a leisurely drive around the country. Back in Washington, he wrote a series of articles about this trip. To the editor-in-chief of Scripps-Howard, they were reminiscent of Mark Twain. Soon Ernie had his dream job: roving reporter.

For seven years, during some of which the Pyles literally did not have a home, Ernie wrote six columns a week. He would drive around for a few days with his wife, who came to be known as "That Girl," then hole up in a hotel room to write several columns at once. Thus he gained a following and entered the consciousness of the nation. Like Studs Terkel, he interviewed all kinds of people from lepers and death row inmates on up. He presented himself as a little guy, a man of the people, but his stories weren't political. They were compassionate, reassuring, honest, intimate. Teenagers loved him. Old people loved him. Everyone felt that they knew him.

But he was worn out, and his alcoholic, melancholic, drug-abusing wife was in perpetual crisis. In 1940, in despair over their marriage, the Pyles moved to Albuquerque and built a house with a white picket fence overlooking the Rio Grande. Jerry settled in. Ernie took off for England and the Battle of Britain.

During the next two years, while continuing to write his column, he divorced Jerry, committed her to a sanitarium in Colorado, returned overseas, joined an infantry troop in Algiers, and then remarried by proxy.

In describing the everyday events of wartime, Ernie Pyle took as his point of reference the ordinary soldier. His portraits were not composites. He named names and gave addresses. "Sergeant James Bernett, 1541 Cheyenne Street, Tulsa, Oklahoma, was driving our jeep . . . ," he wrote. When a false alarm forced Bernett to slam on the brakes, catapulting another soldier out of the jeep and onto the gravel, "Sergeant Bernett and I got the snickers. That can happen sometimes when a person is pitifully cold and also wonderfully relieved. We couldn't keep from laughing . . ."

He wrote about loneliness and despair and fear, about killing and about corpses. His dispatches, collected into a volume entitled *This Is Your War,* became a best seller and won a Pulitzer Prize. Not only was he rich, he was famous, a state he thoroughly enjoyed ("When you hit a point where you're recognized every time you step out, you can't help but feel sort of sparkly inside . . ."). He continued to follow the troops.

He was at Anzio and Saint-Lô, at Normandy the day after the invasion, and in Paris on the day of its liberation. He loved the army, and yet he didn't romanticize it. And he didn't turn from the awfulness of war. He wrote about mistakes. He was once bombed by our own troops in an instance of friendly fire. He knew what it meant to be in a bombing raid, and he confided to a friend that if it ever happened again, he thought he would lose his mind.

He also celebrated moments of fraternity. He could bring a lump to your throat, yet you didn't feel manipulated. You felt that he was simply telling you the truth. He made the war so real that some of his columns—op-ed, by today's standards—ran on the front page.

"I never heard anybody say anything patriotic like the storybooks have people saying," he wrote. But he thought he detected among the soldiers a "plain, ordinary, unspoken, even unrecognized, patriotism." He also described the way war wearied the spirit. "For me," he wrote, "war has become a flat, black depression with highlights, a revulsion of the mind and an exhaustion of the spirit."

In September 1944, he returned home. He didn't stay long. Weary though he was, he felt that he had to report on the war in the Pacific. But he had an ominous feeling about it. "You begin to feel that you can't go on forever without being hit," he told an interviewer. "I feel that I've used up all my chances. And I hate it."

He thought that, compared to the men in the foxholes, the sailors led a cushy life, and he said as much. Not surprisingly, his reports from the Pacific did not go over well. "Sometimes I get so sad and despairing and homesick I can hardly keep from crying," he wrote to a friend. On April 18, 1945, Ernie Pyle was killed on a small island four miles west of Okinawa. He was buried there among other American soldiers. "That Girl" caught a severe case of flu and died seven months later.

His legacy is a peculiar one. He made the grinding "dailiness" of war a reality. His war was more gritty than glorious, more personal than tactical, more dispiriting than inspiring. Yet even as he explored the ambiguities of war, he made ordinary foot soldiers into heroes. His work, wrote the poet Randall Jarrell in 1945, was "an unprecedented aesthetic triumph. Because of it, most of the people in the country felt, in the fullest moral and emotional sense, something that had never happened to them, that they could never have imagined without it—a war."

To somebody in my business, Ernie Pyle is also important for another reason. He epitomized the concept of "propaganda"—a word that has become pejorative. I use that term in its original, positive sense. Propaganda is the way we wage a war of ideas. It is the way we talk up democracy, and it is the way we make the freedoms we value appealing rather than threatening. To many Americans, the desirability of our way of life seems obvious. But as Ernie Pyle understood, not everyone sees things the way we do. Strange as it may seem, totalitarianism has its appeal. Here's Ernie in North Africa in 1942:

The German propaganda here had been expert. The people had been convinced that Germany would win.... German propaganda had also drilled into them the glories of the New Order. Those people believed that life for them under German control would be milk and honey, perpetual security and prosperity. They really believed it. Also, our troops made a poor impression, in contrast to the few Germans they had seen. We admittedly are not rigid-minded people. Our army didn't have the strict and snappy discipline of the Germans. Our boys sang in the streets, unbuttoned their shirt collars, laughed and shouted, and forgot to salute. A lot of Algerians misinterpreted this as inefficiency. They thought such a carefree army couldn't possibly whip the grim Germans.... The Algerians couldn't conceive of the fact that our strength lay in our freedom.

The biggest challenge facing us today is the relationship between the Islamic world and the rest of the world. If we want to deal with the Islamic people, we have to understand the richness of their tradition. And then we have to go to the Ernie Pyles of today and find a way to communicate the wonder of our culture. Who are the Ernie Pyles of today? They are broadcast journalists and moviemakers and information technologists. Let's call on them to infuse our values into movies, into video games, into television and radio broadcasts. Let's make our way of life attractive—not in the phony, off-putting *Baywatch* sense, but in the profound way. That's how we can solve the problem that threatens to divide and destroy our world.

Ernie Pyle's Heroes

In addition to the everyday soldiers he honored in his column, Ernie Pyle had other heroes, most of whom were men of action. Among them were ...

• Race Car Drivers: "I would rather win that five-hundred-mile race than anything in this world," he said at

age thirty-six. After describing the longed-for sensation of winning the Indianapolis 500 in riveting sensory detail, he admitted, "I have dreamed of myself in that role a thousand times."

• Generals: "If I could pick any two men in the world for my father except my own dad, I would pick General Omar Bradley or General Ike Eisenhower," he wrote. He described them as "doubly great because they are direct and kind."

• Pulitzer prize–winning journalist Kirke Simpson, whose 1921 article about the Tomb of the Unknown Soldier at Arlington National Cemetery brought tears to Ernie's eyes. He considered that story a model of good writing, and years later, he was still quoting from it.

ONE MORE WRITER

Ask the editor of a magazine about his heroes and you are bound to hear about writers. Another one that Steve Forbes named was the journalist Theodore H. White. I became aware of him when I read *The Making of the President 1960.* That absorbing book, the first in a series, revealed the underside of a presidential campaign in a way that had never been done. But was writing it an act of heroism? Steve Forbes asserts that it was:

SF: Theodore White invented the genre of reporting not just on the campaign but on what went on behind the scenes. It was a heroic act because, when he started, no one thought this project would work. So he put his savings into it and went out with the candidates on his own. At the time, you might get local reporters to do that, you might even get an occasional national reporter, but, by and large, the coverage was episodic. That isn't the way White did it. He would go everywhere, wherever the campaign took him. Regular reporters thought he was nuts because he wasn't writing for a daily paper. In Manhattan, people felt sorry for him. He had a dirty raincoat and a stubby pencil. He was taking notes constantly and pursuing stories long after deadline. People thought the poor guy was going off on a tangent. No one could conceive of what he had in mind or where it would go. He had a vision that no one else shared.

White's book opened the door on something that had been hidden. He invented a new kind of political journalism and made a major contribution to the national understanding. And he did it on his own, fueled by nothing but the condescending pity of others. Definitely heroic.

A FINAL WORD

It occasionally seems to me that the only people who are not worried are those who don't follow the news. Forbes agreed with me that these are terrifying times. But he put it into perspective:

SF: These are times of peril, but we've had them before. In the last century, we had the two world wars, the Great Depression, the turmoil of the sixties, many periods of what the Chinese called interesting times. We're in one now in which we have to play a global role that is very different from what we were accustomed to during the Cold War. In retrospect, the nineties were, as some have pointed out, a holiday from history. Now we've learned once again that human nature has not changed, that evil still exists, and that there are those who wish us ill and want to destroy what we are.

RD: What can we do? How can ordinary people respond to that?

SF: By recognizing and nurturing our basic values and principles. These include the ideas that we're on this earth for a higher purpose; that there is right and wrong; that you try to do right even if no one is looking; that you try to develop inner strength. The key lies in the seemingly mundane things we do each day. These habits may look utterly unheroic, but they provide continuity and they prepare others—i.e., our youngsters—for the future. Then, when you get a crisis such as September 11, you get a stirring and positive response.

That's precisely what happened. People responded unselfishly. Without a doubt, that's one measure of heroism.

CHAPTER 5

A Conversation With
JOHN HAMRE

On Lenny Skutnik, John Glenn, and Others

Some people, I have observed, conceive of heroism in a distant, almost romantic way. Their heroes tend to be glamorous figures from history or literature—Napoleon or Robin Hood—bathed in the golden light of the past.

Other people, awash in cynicism or simply all too aware that to err is human, claim to have no heroes at all. For them, every flaw is fatal.

And then there are people who find heroism all around them. They see it in their parents and they see it in the paper boy. Their form of heroism is arguably a little mundane. But it is never distant. For these lucky people, heroism suffuses their world. They find it wherever they go.

John Hamre is such a person. He is president and CEO of the Center for Strategic and International Studies (CSIS), a bipartisan think tank that collaborates with organizations from around the world to address international issues involving security, technology, trade, finance, and energy.

Dr. Hamre studied at the Harvard Divinity School but received his doctorate in international politics, economics, and U.S. foreign policy from the School of Advanced International Studies, Johns Hopkins University. Afterward, he worked in the Congressional Budget Office (CBO), where he focused on national security and international affairs. He then became a staff member of the Senate Armed Forces Committee, a position he held for ten years. In 1993, he was appointed undersecretary of defense (comptroller), and in 1997, he became the twenty-sixth U.S. deputy secretary of defense. He joined CSIS in 2000.

Like many people I spoke with, Dr. Hamre chose his heroes from the ranks of people he actually knew. I asked him why. "A hero isn't a remote figure to me," he said. "It isn't somebody who is reported to have done a great deed. It's someone I know. There's no question that there are other heroes. I just don't know them."

One of the first heroes he mentioned was someone I had forgotten, although he certainly had his fifteen minutes. The very opposite of a mover-and-shaker, he worked in the CBO, as did Dr. Hamre. His name was . . .

LENNY SKUTNIK
Everyman

January 1982. Air Florida Flight 90, a Boeing 737 with ice on its wings, took off from National Airport in Washington, D.C., in the midst of a snowstorm. Moments later, it hit a span of the 14th Street Bridge and crashed, nose down, into the frozen waters of the Potomac River. Most of the passengers died instantly. A few survived, flailing about in the water and clinging desperately to parts of the tail.

As passersby gathered on the nearby bridge, rescuers went into action. Firemen on rubber rafts tried to pull the passengers from the water. Rescue workers in helicopters lowered long ropes to them in hopes of lifting them out of the water. One passenger, so benumbed by the cold that her fingers could not clasp the rope, was balanced precariously on a ragged chunk of ice. The helicopter pilot lowered the rope to her again and again, but she was too weak on hold on.

After several attempts, she began to slip off the ice into the river. She was screaming. It was obvious that she could easily die.

And she might have. But one of the passersby had a better idea. Lenny Skutnik, a twenty-eight-year-old clerk in the CBO, imagined that she might be saved. Throwing off his coat, he leaped into the river, grabbed her, and swam to safety.

The story made the news that night, the one bright moment in what otherwise would have been a total tragedy. His story, which President Reagan cited in his State of the Union address a few days later, was all the more moving because Lenny had no particular credentials. He wasn't an athlete or a doctor or an off-duty cop. He was a clerk, earning fourteen thousand dollars a year. He was Everyman. The message was clear: if he could rise above his everyday concerns in such an astounding way, well, you could too.

Like all heroes, Lenny Skutnik possessed an unusual combination of selflessness and daring that enabled him to act when people all around him were immobilized. Why did he do it? His explanation was simple. "I believe it's human instinct," he said. "I knew she wasn't going to make it, so I dove in." Although he may have looked unremarkable, he harbored within himself the most noble of human virtues and was, in fact, extraordinary.

In his book *Lives of Moral Leadership*, the psychiatrist Robert Coles wrote, "We need heroes, people who can inspire us, help shape us morally, spur us on to purposeful action—and from time to time we are called on to be those heroes . . . either in a small, day-to-day way, or on the world's larger stage." Lenny Skutnik heard that call. The enormous publicity that briefly swirled around him was a recognition of that fact.

The Dangerous Side Effects of Becoming a Hero

I know nothing about Lenny Skutnik's life beyond what I have reported here, except that I believe he still works for the CBO. If that's true, he's a lucky man. Because heroes, at least those who are elevated by the media into instant celebrities, sometimes suffer from tragic fates.

Take Bob Long, the engineer who helped rescue nine miners who were trapped underground in July 2002. CNN called him "the man behind the miracle."

Or Robert O'Donnell, the paramedic who was catapulted to fame when he rescued Baby Jessica from a mine shaft in 1987.

Or Terry Yeakey, a policeman who rescued four people when the federal building in Oklahoma City was bombed in 1995.

All three men were acclaimed as heroes. And all three men ultimately committed suicide. It's not easy to be a hero. Few people feel that they deserve the title. Add to that the disruptive effects of fame, which can stir up resentment from others and which can disappear as suddenly as it came, and the post-traumatic stress disorder that often accompanies catastrophic experiences, and you've got a recipe for disaster.

None of that made a major impact on Lenny Skutnik. He went on with his life.

THE PROFESSOR

Another one of John Hamre's heroes was Alfred J. Hotz, his political science professor at Augustana College in Sioux Falls, South Dakota. "He was a hero to me. He was the most creative and dynamic professor I ever had. He was a consultant to the State Department on international relations and he inspired me dramatically," Dr. Hamre told me.

"How?" I asked.

"He saw the potential in me and in my fellow students and he found a way to reach into us to make us bigger than we were."

That ability is a crucial part of the hero's arsenal. The best teachers are heroic not because they sacrifice themselves but because they help their students to become bigger people and to participate in a larger world.

My graduate school advisor, Walter Siefert, did that for me. He showed me that life could be bigger than I had imagined, and that I could bring more to the party by developing my skills. He not only encouraged me, he provided a vision that I was able to follow. For me, he was a hero—the proverbial Mr. Chips.

I'd like to imagine that there's a Mr. Chips in everybody's life, but I know too much about our beleaguered educational system to believe that. Still, I think it's worthwhile to look for a Mr. Chips. It's even more meaningful to become a Mr. Chips, perhaps by participating in a tutoring, literacy, or mentoring program. It's a simple way to be a hero—and you don't have to jump into an icy river to do it.

ON THE NATURE OF HEROISM

What finally makes a hero? Here's John Hamre:

JH: A hero is somebody who's not just brave but wise. A lot of people in the world are wise enough to know what should be done but they don't have the courage to do it. A lot of brave people have confidence and daring, but without wisdom, their courage isn't necessarily meaningful. It's a rare combination that you're looking for.

It also seems to me that heroes never think of themselves as heroes. They see themselves as having an obligation to accomplish good things for others. Heroes genuinely honor the dignity in others. They implicitly ask us to rise above ourselves and to envision a larger reality. Even in Lenny Skutnik, there's a sense of that. Heroes have vision.

That vision is always a positive one, for heroes imagine a better world—and they see untapped potential everywhere. They fill us with confidence and hope because they don't fear the future.

Consider, for instance, the astronaut John Glenn, who became the first American to orbit earth in 1962. Several people, including John Hamre, named him as a hero. I met John Glenn years ago, when I was working with NASA's public information program. Glenn was one of the first seven astronauts. The public loved him. The men in the space program did not. They ostracized him. They perceived him as a goody two-shoes because Glenn did everything by the book. Glenn didn't womanize; he didn't drink; he didn't play practical jokes. Glenn was there to get us into space. He played the game straight.

But that is not what makes him a hero. He is a hero because he risked his life to do something worthwhile that had never been attempted before, and in the process he opened up cosmic vistas for us all.

After that first flight into space, John Glenn was lionized. When Time magazine featured a cover story about his historic flight, they called him "a latter-day Apollo." But as the article pointed out in a quote from Rodgers and Hammerstein, he was also "as normal as blueberry pie." Here's his story:

JOHN GLENN

He grew up in New Concord, Ohio, in a childhood he himself describes as right out of a Norman Rockwell painting. His father was a plumber, car salesman, and World War I veteran who played taps during Decoration Day ceremonies. He also gave Glenn, as he explains in his memoir, a "sense of unbounded possibility" and an "eagerness to experiment."

One day when Glenn was eight years old, his father treated him to an airplane ride. After that, Glenn longed to learn how to fly. World War II provided the opportunity.

As a marine, he flew fifty-eight combat missions, followed a few years later by more missions over Korea. Afterward, he became a record-breaking test pilot. In 1959, he became an astronaut.

His first heroic moment—but not his last—came on February 20, 1962, when he orbited the earth three times in the United States' first manned orbital mission. Today, we remember *Apollo 13*'s voyage to the moon as the most suspenseful space mission. But Glenn's trip in the *Friendship 7* was also fraught with danger, due to wandering gyroscopes and a fiberglass heat shield that threatened to detach itself in orbit. That didn't happen. Glenn piloted the ship manually while pieces of the heat shield whizzed past his window in flames.

His safe landing was celebrated around the world. In Washington, he was asked to speak to a joint session of Congress. Vice President Lyndon B. Johnson, eager to impress on him the nature of the privilege, said, "Usually the honor is reserved for heads of state, but in this case the whole country elected you."

When his friend Bobby Kennedy asked him to run for the Senate from Ohio, Glenn said no. He wanted to return to space. President Kennedy's assassination in November 1963 made Glenn rethink his decision. A few weeks later, in January 1964, he announced that he was seeking the Democratic nomination for the U.S. Senate.

He was prevented from achieving his ambition by a banal bathroom accident. While trying to fix a heavy mirror, he slipped on a tile, hit his head, and blacked out for a couple of minutes. The vertigo that followed forced him to drop out of the race. In 1970, he ran again but lost in the primary.

Finally, in 1974, John Glenn was elected to the U.S. Senate. Although his presidential hopes were dashed in 1984, he served in Congress for four terms and was an excellent senator. Among his other accomplishments, he fought against nuclear proliferation and was a member of the Special Committee on Aging.

Which is not to say that Glenn was perfect. Along with four other senators collectively known as the Keating Five, he was investigated by the Senate Ethics Committee for his role in a savings-and-loan scandal of the late 1980s. He emerged slightly tarnished but was reelected.

His most valiant moment was yet to come. In 1998, after several years of lobbying on his own behalf, John Glenn returned to space for nine days to help determine the effect of space flight on the elderly. He was seventy-seven years old. Although he was roundly mocked for his efforts, he was also widely admired. A pioneer in space, he became a pioneer of aging as well as a hero for anyone who has ever struggled with the concept of growing old.

And if his flight fulfilled a personal goal, it also symbolized something greater: a future in space exploration for people of all ages. His flight was not just heroic; it was visionary.

OTHER HEROIC SENATORS

Being a senator is definitely a heroic job. Of course, some senators are more heroic than others. In addition to John Glenn, Dr. Hamre named three others:

• Ted Stevens, the Republican senator from Alaska

• John Warner, the Virginia Republican who refused to support Oliver North when he ran for public office because he objected, in Dr. Hamre's words, to "the way Ollie North participated in the near subversion of the Constitution when he was working for President Reagan"

• Barry Goldwater, Republican from Arizona. "He was guided by a consistent philosophy and he was just as heroic standing up against dumb ideas coming from his own party as he was from the opposition. Too many politicians are always calculating the political advantage from their comments. Barry Goldwater was not like that," Dr. Hamre said. "It was Barry Goldwater who basically said that the Republican Party ought to lay off gay bashing. That was typical Barry Goldwater. He spoke with honesty and objectivity. He was a man who had a consistent vision."

THE VISION THING

Every once in a while, a person comes along who has the ability to create a vision and to induce people to follow him. Christ created a vision. Moses created a vision. Mohammed created a vision.

Politicians also need to create a vision. Without it, they are nothing more than functionaries. But creating a vision and getting people to follow you is not enough. After all, Hitler created a vision. So did Stalin. So did Osama bin Laden and Saddam Hussein. Those men are amoral and depraved—the polar opposite of heroic, by our standards. But each one had a vision. And each one had enough charisma—or brute force—to convince people to follow him.

To be a hero, then, a visionary must also possess a moral compass and an innate sense of compassion. Otherwise, a vision can be dangerous. The history of the twentieth century is replete with examples.

But a vision can fade. Edwin Land invented the Polaroid camera. What a commotion that device created when it debuted! It's hard to imagine today how miraculous the Polaroid seemed then. But when

Land died, the people who came behind him couldn't sustain his vision. The company still exists, but the innovation and excitement disappeared.

That didn't have to happen. A hero, somebody with ideas and wisdom and energy, needed to step forward to renew that vision. No one did.

A FINAL WORD

"As I grow older," wrote the essayist Joseph Epstein, "I find that I am simultaneously less trustful of heroes and increasingly in need of them. To worship false heroes is quite as foolish as worshipping false gods. . . . On the other hand, true heroes remind me of life's possibilities—of how difficulties can be overcome, of how often perseverance pays off, of how without integrity self-disgust becomes one's regular companion, of how lovely life can be when fear is conquered. . . ."

You can't reach my age—let's just say that AARP has been onto me for a while—without having been disappointed more than once by would-be heroes. But I've also learned that, while no one can be a hero all the time, true heroes maintain their vision and are sustained by it. Their failures along the way only spur them on to greater achievements.

CHAPTER 6

ON HOW TO BE A HEROIC BOSS

Not many people I spoke with listed their bosses as their heroes. John Hamre mentioned two: Bill Perry, Secretary of Defense during the Clinton administration, and Senator Sam Nunn. He named them, he said, because each had the ability to form a cohesive team and to create synergy. Their styles may have been different but they stimulated those who worked with them to do their own best work.

"There are people in life who want weak people around them so they can look better than they are. Not these guys," Dr. Hamre said. "They wanted the strongest people they could possibly get around them. They each created an operating environment that was truly wonderful. I consider that heroic."

So do I. Anyone who is a boss has the opportunity to open doors for his or her employees and to challenge them to excel. But most bosses are blind to the opportunities before them and are simply not up to the task. Bringing out the potential in their employees takes self-confidence, which CEOs generally have in abundance. But it also takes imagination and generosity of spirit, which is woefully insufficient in the business community.

How can you be a heroic boss? You can't do it if you're making an enormous salary while nickel-and-diming your employees. You can't take away all hope for advancement—or boot out older employees once they actually start to use their medical insurance—and think that better parking privileges will make up for it. People aren't stupid.

Although being heroic means one thing if you're the CEO of a Fortune 500 corporation and another if you run an ice cream shop, the basic challenge is the same. If you're a boss, you have to balance your own interests with those of the organization and those of the employees. None of those interests may be congruent. Yet the goals of the organization and of the individual boss can only be achieved if the employees are with you.

The heroic boss does it all by helping the employees rise to the highest level possible. Here are a few ways to do that:

- Do what is right. People respect people who know what's ethical and act accordingly. They don't respect people who don't.

- Be transparent. Let people know as much as you can about your feelings, your views, and your attitudes toward the organization, the workers, the customers, and the processes you use. You may not be happy with everything on that list, and you may have the intention of changing some of them. That's fine. Don't keep it a secret.

- Be compassionate. Understand that as the boss you have many privileges, including an income that is significantly larger than that of your employees. They face challenges, pressures, and tensions that are unlike yours. Your task is to understand this. If you do, you'll be compassionate toward them. And if you're compassionate toward them, they'll recognize that and you'll get a better result.

- Be generous—and I'm not necessarily talking about money. We all know close-minded, narrow people who never let you in on things, who husband information and contacts, who make you feel small. Don't be like that. Demonstrate that you are neither small-minded nor fearful by sharing information—and by putting other people's agendas ahead of your own. As the boss, you have greater resources and more power. That gives you the ability to make a huge difference in the lives of others, often with relatively little effort. Take advantage of the opportunity to step outside of yourself and be a big person.

- Enlarge your goals. In virtually every undertaking, whether you're making an automobile or performing a service within a non-profit organization, you can create a heroic experience by enlarging your immediate goals. Your immediate goal might be selling shoes. Don't let that limit your vision. You can use that experience as a way to train young people, not just to sell shoes but to be successful in any organization. You can set up a mentoring program. You can direct a portion of the proceeds to charity. You can sponsor a volunteer program.

  By setting a goal that has a redeeming social feature to it and goes beyond the immediate objective of the business, you give your employees a chance to do something for others. At the same time, you turn an ordinary business, be it a shoe store or an international conglomerate, into a meaningful enterprise that does good in the world. That's the kind most people want to be involved with. Everyone wants to be part of a larger universe. As the boss, you can make it happen.

In tough economic times, being a heroic boss involves sacrifice. But there is much to be gained from making that sacrifice, and not just in the workplace. If the heroes who make the biggest impact are the ones who are near at hand, the boss is in a unique position to better the lives of a specific group of individuals and, by extension, to improve society. It is a hero's challenge.

CHAPTER 7

A Conversation With

ORRIN HATCH

*On Vernon Law, Irving Brown, Elizabeth Glaser,
and Others*

I am a pushover for an old-fashioned American success story. That is one of the reasons I like Orrin Hatch, Republican senator from Utah. His father was a hardworking union man, a metal lather who struggled to support nine children; his mother was an avid reader with an eighth-grade education who insisted that her son study music. It was a symbol of something better, a world of beauty away from want, but it was also an attainable reality. Despite their poverty, they shelled out $18.75 every year to buy Orrin a student pass to the Pittsburgh Symphony Orchestra. "I would go to every concert," Hatch told me. "It was an ordeal because I'd walk two miles, take a streetcar for forty-five minutes, and then walk back up to the Syria Mosque, sit in peanut heaven, listen to the concert, and reverse the process going home. I got home usually after midnight—and it was a very, very good thing for me."

Later on, Hatch worked as a janitor and a salesman to put himself through college. I like that. I like to think that even today it is possible for "a kid from the wrong side of the tracks," as Hatch has described himself, to rise to the highest level of government.

And I like the fact that he doesn't always hew to the party line. For instance, although he is strongly pro-life, he angered the anti-abortion establishment by coming out in favor of stem-cell research. And although he is well known as a conservative, he has from time to time collaborated with—and even befriended—überliberal senator Ted Kennedy. I admire that kind of flexibility. Democracy demands it.

Finally, I can't help admiring the fact that the Republican senator from the state of Utah is a songwriter with hundreds of songs and seven CDs to his credit. He has even had his compositions recorded by the likes of Donny Osmond and Gladys Knight, who pronounced Orrin Hatch an honorary Pip. As a seasoned PR man, I can tell you: That's the kind of honor money can't buy.

A Series of Heroes

And here's another interesting fact about Orrin Hatch: He has a wide array of heroes. Some matched my expectations. Some did not.

The former category includes his parents; his brother Jess, a World War II flyer who died in the bombing raid that destroyed the vital Ploesti oil fields in Romania; two women he knew growing up "who grandmothered me to death"; and a ballplayer and fellow Mormon he met as a teenager.

Hatch's heroes also include a labor leader, a Hollywood activist, and a trifecta of politicians, one of whom is a certified liberal.

What attributes do these disparate types have in common? One, I noticed, was that they were all people Orrin Hatch knew personally—starting with . . .

VERNON LAW
The Deacon

Imagine that you're a teenage boy (not a pleasant thought, I know). Now imagine that a major league ballplayer moves to town, attends your church, comes to your home for dinner, and starts spending enough time there to call your folks Mom and Pop. Unless that ballplayer is pretty low to the ground, he's going to become your hero.

That's what happened with sixteen-year-old Orrin Hatch and pitcher Vernon Law. One of a dozen children, Law was twelve years old when he became a deacon in the Church of Jesus Christ of Latter-day Saints. By eighteen, he was an experienced teacher, an ordained priest, and a married man. He was also such a gifted athlete that when Senator Herman Welcker of Idaho saw him pitch, he called his friend, Bing Crosby, part owner of the Pittsburgh Pirates, and convinced him that Vernon Law should join the team. In 1948, Vernon Law and his brother Evan became Buccaneers.

Two years later, he and his seventeen-year-old wife VaNita moved to Pittsburgh and met the Hatches. "We became instant friends," Hatch recalls.

Law was a fine ballplayer. His championship season was 1960, when he won two of the four games in the World Series against the Yankees and was given the Cy Young Award.

But it wasn't solely his athletic ability that made him a hero in Hatch's eyes. Law embodied the virtues that Hatch had been brought up to admire. He didn't smoke; he didn't drink; he didn't use foul language. In fact, Vernon Law was considered so straight-laced that he was once thrown out of a game in order to protect him from even hearing the salty language of the other players. Law kept a spiral notebook filled with inspirational quotes—"Words to Live By," he called it—and he was so devout that he would pray on the mound. His teammates called him Deacon.

"They respected him because of the way he lived," Hatch says. "Of course, he was a great athlete who kept himself in terrific condition at all times. He was such a fine, upstanding, solid, decent man that he was a great influence on me. He lived his religion and did all the things you expect a really good person to do. He set a good example for me and for hundreds of thousands of others as well."

Law retired in 1963 but returned the following year. In 1965, he received the Lou Gehrig Award for comeback player of the year. He retired permanently two years later.

Vernon and VaNita Law also raised six children: Veldon, Veryl, Vaughn, Varlin, VaLynda, and Vance, also a major league ballplayer.

Is Vernon Law a hero, then, or just a role model? In the literature of heroism, the difference between the two has been much debated. In real life, the distinction is vague at best, and perhaps irrelevant.

"When you're through learning, you're through."—VERNON LAW

The next hero Hatch told me about differed from Vernon Law in every respect but one: love of baseball. Hatch called him "one of the greatest heroes this country has ever had—and yet very few people know who he was." His name:

IRVING BROWN
The Scholar Pumpernickel

Before he became a conservative Republican, Orrin Hatch was a liberal Democrat. It makes sense that one of his heroes should be a man who made a similar journey. Irving Brown (1911–1989) was a labor leader and a Communist who ended up on the other end of the political spectrum and was awarded the Presidential Medal of Freedom by Ronald Reagan in 1988.

Nor is it entirely surprising that Hatch should name a labor leader as one of his heroes. True, the status of the labor movement is much diminished from what it once was. In the eyes of many, particularly on the ideological right, labor unions have become just another special interest group. But Orrin Hatch grew up in a union household. So although he may despair of the labor leaders of today, he also knows how important they can be.

But to describe Irving Brown as a labor leader fails to capture the wonder of the man, the breadth of his experience, or the significance of his work. He had a big grin; an expansive personality; endless energy; a love of adventure; a thorough appreciation of good food, good wine, and good conversation; and a knack for learning languages—a useful skill for a man who operated on the world stage, even if he did speak those languages with a Yiddish accent.

Born in 1911 in the Bronx, Irving Brown was the son of a Russian immigrant named Fannie and a milkman named Ralph, who held a minor position in the Milk Wagon Drivers Union. When he was twelve years old, the New York Yankees moved to the Bronx and Irving began to dream about becoming a third baseman. For a brief period, he even found a home in the minor leagues. But he turned in another direction. He went to NYU and in 1929 joined the Communist Party. He dropped out almost immediately when he learned that his mentor, Jay Lovestone, the head of the American Communist Party, had gone to Russia and been publicly denounced by Joseph Stalin.

Now, Lovestone was an interesting guy. A Lithuanian immigrant fourteen years older than Brown, he had been a committed Communist for ten years. After being expelled from Russia, he began to drift, first forming his own anti-Stalinist faction within the party and eventually becoming not just anti-Soviet, but anti-Communist. He ended up working with the International Ladies Garment Workers Union (the ILGWU) and the worldwide labor movement. His aim was to bring down the Soviet Union and to keep trade unions out of the hands of the Communists. His right-hand man was Irving Brown.

Over the years, Brown worked not only with Lovestone, but with George Meany, the AFL-CIO, and the CIA. During World War II, he worked undercover with the French resistance. After the war, he remained in France for seventeen years. It was his mission to prevent trade unions from being taken over by the Communists. He was particularly successful with the French dockworkers. This long struggle waged by the labor movement against the Communists was secret and fraught with danger (or, as Brown put it, "no *salon de thé*"—no tea party). His life was often in peril. Condemned on the right as a Communist sympathizer and on the left as a CIA stooge, he was frequently threatened and occasionally beaten, but he never lost faith in the importance of his work.

After the war, Brown and Lovestone formed the International Confederation of Free Trade Unionists, an anti-Communist group which in the fullness of time gave rise to the Solidarity movement in Poland. Brown became international vice president of the AFL-CIO in charge of foreign policy and chief United States representative to the International Labor Organization (ILO), a UN group. He also helped create the National Endowment for Democracy, which battled Soviet disinformation back in the days when the Soviet Union still existed and, since then, has done its bit to support pro-democratic forces.

And he did it all with panache. The *Reader's Digest* once described him as "an entire diplomatic corps and a one-man OSS." Indeed, he was so swashbuckling and so wily that his colleagues in the CIO compared him to the Scarlet Pimpernel. However, since he was not a dashing French aristocrat fighting the forces of Robespierre, but an audacious Jew from the Bronx, that designation did not quite fit. They called him instead the Scholar Pumpernickel.

He was also fun to be around, especially if your idea of a good time is to talk deep into the night. "He was a real intellectual who knew all of the Left Bank intellectuals from Simone de Beauvoir to Jean Paul Sartre to Raymond Aron, the conservative political scientist, whom he loved the most," Hatch told me. "Whenever I got to Paris, I would stop and see Irving. He'd take me to one of these little bistros that turn out to be better than the five star restaurants and we'd just sit there and philosophize most of the night and chat about freedom and the fight against communism. He was a great leader. He was fearless. He was truly one of the most heroic men I've ever met in my life."

As AFL-CIO president Lane Kirkland said, "No other individual did more than Irving to protect and advance workers' rights in every nation around the world."

Irving Brown makes an exciting hero: dramatic, adventurous, an unforgettable player on the world stage. Elizabeth Glaser is a very different kind of hero. She also addressed a worldwide issue, but her problem began on a strictly personal level, with her family.

ELIZABETH GLASER
AIDS Activist

Elizabeth Glaser should have had a long and happy life. She moved to Los Angeles in 1973 and got a job as an elementary school-teacher. In 1975, still smarting from an early marriage that had ended in divorce, she told her therapist that she didn't need a man. Later that same day, she stopped at a traffic light and noticed the man behind the wheel of the car next to her. In her memoir, *In the Absence of Angels,* she remembered thinking, *"Oh, my god, that is the cutest guy I've ever seen."* (Italics hers.) He noticed her, too. One thing led to another, and twelve days later, they were in love. At the time, Paul Michael Glaser was a little known actor hoping to hit the big time with a show that had yet to air. A few months later, they were living together and his new show, *Starsky and Hutch,* was a smash. It was a fairy-tale romance—with a tragic ending.

By 1981, they were married and having their first child, a daughter named Ariel. It was a difficult delivery. Elizabeth hemorrhaged and received a transfusion of seven pints of blood. Three weeks later, she read an article that suggested that the virus responsible for AIDS might be spread through contaminated blood. Panicked, she called her obstetrician. He reassured her. And sure enough, she recuperated and the baby seemed to be thriving. In October 1984, she gave birth to her second child, a boy named Jake.

But in 1985, her daughter developed serious digestive and other medical problems that just didn't go away. Many months and medical consultations later, Ariel was diagnosed with AIDS. A few days later, Elizabeth and her infant son, both symptom-free, were found to be HIV-positive. She had indeed contracted AIDS from the blood transfusion. By breast-feeding she had inadvertently passed the virus on to her daughter. Her son became infected in the womb.

The prejudice against people with AIDS was monumental in those fearful days. Elsewhere in the country, people with AIDS had literally been burned out of house and home by terrified neighbors. For that reason, the Glasers hoped to keep the devastating diagnoses a secret. And for several years, they succeeded. At the same time, Elizabeth was trying desperately to find treatment for her daughter. It was not easy because treatments that were prescribed for adults often were not approved for children, a generally overlooked subset of the AIDS population.

As her daughter struggled, Elizabeth began to speak about the failure of the government to recognize the problem and the pitiful lack of funding for AIDS research—and for pediatric AIDS in particular. As a member of the Hollywood celebrity circuit, she had access to powerful people. But the first time she went to Washington, D.C., she was stunned by the level of ignorance she encountered. She realized that no one was lobbying on behalf of children who were infected with the virus. "I felt a mantle of responsibility descend upon my shoulders," she wrote. "It was a frightening and unforgettable moment."

Seven-year-old Ariel's death in 1988 galvanized her. She sat down with two friends, also young mothers, and created a nonprofit organization called the Pediatric AIDS Foundation, the purpose of which was to encourage research on the transmission of the virus and the treatment of children with AIDS. She knocked on plenty of doors that year, including those of the White House. When Ronald and Nancy Reagan met with her, they seemed empathetic. "We were convinced that we were on the threshold of major and significant political change," Glaser wrote. "We were wrong. . . . Time went by and nothing happened."

Finally, she met with an aide from Democratic senator Howard Metzenbaum's office. He directed her to talk to the senator across the hall—Orrin Hatch, the conservative Republican from Utah, who had already worked with Metzenbaum on legislation concerning abandoned HIV-positive babies. Orrin Hatch, she remembered, looked "as clean-cut as an FBI agent." And she noted that "Orrin and Howard agree on about one out of a thousand bills." Nonetheless, the conservative Republican and the liberal Democrat agreed to host a fundraiser for the Pediatric AIDS Foundation. With Alan Alda as master of ceremonies and Cher as the star attraction, the benefit raised over a million dollars.

In 1989, the Glasers heard that the *National Enquirer* was on the verge of publishing an article about them. To make sure that they got to tell their own story, they called the *Los Angeles Times* and went public. In doing so, Elizabeth helped bring the issue into the spotlight. She lobbied long and hard, even addressing the 1992 Republican National Convention. "If I didn't have AIDS, if I hadn't lost my daughter to it, if my son didn't have it, if my life wasn't so sad, I would be very fulfilled by what I'm doing," she said.

On December 3, 1994, she died, leaving behind her husband, Paul, and her son, Jake, who, I'm pleased to note, is thriving.

As for the organization she founded, now called the Elizabeth Glaser Pediatric AIDS Foundation, it continues to raise both money (over $130 million so far) and awareness. As a result of research it has funded, we know a great deal more about how to treat children with AIDS and how to prevent them from contracting the virus in the first place, even when the mother is HIV-positive—an essential piece of information that could have saved both of Elizabeth's children from becoming infected.

Why was she a hero? "Elizabeth was a hero to me because she was HIV-positive; she had already lost her daughter; her son, Jake, was positive and yet she gave everything she had to try to help these kids with pediatric AIDS," Hatch says. "I really respected her."

THE POLITICIANS

Vernon Law, Irving Brown, and Elizabeth Glaser are admirable people. But they are not the heroes I would have expected a senator—and especially such a conservative one—to choose. I had to ask directly:

> RD: Are there any politicians you consider heroic?
> OH: Since running for office, I've had a lot of heroes. Ronald Reagan was probably the biggest. He was of immense help to me. The first time I ran for office, filing on the last possible day in 1976, I had zero name recognition. *US News & World Report* listed my opponent as the only incumbent running that year who could not be beaten. But by the time I won the primary and Reagan endorsed me, 95–96 percent of the people in Utah knew who I was. I loved Gerald Ford, but I was so committed to Reagan because of his conservative political stance and because

he was probably the most articulate Republican at the time. I endorsed him early on in the campaign and we became good friends. He was a very, very good person.

I might add that Barry Goldwater was a great hero to me. He wrote *Conscience of a Conservative*. As an undergraduate at Brigham Young University, I was a liberal Democrat. But by the time I entered law school in 1960, I couldn't stand it anymore. I felt like they were completely caught up in building more and more government, controlling more and more lives, taxing more and more people, and just spending and spending and spending. I couldn't tolerate it. I admired Goldwater as a straight-talking, straight-shooting, honest man and so he had a tremendous influence me.

And Hubert Humphrey was a hero. He and I differed on many critical matters, but I liked his compassion. This was a case of a person from the other party who had a big heart. He befriended me and I befriended him. On one occasion, a sick little boy from Utah visited me. I brought him to a committee hearing and asked Hubert if he minded if he sat with me on the dais. Heavens no, Hubert said, he can have my seat. Hubert was dying of cancer at the time. But afterwards he said, "It's one thing for somebody my age to die of cancer, but for a little beautiful boy like that . . . ." He got all teary-eyed. We were very close and I respected him greatly.

RD: You've listed a wildly varied group of people as your heroes.

OH: There are others, of course, who get high marks from me. There was a great philosophy teacher at Brigham Young University named Truman Madsen. He was so intellectually astute. I loved philosophy and especially the religious side of philosophy, and he was absolutely without fear as a teacher. He was a great influence in my life.

When I got through law school, one of my greatest heroes was a man I became a partner with named Robert Grigsby. He is a strong Catholic who really lived his religion and was in my opinion one of the top trial lawyers in America, a tremendously ethical and upright and accomplished trial lawyer. He is a very, very good human being and he meant a lot to me.

RD: What draws all these people together?

OH: In their own ways all of them were fearless, they were organized, they were intellectually superior, they had anchored beliefs that they lived up to, they set good examples, and they worked hard. They were dedicated to their beliefs and worked exhaustively to implement their beliefs, and they had fears but they were not afraid. Nothing could stop them. In each case they were morally and spiritually upright.

RD: I understand the importance of being fearless. But it's interesting to me that in the list of qualities you associate with heroism, the second one you mentioned was being organized.

OH: Well, these were people who knew what they were doing. They had a plan and they implemented it. Most of them were pretty well-organized.

They were also able to pick the people who worked with them and they weren't afraid to take advice from those who knew more than they did. In other words, there was an element of humility.

RD: That's not something we generally associate with heroism.

OH: I think that the great leaders and heroes of this world are people who deep down are profoundly humble, although it might be one of the last qualities you'd think to mention about them. If people aren't humble, you can't teach them anything. But the people who are humble will learn. They're teachable. That's why humility is such an important trait.

RD: Any other qualities you would list?

OH: Honesty and humility are two of the great qualities that every one of those heroes had. And it's essential to have a moral or ethical compass. Not all great leaders have one that fits with mine. But to a degree they've got to have a moral and ethical compass. Great leaders live their beliefs. They do what they know is right—and let the consequences follow.

For most of us, letting the consequences follow is the hard part. If you're a politician, it can mean losing an election. But even if you're an ordinary office worker or a waitress, merely going on record with your opinions can be dangerous. (That's why politicians who are primarily worried about getting reelected tend to avoid press conferences.) Heroism means putting your reputation or your paycheck or even your life on the line.

I am reminded that while heroism can have many expressions, both seen and unseen, it is never a minor virtue. And that's true no matter where you are on the political spectrum.

CHAPTER 8

A Conversation With

JOEL KURTZMAN

On Harry S. Truman and the Hero's Journey

Over the past two decades, the commonly understood definition of the hero has taken on new meaning, thanks to the influence of Joseph Campbell. His PBS interviews with Bill Moyers in the 1980s stirred up a fresh interest in mythology and rescued it from a horrible fate—being cooked to death by academics. Campbell infused the subject with life. He also popularized the concept of the hero's journey, maintaining that it applies not only to mythological heroes, but to each one of us.

According to Campbell, the adventure begins when the hero (or heroine) is "called," often by chance and on a moment's notice, to something outside of ordinary experience. By responding, he leaves his accustomed world behind and steps into the unknown, where dangers abound. Like Jonah in the whale or Daniel in the lions' den, he may have to escape from a threatening situation. When he does, he leaves his old self behind and emerges victorious—only to discover that his problems are far from over.

To prove himself, he may have to fight a dragon or descend into the underworld or perform a task that looks impossible. Obstacles, both inner and outer, block his progress, and he is sure to stumble. Undaunted, he persists. At last he triumphs and returns to ordinary life, where—who knows?—he may receive another call.

But notice that there is another possibility. The would-be hero might fail to answer the call. The moment might pass.

We celebrate heroes because they respond. They don't suppress their inner voices or pretend not to know what's going on or sink into their Barcaloungers to contemplate their options. They don't succumb to fear. So things keep rolling along for them. In their businesses, in their families, and in the societies in which they live, problems get addressed and sometimes solved.

I was hoping one of my brilliant friends would bring this concept up. Joel Kurtzman finally did. A California boy who went to Berkeley in the late 1960s and early 1970s, he later studied economics at the University of Houston and Rice University and became a global economist at the United Nations.

After that, he worked as a business editor and columnist at the *New York Times* and subsequently edited the *Harvard Business Review*. Now he works at PricewaterhouseCoopers as lead partner for a branch of that organization called Thought Leadership. He's written or edited eighteen books, primarily about business and the economy. (My favorite: *The Death of Money*.) He also reaches out to other people when they need help, even without being asked. I have seen him do it. He has done it for me.

In our discussion of the hero's journey, he brought up an aspect of heroism that needs to be acknowledged. "Let's not be naive and think that heroes are always rewarded for their actions," Kurtzman told me. That is not necessarily what happens.

Take Winston Churchill. After his brilliant leadership during World War II, Churchill was promptly turned out of office. Not exactly a reward for exemplary service.

Or think about the three women named *Time* magazine's Persons of the Year for 2002. The magazine referred to them collectively as . . .

THE WHISTLE-BLOWERS

People who become firefighters want to be heroes. That is not why people go to work for large businesses. They're not thinking about becoming heroes. They want to make money.

But heroes can spring from the most barren soil. That's what happened at Enron, a company that fell apart beneath an avalanche of crooked accounting schemes, burying the retirement savings of countless hardworking people. When Sherron Watkins, a company vice president, realized there were problems with the smoke-and-mirrors accounting, she did something about it. Instead of keeping her mouth shut, she went directly to Chairman Kenneth Lay. He continued to assure Enron employees that the company was financially solid. A few months later, Enron imploded, just as she had predicted.

At Worldcom, Cynthia Cooper saw that the books had been cooked to the tune of $3.8 billion. She fearlessly let the board know about the accounting fraud.

And then there's the FBI, where Coleen Rowley knew that something was amiss—and it was keeping her awake at night. In the wake of intelligence failures concerning September 11, she wrote a thirteen-page indictment of that organization that might have ended her career. Then she gave it to the director of the FBI and the Senate Committee on Intelligence.

It wasn't easy for these women to do what they did. Whistle-blowers are not always admired, which may explain why hardly anyone wants to be one. "Seventy percent of people who see something wrong don't do anything about it, because it's an incredibly stressful process," said Louis Clark, executive director of the Government Accountability Project, in an article published in the *New York Times*. "They don't want to be made into martyrs or commit career suicide."

Watkins, Cooper, and Rowley took that chance. Once they heard the call—once they knew in their hearts that something was deeply wrong—they had to respond. All three women stood up for the integrity of their organizations by contacting the higher-ups and making sure that those in a position to make changes had the facts.

Once their role became public knowledge, they were hailed as heroes. Naturally, they rejected that label. "We don't feel like we are heroes," said Cynthia Cooper. "I feel like I did my job." Around the country, praise was heaped upon them.

Not so within their organizations. Although all three had supporters, corporate culture by nature values loyalty above all else. It views whistle-blowers as traitors and punishes them accordingly. So Sherron Watkins was demoted and ostracized. After a year, she quit.

Cynthia Cooper was so stressed by the way her colleagues treated her that she lost thirty pounds (a nearly impossible feat in my experience). Coleen Rowley was compared to Robert Hanssen, a convicted spy.

These three women jeopardized their careers and undoubtedly lost a few friendships. Shunned and ignored by many of their colleagues, they gained little more from their heroic actions than a conscience at ease and their pictures on the cover of *Time*. I was glad they got that recognition. I wish they had gotten more.

Yet being a hero involves accepting risk. And more often than one would like to think, it involves failure. "The Warsaw Ghetto was filled with people who acted heroically," Kurtzman said. "But in the end it burned and collapsed. Heroism resides in the act and not the outcome."

Ultimately, then, heroism has to be its own reward. Here's part of the conversation Joel Kurtzman and I had on the subject:

JK: Being a hero is a long arduous journey that is fraught with difficulties. The ancient mythology about the hero's path is not the same as the story line of *Terminator 3*. There are all kinds of turns in the road, all kinds of challenges.

RD: And surprising things can occur in the wake of heroic action.

JK: That's because heroism changes things around you. When you raise up your head to say something is wrong here, or when you lead a group against a powerful foe, real forces will try to suppress you. And the outcome is in doubt. It's not like the movies. That's why it's unusual for people to make heroic gestures.

RD: And, as you pointed out, recognition can be a long time coming.

JK: In some cases, people are vindicated years later, sometimes after their deaths. Look at Vincent van Gogh. He never received any recognition in his own lifetime. He sacrificed for his art, took a lot of criticism, and was scorned. But he changed the way we look at landscapes. He changed the way we see.

RD: What do you think makes the difference between people who have the inner strength to maintain their vision and people who fall away?

JK: That's a good question. It's just that: a certain type of inner strength. First of all you have to have a sense of truth, an understanding of right and wrong in a broad context. You have to have the ability to see what's wrong. And you have to have the ability and the strength to act on it. That seems to be innate in some people and in other people it doesn't seem to exist at all. In the case of companies where betrayal of trust has been an issue, in most instances only one or two people stand up. The majority go along. True heroism is rare.

And I think there's a difference between acts of conscience and authentic heroism. Heroism transforms things. In the smallest instance it transforms the individual; in the largest it transforms society.

RD: I wonder if you could tell me who your personal heroes are.

JK: Well, I know it sounds silly, but I have to say Harry Truman is one of my personal heroes. He was a person who, when faced with opposition, when faced with corruption, stood up again and again and did the right things.

It didn't sound silly to me. I have been curious about the man ever since I was little and my brother asked me, "What does the S in Harry S. Truman stand for?" It did not stand for anything, my brother told me triumphantly. (I later learned that Truman's parents, hoping to satisfy both sides of the family, gave him that solitary letter in honor of his two grandfathers—the one whose middle name began with S and the one whose first name began with S.)

Harry S. Truman (1884–1972) was a nonheroic type if ever there were one. But then, as Daniel J. Boorstin has pointed out, Americans tend to distrust the heroic type. "Most forms of government depend on a belief in a divine spark possessed by a favored few; but American democracy is embarrassed in the charismatic presence. We fear the man on horseback, the demigod, or the dictator . . . ," he writes. "Our most admired national heroes—Franklin, Washington, and Lincoln— are generally supposed to possess the 'common touch.'"

That was certainly true of Truman. He was often considered common, a sorry substitute for the patrician Franklin D. Roosevelt. But he was honest, courageous, and decent, with a self-deprecating wit and a solid set of values that kept him from mudslinging, even in campaigns everyone was certain he would lose. He made big, unpopular decisions and was often unpopular himself. But unlike more glamorous figures whose heroic auras have faded over time, Harry Truman has grown more heroic in retrospect. Here's his story:

HARRY S. TRUMAN
The Man from Independence

He was slow in getting started. He didn't go to college. He didn't get married until he was thirty-five. His last business—a haberdashery—failed. At thirty-eight, he was deep in debt and living with his imperious mother-in-law, who was certain that her daughter, Bess, could have done better. His prospects looked dim, which surprised no one. As one of his schoolteachers admitted years later, "Nobody thought that he'd go far at all."

Kind of a Sissy

Born in 1884 in Missouri, the son of a farmer and mule trader, Harry S. Truman grew up in a home filled with books and music. A voracious reader, he claimed that by age fourteen he had read all three thousand books in the local library—"including the encyclopedia." But he wore glasses—a rare thing for a child at the time—and was forbidden to fight for fear of breaking them. He described himself as lonely and "kind of a sissy" as a child. Yet he also asserted that "I had just the happiest childhood that could ever be imagined." That's classic Harry Truman. Regret and self-pity were not part of his nature. He was that rare thing—a realist with a positive outlook.

For instance, when he was fifteen, he stopped taking piano lessons because he decided that he wasn't good enough to be a professional. "I wouldn't ever have been really first-rate," he said. "A good music-hall piano player is about the best I'd have ever been. So I went into politics and became President of the United States."

In high school, he hoped to go to West Point. But his bad eyes denied him admission, and his father's finances kept him from being able to attend any other college. He knocked around for a while, working in the mail room of the *Kansas City Star*, as a timekeeper for the Santa Fe Railroad, and as a clerk in a couple of Kansas City banks. He even joined the National Guard. In 1906, when his father asked him to help run his grandmother's farm, he became a farmer, occasionally moonlighting as a postmaster and a road overseer. He became a partner in a lead mine and later in an oil business. Nothing caught fire with him.

War and Peace

When Woodrow Wilson declared war against Germany and its allies in 1917, Truman memorized the eye chart and was sent to France with the 129th Field Artillery. He rose to the rank of captain and was beloved by his men (and by their mothers, whose letters he always answered). But the peacetime army did not appeal to him and in April 1919 he sailed home. Two months later, he married Bess Wallace. He had been in love with her since Sunday-school days.

That same year, he and an army buddy opened a haberdashery. When the store failed three years later, he thought about declaring bankruptcy but decided against it. It took him fifteen years to pay off his debts. At age thirty-eight, he still hadn't found his way.

Answering the Call

That was when Michael Pendergast, whose brother headed the Democratic machine that ran Missouri politics, suggested that Truman run for Eastern District judge, an administrative position. With the support of the Pendergast machine, Truman won the election. His hero's journey had begun.

Obstacles popped up almost immediately. When he ran for re-election two years later, he lost by 877 votes, in part because the Ku Klux Klan campaigned against him. He then found a job as a salesman for the Kansas City Automobile Club and took a few classes at the Kansas City Law School. A couple of years later, he ran for presiding judge and won. As a jurist, he developed a reputation for integrity and for keeping his campaign promises.

But his connection with the Pendergast machine damaged him. The Pendergasts were involved in prostitution, gambling, even murder. Their reputation was so bad that in 1934 they couldn't find a candidate to run for the U.S. Senate because no one wanted to be associated with them. Truman was their fourth choice. He said yes.

"And oh, the newspapers made quite a bit of fun of me . . . ," he remembered. "They made quite a big to-do about a little country judge who wasn't even a lawyer running for the U.S. Senate." But he was a tireless campaigner. "I went into sixty counties . . . ," he said. "I'd tell people that I was a farmer and a failed businessman and that I understood the problems that the common people were facing because I was one myself, and they could see that despite what the newspapers were saying, I didn't have horns and a tail."

In Washington, the "Senator from Pendergast" was well liked and effective. Yet six years later, that association cast a pall over his prospects for reelection. In a three-way primary, Truman was considered the sure loser. His chances of being nominated, according to the *St. Louis Post-Dispatch,* were "nil. He is a dead cock in the pit." Even the Roosevelt administration did not support the Democratic incumbent.

He campaigned on the issues, including civil rights, of which he was an early supporter. The campaign was a dirty one. He was even accused of being Jewish because his grandfather's first name was Solomon. "I'm not Jewish," Truman said. "But if I were I would not be ashamed of it." (Still, as if we needed more proof of the fact that heroes have feet of clay, a hitherto unknown diary of Truman's, discovered in 2003 on the shelves of his library in Independence, revealed that he was not free of anti-Semitic thoughts.)

Truman was reelected. Back in the Senate, he was greeted with a standing ovation.

Becoming President

In 1944, with Franklin Roosevelt running for his fourth term and World War II still raging, Truman was nominated for vice president. Eighty-two days into the new term, Roosevelt died. Truman was shaken. "I felt like the moon, the stars, and all the planets had fallen on me," he said. No one thought he was equal to the task of replacing a beloved commander-in-chief.

But Truman was up and running. His famous sign, "The buck stops here," wasn't just PR. He had the ability to make decisions, even when his positions were not popular, even when they challenged an important constituency, even when they meant life and death.

So it was Harry Truman who helped established the United Nations, negotiated the German surrender, attended the Potsdam Conference with Winston Churchill and Joseph Stalin. It was also Harry Truman who made the contested decision to drop the bomb on Hiroshima and Nagasaki, thereby ending the war.

And it was Harry Truman who fought the first battles in the Cold War; established the Truman Doctrine, which opposed Communist aggression; and backed the Marshall Plan. He resisted the CIA, opposing a coup against the democratically elected government of Iran, only to be reversed by his successor in office, Dwight Eisenhower. He fought vigorously against communism, and later on, he fought red-baiting at home, calling the House Un-American Activities Committee the most "un-American activity in the whole government." He desegregated the armed forces. He proposed new civil rights legislation as well as a national health plan. He initiated the Berlin Airlift. And unlike his own State Department, he supported recognition of the State of Israel.

"Dewey Defeats Truman"

Still, he was not Franklin Roosevelt. When he ran for president in 1948, pollsters, columnists, and commentators agreed: The winner would be New York governor Thomas E. Dewey, despite his stiff demeanor. ("You have to know Mr. Dewey well in order to dislike him," the wife of a Republican politician famously said.)

The people ignored the pundits and gave Truman 303 electoral votes to Dewey's 189. Truman beamed when he picked up the early edition of the *Chicago Tribune* with its premature headline, "Dewey Defeats Truman." That photograph became iconic.

In his second term, he survived an assassination attempt and went to war in Korea. Later, he courageously fired General Douglas MacArthur for compromising his efforts to negotiate with the Chinese. I have spoken to people who cheered that decision, who remember MacArthur as arrogant, self-serving, and eager to widen the war. But not everyone saw it that way at the time. According to a Gallup Report, 69% of the people polled preferred MacArthur to the President, who received only 29% of the vote.

Throughout his presidency, Truman acted firmly. Were some of his decisions wrong? Sure. Even he admitted it. One decision that rankled him in later years: his appointment of Tom C. Clark (father of Ramsey Clark) to the Supreme Court.

More controversial to this day was his decision to drop the bomb on Hiroshima and Nagasaki. The jury is out on whether it was a good idea, because it saved countless American lives and shortened the war, or a bad idea, because it launched the nuclear age and killed hundreds of thousands of innocent people, perhaps unnecessarily. Some argue that Japan was, in fact, ready to surrender or that a demonstration bomb on a deserted island should have been dropped first. Truman himself never doubted the wisdom of his decision.

In 1952, when his second term ended, he returned to Independence, Missouri, where he took his daily constitutionals and lived (in his mother-in-law's house) until his death in 1972.

Harry Truman's Heroes

When Harry was ten years old, his mother gave him a four-volume collection of essays entitled Great Men and Famous Women. *He devoured it. He was particularly impressed by the stories of two beloved American heroes: populist Andrew Jackson, whom his daughter Margaret called "his greatest hero," and Confederate general Robert E. Lee, who was admired by generations of Americans for being gracious in defeat. Nor were these solely the heroes of childhood. In adulthood, he savored their multivolume biographies, and he kept a statue of Jackson in the Oval Office.*

An American Odyssey

What makes Truman a hero? Integrity is part of it. He had moral stature and the confidence to make independent decisions. He was kind and modest, energetic and intelligent. When he became president, he was not a member of the inner circle. Yet he seized the reins of government without hesitation. And unlike certain presidents I could name, he was well-read and extremely knowledgeable.

But he was also a human being. When a music critic panned his daughter Margaret's recital, he wrote an angry letter offering to beat up the man. The letter hit the tabloids, and Truman was accused of being uncouth, incompetent, mentally unstable, and common—"very common." He was unfazed. As he told Margaret and Bess (whom he called "the Boss"), "Every man in this United States that's got a daughter will be on my side." Above all, he was a shrewd politician.

Very much a hero in the classical sense, he suffered many defeats, pursued high adventure, and lived his life trying to follow advice he underlined in a copy of Marcus Aurelius's *Meditations*: "If it is not right, do not do it; if it is not true, do not say it."

David McCullough, author of the definitive biography of Truman, had this to say about him: "He was the kind of president the founding fathers had in mind for the country. He came directly from the people.

He was America....There was something almost allegorical about it all: the Man of Independence and his Odyssey."

ON *THE ODYSSEY* OF HOMER

And then, of course, there was Homer's *Odyssey,* a story everyone can identify with, even though it was written over twenty-five hundred years ago. Odysseus, who knew nothing about mythologist Joseph Campbell and his theories, does not even want to go on an adventure. When he is asked to fight in the Trojan War, he tries to wiggle out of it. He goes off to war despite himself. Afterward, all kinds of calamities befall him. He falls asleep at the wrong time (in the cave of the winds); he is forced to navigate his ship between the twin dangers of Scylla and Charybdis; he is waylaid by Calypso and loses seven years of his life to that relationship; he is attacked by monsters. But he is also crafty and determined, and he ends up where he wants to be: back in Independence—er, Ithaca—with his wife, Penelope.

The Odyssey is one of my favorite books. It is also one of Joel Kurtzman's. Here's part of our conversation about it:

> JK: Growing up, I admired biblical heroes like Moses and fictional heroes like Superman and mythological characters. Of all the mythological characters, the one I admired most was Odysseus. *The Odyssey* is one of the most important books I've ever read.
>
> RD: What is it that appeals to you?
>
> JK: What's so amazing about that book is that it does not paint heroism as something in which the hero is surrounded by cheering crowds. In fact, when Odysseus returns home after twenty years of wandering, no one recognizes him except his nurse and his old dog.
>
> RD That's a touching scene.
>
> JK: His wife is surrounded by the suitors, as they're called in the book, and parties are going on. Odysseus is forgotten,

except by the dog—and the dog dies. He has to build recognition slowly for what he has done. It's a more complete picture of heroism than a movie in which the hero receives ticker-tape parades and cheers. Odysseus's homecoming offers a sobering and realistic view. It says that the place to which you ultimately return is the place that you started out from. It says that the journey is filled with danger and can go wrong at any time. And the reward is not necessarily acclaim. It's simply a repossession of the place that you started from. As a result there's a lot of elegance in the journey. I think that's the reward: elegance.

Truman had it. There is a certain elegance in the way that, as an old man, he took his walk every morning around his house in Independence. He was in some ways the same man he started out as—except that he changed the world. Now to change the world and remain the same person you were when you began is a tremendous achievement because, as you know from *The Odyssey*, one of the dangers on the hero's journey is temptation.

RD: Yes. That comes up in the section about the Sirens. Odysseus tied himself to the mast so that he could hear them singing but wouldn't be able to succumb to their wiles. He didn't lose sight of his goal, which was getting home to Penelope. I think that sets a wonderful example.

JK: The real temptation, whether it comes from the Sirens or elsewhere, is to change who you are. That's probably the biggest pitfall. That's why I like the story of Truman so much. He had all the trappings of power—and not just the trappings. He was the driving force behind everything from the United Nations to the postwar Marshall Plan to the Truman Doctrine to the concept of containment and on and on and on. Yet in the end he was the same person. He never succumbed to vanity, and vanity is probably the first temptation of that kind of history-making journey.

The whole system as we have it set up today makes vanity a big temptation because we have the apparatus of the media. To resist that and still change either your circumstances or the world is an extraordinary thing.

RD: It is also a rare phenomenon. Many people come to see me because they want to be famous. That's not the hero's way. The hero wants to make the world a better place.

CHAPTER 9

ON MY DAD AND OTHER HEROES

Ask people about heroes, and you will hear a small number of names again and again. Martin Luther King, Jr. comes up a lot. So does Mother Theresa. And so do Mom and Dad, often for reasons that aren't clear to anyone other than their progeny.

The psychology behind that phenomenon is pretty obvious. Parents are more than our first role models. They are our first superpowers, our first gods. Towering above us, these exalted beings hold our fate in their hands. They reward us, punish us, protect us, mystify us, and sacrifice for us. When we are small, they are heroes of the first rank. But as the years go by, they fall from grace in our eyes. To establish our own identities, we are forced to rebel and to look elsewhere for heroes.

But for many people, the deep-down longing for heroic parents persists. Even if our parents are almost entirely lacking heroic qualities, we honor their quieter virtues and cherish the few stories that cast them in a noble light. It's no wonder that many people, given the chance to name their heroes, pick their parents first.

Of course, some parents really are heroes. Take, for example, my dad. His name was Sigmund John Dilenschneider, otherwise known as Dil. He was born in Pawtucket, Rhode Island, the son of a weaver. He grew up with virtually no money. When his friends went to college, he went to work and saved what he could. He didn't get to college until he was well into his twenties, years after his friends had moved on to other things. He graduated from the Wharton School in Philadelphia, where he met my mother. But this was in the midst of the Depression, and money was tight. Even after they got married, they couldn't live together because he couldn't afford an apartment.

Finally my dad got a job at a newspaper and his career began. He worked for the *Philadelphia Inquirer* and the *Philadelphia Bulletin.* Then he moved to New York and got a job with Scripps-Howard. He ended up in Ohio, working for the *Cleveland Press* and finally the *Columbus Citizen.* That's where he was when the story I'm about to tell took place. I was very young at the time, but I remember it well.

It began when the phone rang. To my surprise, my dad took the call in the basement. Unbeknownst to him, I was huddled beneath the basement steps in a favorite hiding spot of mine, listening to the whole thing. I don't know how much I understood at the time, but I'll never forget the drama and tension surrounding the whole event. Later on, my parents filled me in on the details.

The call came from a local department store called Cousins & Fern. Cousins & Fern was then a major retailer in Columbus, Ohio. Its advertising support kept the paper alive. But they had a problem: The store's CEO or founder, I don't remember which, had just committed suicide. The person on the phone wanted my dad to keep the story out of the paper.

My dad said he couldn't do that. He promised to present the story respectfully and not trumpet it across the first page. But they had to treat it as news, he said, because it was important. He reiterated that point a couple of times. A long silence followed. It turned out the guy on the other end of the phone had threatened to withdraw all the Cousins & Fern advertising if my dad published the story.

This could easily have destroyed the paper. But my dad didn't flinch. He said, "I'm sorry, I've got to do it, and I hope you'll be able to understand why I've got to do it, and I hope we'll retain your advertising." Then he hung up and went upstairs. I followed.

The next day, two things happened. The story ran in the paper, just as my father had said it would. And Cousins & Fern withdrew all of its advertising.

Freedom of speech wasn't a meaningless phrase to my father. A newspaperman through and through, he wasn't willing to compromise on that. To this day, I am tremendously proud that he took that stance.

Fortunately, he didn't have to pay the consequences, though he was willing to. Two or three days later, a guy named Fred Lazarus, the founder of the Federated Department Store chain, called my father and asked him to come over to his office. My dad went. As he told the story, he and Fred Lazarus sat on an elegant French couch and sipped demitasse coffee from delicate China cups. Fred Lazarus said he was surprised that Cousins & Fern had decided not to advertise in the paper any longer. That meant Lazarus could increase his own advertising commitment to the paper. In fact, he said, he wanted to put Cousins & Fern out of business. Which is precisely what happened. Lazarus doubled his advertising commitment; my dad's paper was safe; Cousins & Fern folded; and Lazarus went on to become Federated.

That wasn't the only time my father stood up for freedom of the press. There was always the issue of which columnists were going to be published in the paper. Scripps-Howard had an annual meeting at which all the papers came together and decided which candidates to support in the next election. Their politics were middle-of-the-road. The *Dispatch,* which was the other paper in town, was highly conservative—they were so tight they squeaked—and my dad always felt it was important to represent another point of view. Accordingly, he filled the pages of the *Citizen* with liberal columnists. In a conservative town like Columbus, that was not a popular thing. But it was his view that a newspaper should offer alternative points of view, and he didn't care if he took a lot of criticism as a result.

I must note another heroic aspect of my dad: Even when he was provoked, he made a point of getting along with everyone who worked for him. One time, the pressmen went on strike. Those were the days of hot linotype. Using hot type was a noisy, dangerous process. The Linotype operators wore gloves in case they caught the hot type. You had to have gloves. One day, my dad, who represented management, went down to the composing floor and one of the Linotype operators threw some hot type at him. It bounced off his chest and shoulder and fell to the floor. When it stopped sizzling, he picked it up and handed it back to the Linotype operator. He said to him, "You might want to remelt this lead because if we don't, it's going to cost us money and we won't be able to give you the raise you deserve." The guy was trying to start a fight. My wise father refused to take the bait. He believed in civility—and negotiation.

He was quite a figure. He was a religious man who never had a bad thing to say about anybody. He reached out to people all over the community and was always involved in civic activities. He was a strong believer in education.

He was not a big spender. He had only one suit—a blue one, which he wore every day because he couldn't afford another. On Saturdays, he would take the suit to Swan Cleaners for a dry cleaning. At some point, my mother would announce that his suit was getting shiny, and he would buy a new one. In my memory, there was never an overlap between the old suit and the new one. My father was always a one-suit man. The old one, suffering from advanced old age, was retired. The new one immediately took its place.

My dad was also heroic as a father. For example, I wasn't a very good baseball player. Because he knew baseball mattered to me, he got me some special instruction, bought me a better mitt, and did everything he could to help. When I was hitting, he was there celebrating. When I was not hitting, he would never say a word. I remember one of the most devastating moments of my life. I was at bat, and I struck out. And as I walked back from the plate, I saw my father parked in the car about fifty yards away from the ballpark. He had seen me strike out. But he never mentioned it, never humiliated me. He was that kind of guy. I try to keep his example in mind.

My dad wasn't emotionally expressive, and he didn't tell my brother and me what to do. He helped us reach our own conclusions. He encouraged. He helped us develop our own talents, and he gave us the tools to do it. He also took great pride and pleasure in our achievements. That made a big difference. I don't know if that's heroic or not, but it made me feel pretty good and proud to call him my father.

On the day when I left home for my first job, my dad performed one of his most heroic actions: He came home for lunch. Now, I have to say that my dad was always working. He put in long hours at the paper. He never came home in the middle of the day. But on the day when I was preparing to leave Ohio and go to New York for my first real job, he came home at noontime. It was highly irregular. He sat down at the kitchen table with me and we had tuna fish sandwiches. For a few minutes, we hardly said anything. Then he looked at me and said, "This is a big thing that's going to happen now. You're going to go off, and I want you to be very successful and do what you want to do. But I want you also to know that if things don't work out, I'm here for you. All you have to do is call me." He meant it. And I knew it. A stranger might not fully understand this, but when my dad came home for lunch that day, it was a heroic gesture. It fortified me at a critical moment in my young life. I hope to provide the same sense of support for my kids some day.

DOMESTIC HEROES AND HEROINES

My father has always been one of my great heroes, but somehow I had not imagined that so many people would feel the same way about their parents. I have learned otherwise. It's not simply that people admire their parents. They see the extraordinary in them, and they are inspired by it.

Marilyn Carlson Nelson, the great lady who runs the huge global hospitality company, Carlson Companies, told me that one summer when she was four or five years old, the polio epidemic was everywhere and people were terrified. Her parents were determined to protect their children. "So my mother and my aunt took my sister and myself and my cousins way up to northern Wisconsin," she said. "They took us out to a cabin on an island and we stayed there for months. They had to row a boat the length of the lake not only to get groceries but to get ice, because there was no power out on the island. The objective was to keep us away from exposure to polio because there was no vaccine at the time. They kept us there until after the first frost."

In the fall, Marilyn returned home and learned that polio had, indeed, visited the neighborhood. One neighbor died. Another was paralyzed for life. Her mother's love and sacrifice had protected her, not just theoretically but in fact.

Monk Malloy, president of the University of Notre Dame, also named both his parents among his heroes. They did not pull anyone out of an icy river or walk into a raging inferno. But "they worked hard to support a family and to be good citizens and to be active in their church. In a sense, they devoted their whole life to myself and my two sisters. And they'll never be publicly acknowledged and books won't be written about them, but people like them provide the underpinning for civilization and for a society that promotes the common good. I think of them as domestic heroes and heroines." I like that phrase. I like that concept.

PARENTS IN OLD AGE

Finally, parents are heroes when we are small and they are in their prime. Later, we come to see them as human beings, not heroes. But decades later, when we are fully functioning adults and they have become old, I have noticed that they occasionally regain their former status, not in the old way but in a new way. They become heroes once again, admired for the bravery with which they confront physical frailty, compromised memories, the indignities of old age, and the imminence of death.

Take, for example, my mother. At ninety-eight years of age, she has been through difficult, painful times, both emotionally and physically. Seven years ago, she had to have her hip replaced. An infection set in during the operation and led to six more operations—not an easy experience for a woman in her nineties. Those operations drained her. But when she was getting physical therapy, she would still say, "Look, I'm able to walk four steps; I'm able to walk five steps." Her attitude was always positive.

Now she has a full-time attendant because she literally cannot get out of bed or sit up in a chair alone. I see how tough it is. Yet she never complains. She is always upbeat, asking me about what I'm doing, never complaining about herself. Her ability to push her problems aside and focus on others is nothing less than heroic.

If you have a parent who is heroically combating old age with dignity and grace, you can consider yourself fortunate—even if you do have to spend long hours deciphering the complexities of medical insurance or listening to the same old stories again and again. Some of those stories may simply rehash old grievances or long-ago gossip. But if your family is anything like mine, a few of them rise to another level. They aren't just a family saga. They are your heroic heritage.

CHAPTER 10

A Conversation With
THE REVEREND EDWARD A. MALLOY

On Jimmy Carter,
The Reverend Theodore M. Hesburgh,
Walker Percy, James E. Burke, Aaron Feuerstein,
and Pedro and Violeta Chamorro

Anybody who's known me for longer than five minutes knows that I am a proud alumnus of Notre Dame. It's an essential part of my identity, and over the years I have strengthened my connection to the university. So I have known the Reverend Edward A. Malloy, president of Notre Dame, for a long time.

Widely known as Monk, a nickname he acquired in the fourth grade, Father Malloy was ordained as a priest in 1970; earned his Ph.D. in Christian Ethics from Vanderbilt; became a member of the Notre Dame faculty in 1974; and was appointed president in 1986. He has won all manner of awards, including one from the National Association of Basketball Coaches, but he has never sought the limelight. He's one of those people who steps back so that other people might step forward. It's a trait that marks him in my mind as a hero.

THE COURAGE OF THEIR CONVICTIONS

"I find it easiest to think about heroism in terms of individuals," Father Malloy said. We began by talking about the greatest American hero: Abraham Lincoln.

MM: I've read a lot about Lincoln's life and his circumstances, about his decision-making, and about the difficult choices he made. Within his range of God-given talents and experience, he identified a set of goals and priorities that were partially personal but mainly served the common good. In the face of criticism, depression, misunderstanding, and times in which everything looked hopeless, he stuck to his principles. He was a man of conviction and courage who paid the ultimate price when he was assassinated. Heroes are people like Abraham Lincoln who live by values that they are convinced are worth pursuing; who have the courage of their convictions even in the face of opposition; and who are willing, in some circumstances, to stick to those convictions even at the risk of their lives. It's hard to be heroic unless you have deep values. There have to be things worth sacrificing for and worth dying for. If you're just a plaything of fashion, there's nothing that's actually worth sacrificing for.

RD: I agree. Sacrifice is an essential element of heroism. I wonder if you could say more about it.

MM: I think there's a deep religious sense to it. I would say, as a Christian, that the heart of the Christian mystery is life springing out of death. It's a world view in which sacrifice and hardship are necessary parts of life. Nobody can avoid them, no matter how rich you are, no matter how attractive you are, no matter how talented you are. At some point, everybody has to face the reality of illness, disappointment, and failure, as well as the realities of the world around us, our inability to control relationships, our inability to make things turn out right for our children. Those are elemental conditions.

Heroes are people who say that it's worth sacrificing in order to create a better life for others. They are willing to forego their own pleasure for the well-being of their children. They are willing to share their goods with the beggar or to go without sleep to take care of someone who is sick. They are willing to assume those burdens. The heroic people in life, more often than the average person and more regularly than is usual, willingly pay that price. And there is a positive force, not just merit, that can be unleashed by a willingness to sacrifice with forethought and consciousness.

There's another point I'd like to add. I believe in the tradition of icons—people who are declared religious saints or presented to young people for emulation. Some of the most recognizable heroic figures, like Gandhi or Martin Luther King, Jr., or Abraham Lincoln, were assassinated for reasons clearly connected to what they were about. I don't think we need to expect that a person's heroic qualities will necessarily lead to death. But I think all of us can be schooled in the qualities of heroism by reflecting upon these examples.

Archetypal heroes such as the ones he named almost always die for the cause, whatever it may be. But not all of Father Malloy's heroes died a martyr's death. For instance, one of his heroes is Jimmy Carter, maybe the best former president this country has ever had.

JIMMY CARTER

You can argue about Jimmy Carter's presidency. His victory in the 1976 election over the incumbent Gerald Ford, who was appointed vice president when Spiro Agnew shuffled off in disgrace and became president when Richard Nixon resigned, was a reflection of disgust over Watergate. Carter was a strong advocate of human rights. But his term in office was marred not only by high inflation and long lines at the gas station but by the capture of fifty-two hostages from the American Embassy in Iran. Carter's failure to free the hostages led to his defeat in 1980. After 444 days in captivity, they were released on the day following Ronald Reagan's inauguration. It must have been a humiliating moment.

And yet, that's when Carter's story becomes heroic. Instead of hitting the golf course, he returned to Plains, Georgia, and set about trying to help people and to change the world. In 1982, he published his presidential memoir (*Keeping Faith: Memoirs of a President*) and founded the Carter Center. Through that organization, he has monitored elections, acted as an international mediator in places like North Korea, Haiti, and Bosnia, and worked to promote democracy and human rights. The Carter Center has also sponsored a variety of health initiatives focusing on problems like river blindness and Guinea worm disease, which has subsequently been reduced by 98 percent in Africa and Asia. And the list goes on and on.

Carter's domestic efforts are equally impressive. He is probably best known for his work with Habitat for Humanity, an organization that builds new homes for the needy. Besides all that, he is a professor at Emory University, a Sunday-school teacher, and a prolific writer (fourteen books since 1975 and counting). He was awarded the Notre Dame Award in 1992 and the 2002 Nobel Peace Prize.

President Carter meets Father Malloy's definition of heroism by using his abilities to the utmost, choosing goals that serve the common good, and being persistent. "People underestimate the potential of a former president," he told an interviewer in 1991. Noting that he had access to leaders in all fields, he explained that it was easy for him "to dramatize a particular problem, and to reach the news media, and therefore reach the consciousness of the people." Unlike other former presidents, Carter maximized those abilities, devoting himself to the most intractable problems in the world's most troubled hot spots. He has dealt with the Muslims and the Serbs, the Israelis and the Palestinians. His appetite for frustration and disappointment seems limitless. Yet he has carried on.

Carter's example is instructive, and not just as a model former president. Anyone on the verge of retirement needs to take a look at the way Jimmy Carter has chosen to live his life.

EDUCATORS

Consider, for a moment, the annual Academy Awards. The exuberant winners typically thank a long list of people. Yet they invariably omit one category: educators. The high school drama coach, the acting tutor, the ballet teacher, the singing instructor, the adjunct who taught that history of cinema course: these worthies barely rate a nod.

Many books could be—and have been—written lauding heroic teachers. This is not one of them.

Instead, I'd like to point out that, strange as it may seem, teachers are not the only heroic educators. Administrators—and is there a less appealing word in the English language?—can also be heroic. One stellar example is Father Malloy's predecessor, the Reverend Theodore M. Hesburgh. As president of Notre Dame (which is not the only reason I consider him heroic), he changed the nature of Catholic education and involved himself in a profound way with the problems of the world. According to Father Malloy, Hesburgh was "a great American icon" and "a citizen of the world." That opinion is shared by many, including myself. Father Ted is one of the great figures of the 20th century.

THE REVEREND THEODORE M. HESBURGH, C.S.C.

He grew up in Syracuse, the second of five children in a middle-class family that took its religion seriously. "My sisters and I all went to Catholic schools," he wrote in his autobiography, *God, Country, Notre Dame.* "Encouraged to be 'religious,' we never missed mass; some of us went every day. We never ate meat on Friday. We never lied, stole, or cheated—at least we never got away with any such sins. And we never, never talked about sex—in any way, shape, or form. For me, the highest calling in life was to become a priest." He was six years old when he made that decision, and he never wavered.

After being ordained as a priest during World War II, he asked to become a chaplain in the military but was ordered to get his doctorate instead. In 1945, he began teaching at Notre Dame. In swift succession, he became chairman of the Religion Department, executive vice president, and, at age thirty-five, president of the university.

Over the next thirty-five years, from 1952 to 1987, Father Hesburgh oversaw the transformation of Notre Dame from a mediocre school with a championship football team into a world-class university. Under his stewardship, its endowment increased from $9 million to $350 million; its student body almost doubled in size; its campus expanded from forty-eight buildings to eighty-eight; its curriculum was intellectually strengthened; its academic standards improved; and it went coed.

If you were at the university, and I was there when he was there, you always had a sense that Father Ted was around. Yet he was a significant player on the world stage, and his activities extended far beyond the academy. A strong activist on behalf of human rights, he was a member of the U.S. Commission for Civil Rights from 1958, when he was appointed by President Dwight D. Eisenhower, until 1972, when he was removed by President Richard M. Nixon. He was involved in the formation of the Peace Corps. He campaigned vigorously for the peaceful use of atomic energy. He helped bring democratic elections to Central America and did his best to bring peace to the Middle East, an endeavor that has so far defeated one and all. To my knowledge, he never turned down an assignment from the White House or anybody else to do the right thing. He played a role in virtually every social justice cause of the last century.

He boasts that, since his ordination, he has missed saying mass only once. And he has done all that while working as an administrator.

What makes people like him tick? It's not a matter of compassion. Father Ted is very compassionate. But as he told PBS's Gwen Ifill, compassion "doesn't really get anything done."

Commitment is the essential ingredient. Heroes like Father Hesburgh have a higher level of determination and tenacity than other people. They're tough in that way. They believe they can make a difference and they don't give up.

And I am convinced that they literally have more energy than the rest of us.

Heroes have one more quality that Father Hesburgh exhibits: good humor. He is, in his own words, a "Christian optimist." I don't think that's an accidental quality. Heroes have the amazing ability to read the paper and still maintain hope. Their spirits are high.

I am reminded once again of the words of Ralph Waldo Emerson. Persistence, he believed, was the most characteristic trait of heroes, but it wasn't the quality that he most appreciated. "That which takes my fancy most, in the heroic class, is the good humor and hilarity they exhibit," he wrote. Not long after retiring, Father Hesburgh and his second-in-command, Father Ned Joyce, set off to explore the world in everything from a recreational vehicle to the *Queen Elizabeth II*. Hesburgh chronicled the journey in a book entitled *Travels with Ted and Ned*—the work of a man who doesn't take himself too seriously.

WALKER PERCY

Walker Percy, the philosophical novelist who was also a convert to Roman Catholicism, is another of Father Malloy's heroes. "Like a lot of creative artists, he had a tentacle out to sense what was going on in society, what the concerns should be, what the superficialities were," Father Malloy said. "Creative artists pay a personal price. They have no idea if the creative act that they devote their time to is going to find an audience, or if they are just spinning in the wind."

Walker Percy eventually did find an audience. But he didn't have an easy time in life. His early life was marked by tragedy. And unlike Father Hesburgh, who never wanted to be anything other than a priest, Percy came to his calling in a roundabout way. Born in 1916 in Birmingham, Alabama, he was a child of privilege who grew up with such classic boys' books as *Treasure Island*, Kipling's *The Jungle Book*, and Conrad's *Lord Jim*. Percy was eleven years old when his father shot himself in what was in all likelihood a suicide.

When Percy was fourteen, his mother took him and his younger brothers to Greenville, Mississippi, to visit his charismatic second cousin, William Alexander Percy. Uncle Will was an accomplished lawyer, poet, war hero, and memoirist who had just returned from Bora-Bora. "He was the fabled relative, the one you liked to speculate about," Percy wrote.

Two years later, his mother drowned in an automobile accident, probably also a suicide. Uncle Will took over the job of raising the boys. That meant giving up his fantasy of returning to the South Seas and also, according to Percy, "giving up the freedom of bachelorhood and taking on the burden of parenthood without the consolations of marriage. Gauguin chucked it all, quit, cut out, and went to the islands for the sake of art and became a great painter if not a great human being. Will Percy not only did not chuck anything; he shouldered somebody else's burden."

Uncle Will introduced his charges to Shakespeare and Keats, to Bach and Stravinsky, to opera, and to the world of intellectuals. Visitors to the household included William Faulkner, the psychiatrist Henry Stack Sullivan, and a neighborhood boy named Shelby Foote, who became Percy's lifelong best friend.

A popular student, Percy graduated from high school as the winner of a poetry prize. At the University of North Carolina, he studied science and became known for his cynicism and skepticism, especially toward religion. One of his roommates attended mass every Sunday and was ruthlessly mocked for it. A friend described Percy in his undergraduate days as "devoutly agnostic."

After college, Percy enrolled at Columbia University's College of Physicians and Surgeons. He wasn't certain what he would specialize in, but the front-runners were pathology and psychiatry. It wasn't to be. His heart wasn't in it. And circumstances conspired to give him a way out. In 1942, just as he was beginning an internship at New York's Bellevue Hospital, his Uncle Will died of a cerebral hemorrhage at age fifty-six. Within six months, Walker was diagnosed with tuberculosis and sentenced to bed rest, the prescribed cure at the time. Years later, he told an interviewer, "I was the happiest man ever to contract tuberculosis, because it enabled me to get out of Bellevue and quit medicine."

But first he suffered through intermittent bouts of TB and long convalescences at various sanatoriums. When he was healthy, he dated widely. When he was ill, he read widely, focusing on authors like Thomas Mann, Fyodor Dostoyevsky, Thomas Aquinas, and St. Augustine. He was looking for answers. But he felt lost. "The day I turned thirty [May 28, 1946] was one of the worst days of my life," he remembered. "I just thought I was never going to amount to anything."

That summer, he drove out to New Mexico with Shelby Foote and spent a few months mulling over his situation. He decided to give up medicine and become a writer. He also flirted with the idea of converting to Catholicism—an idea that Shelby quickly shot down. "Walker," he said, "you are in full intellectual retreat."

That fall, Percy married Mary Bernice Townsend, known as Bunt. A year later, in December 1947, he converted to Catholicism. Thus he turned his back on medicine, rejected the beliefs and attitudes of his youth, and embraced a more complicated fate.

Some writers have immediate success. Walker Percy was not among them. His first novel, pronounced "boring as hell" by his brother, was never published, and Percy eventually burned the manuscript. His second novel, based on his experiences as a TB patient, also went unpublished.

Along the way, he and Bunt acquired two daughters: Mary Pratt, whom they adopted in 1948, and Ann Boyd, whom Bunt gave birth to in 1954. One day they were all outside when Percy, walking with a gun, spotted a poisonous snake and killed it. The shot, as they say, rang out. But little Ann Boyd didn't blink. The Percys soon discovered that she was almost entirely deaf. The way Walker Percy and his wife dealt with that over the years was as heroic as anything he ever did.

Meanwhile, with his fiction going nowhere, he started writing— and gaining recognition for—his philosophical essays. But he still longed to be a novelist. Throughout the late 1950s, he labored over what was to be his first published novel. *The Moviegoer* was published in 1961. Described as an existential novel, a novel of ideas, it won the National Book Award that year, beating out, among other competitors, Joseph Heller's *Catch-22*.

Percy went on to write five more novels as well as essays and articles on philosophy, language, psychiatry, the South, and other topics. In his work, he ruminates on big themes—alienation, despair, the relationship between science and faith, the nature of the self. (He professed a fondness for *The Incredible Hulk,* a television program about a seemingly ordinary guy who harbors within himself a whole other self.) Above all, he was concerned with the search for meaning—and that, to me, is where the essence of his heroism resides. As he wrote in *The Moviegoer*: "The search is what anyone would undertake if he were not sunk in the everydayness of his own life. To become aware of the possibility of the search is to be onto something. Not to be onto something is to be in despair."

Percy's work is about the loneliness of the self and the quest for something greater: That's always what the hero seeks. In his youth, Walker Percy had the kind of experiences that cause many people to close down. He overcame them. He figured out who he was. And he set about projecting his thinking and his perceptions to others.

Is there anything heroic in that? There is. The feelings Percy elucidates are common to us all, yet most of us turn from them. Percy faced them full-on. To read Percy is to be struck repeatedly with feelings you recognize yet may never have seen articulated so profoundly before. His work is truly illuminating. It is also deeply spiritual. I can see why a man of the cloth would be interested in him.

But Father Malloy also saw a personal level of heroism in Walker Percy. "By the time that I met him in person, he knew he was dying of cancer. I thought he was very courageous in the face of his own mortality," Malloy said. "He continued to do the things that he thought were important and he wasn't overly preoccupied with his own condition. That's a good model for rising to a challenge."

Not being overly preoccupied with one's own condition: Now that I think of it, that's another quality that heroes share.

ON BUSINESS

Not everyone I spoke with mentioned people in the arts as heroes. I was thrilled that Father Malloy did. But then I asked him the hardball question: Are there heroes in business? He named two people whose stories are worth remembering. The first is James Burke, former CEO of Johnson & Johnson.

JAMES E. BURKE
The Tylenol Crisis

If you are old enough to recall the distant days of September, 1982, you probably remember the Tylenol crisis. It began in and around Chicago with seven puzzling cases of sudden death: a twelve-year-old girl who complained of a cold and died less than two hours later; a twenty-seven-year-old man with minor chest pain who took a Tylenol and died later that day; his grief-stricken younger brother and sister-in-law, who came to his house that evening with other family members and died shortly thereafter; a twenty-seven-year-old mother who had just given birth to her fourth child; a thirty-one-year-old woman; and a thirty-five-year-old stewardess who died with an open bottle of Tylenol nearby. What made these seemingly healthy young people die so suddenly?

A couple of off-duty firefighters listening to police radio reports found the first clue. They noticed that in two cases Tylenol was mentioned. "This is a wild stab," one of them said. "But maybe it's Tylenol."

It soon developed that every one of the victims had ingested a capsule of Extra-Strength Tylenol. And each capsule was laced with enough cyanide to kill well over a thousand people.

When the news got out, which was almost immediately, people panicked. Over seven hundred called one area hospital. Throughout the Midwest, people were hospitalized just in case their symptoms might be due to cyanide poisoning.

For Johnson & Johnson, the company that produced Tylenol, this was a crisis that threatened to sink the entire brand. The company could have simply denounced the killer and disclaimed responsibility. After all, the product had been tampered with well after leaving the factory. Johnson & Johnson clearly had nothing to do with it.

Nevertheless, it would be hard to imagine worse publicity. Adman Jerry Della Femina thought that Tylenol would never recover. "I don't think they can ever sell another product under that name," he said. Any advertising person who could solve this problem, he said, could probably "turn our watercooler into a wine cooler."

Yet Tylenol survived. Credit for that miracle is usually given to James E. Burke, CEO of Johnson & Johnson. He understood the nature of the problem and responded with compassion, honesty, transparency and, most of all, integrity. He stopped all advertising and production. He posted a one hundred thousand dollar reward for the killer (who has, incidentally, never been found). He cooperated with the police and the FBI as well as with the media. He sent additional warnings to half a million doctors, distributors, and hospitals. And he recalled all bottles of the painkiller with the same lot numbers as those the victims had taken.

Then he started to wonder: What about the other lots? Although the problem was apparently regional, Burke considered recalling every lot, all the Tylenol in the nation. Of course, that would entail an enormous loss for the company, and it might even encourage the killer. The FBI and the Food and Drug Administration advised him to wait.

But waiting didn't feel right. Burke made the decision to recall all thirty-one million unsold bottles of Tylenol. It cost the company at least one hundred million dollars. Two days later, the company also offered to exchange Tylenol tablets for capsules, at an additional loss of millions of dollars.

Previously, Tylenol had commanded 37 percent of the market. Their market share dwindled to a fraction of what it had been. A few weeks later, the company reintroduced Tylenol in tamper-resistant packaging complete with reassuringly glued flaps, plastic wrap, and tight foil seals: the very safeguards that drive us nuts today. Unfortunately, they're there for a reason. That became all too obvious in 1986, when yet another tampering incident killed a woman in

Yonkers, New York. Once again, Burke took decisive steps. Johnson & Johnson not only removed all capsules from the market, they stopped selling their entire line of over-the-counter Tylenol capsules.

Today, Jim Burke is venerated, a rare example of a CEO who, when faced with a choice between protecting the company and protecting the public, did the right thing. Did he act alone? Of course not. Johnson & Johnson is a major corporation, and plenty of people were involved, including one who had the satisfaction of sending Jerry Della Femina a watercooler filled with wine.

But Burke was the CEO. It was his leadership that saved innocent people from losing their lives—even at the cost of losing his shirt. Which, as it turned out, he didn't lose at all.

Nor is the Tylenol episode the sole example of Burke's concern for others. In 1989, he left Johnson & Johnson to become chairman of Partnership for a Drug-Free America. But that endeavor, no matter how noble, is not what people remember when they think about Jim Burke. They remember his behavior during the Tylenol crisis, when he put public safety ahead of corporate profits.

Another heroic CEO, equally well known in the annals of business, made an equally heroic choice: He protected the people who worked for him. This is his story:

AARON FEUERSTEIN
The Hero of Malden Mills

As the third-generation CEO and owner of Malden Mills Industries, a fabric company in Lawrence, Massachusetts, founded a century ago by his grandfather, Aaron Feuerstein has weathered a number of crises. Two stand out.

In 1981, the company faced bankruptcy. Determined to keep it from going under, Feuerstein invested millions of dollars into creating a new fabric. Polartec® and Polarfleece® revolutionized outdoor clothing and turned the business around, transforming it from a domestic operation into an international concern.

The second crisis occurred on the night of December 11, 1995, when something exploded at the mill and flames swept through the complex, destroying three of the mill's ten buildings. As Feuerstein watched, he made a pledge. "This is not the end," he said. And he meant it—not only for the business, but for the three thousand out-of-work employees. He decided to pay the workers their full salaries for three months and to extend their health benefits three months beyond that. He also offered education and job training.

Why did he do it? He could have retired; he was in his seventies. Or he could have taken the insurance money and moved overseas to a place where wages are significantly lower. The company had faced a similar decision in the 1950s, when they considered moving to the South, where workers earned significantly less. Instead, the company stayed in Massachusetts, moving from Malden, where the company was founded, to Lawrence, where it remains today. After the fire, it would have been easy and profitable to relocate the mill.

But Feuerstein has a conscience. An observant Jew whose father started a synagogue in nearby Brookline in 1930, he felt a responsibility to the men and women who worked for him. "I consider our workers an asset, not an expense," he explained after the fire. He also felt a responsibility to the small communities where those workers lived. "It would have been unconscionable to put 3,000 people on the streets and deliver a death blow to the cities of Lawrence and Metheun," he said. "Maybe on paper our company is worth less to Wall Street, but I can tell you it's worth more. We're doing fine." He often quoted the first century Talmudic scholar Hillel: "In a situation where there is no righteous person, one must try to be a righteous person."

Needless to say, Feuerstein inspired huge loyalty and affection among his employees. Once things were up and running, production not only improved, it bypassed its previous maximum. "Our people became very creative," Feuerstein said. "They were willing to work 25 hours a day."

Feuerstein also rebuilt the plant, replacing a century-old factory with a building that was technologically advanced and environmentally friendly. It was the first mill constructed in New England in over a century.

But providing for his workers and rebuilding the facilities cost hundreds of millions of dollars, and Malden Mills, having lost many customers while it was re-building, never entirely recovered from the disaster. As of this writing, it has filed for Chapter 11 and has had to let a few workers go. It has also received enormous support. Unbidden, strangers from around the country have sent checks to save the company. By the time this book is published, I am confident that Malden Mills will be on firmer ground.

But even if it were to go under, Aaron Feuerstein would still rank as a hero because he put his workers first. "Everything I did after the fire was in keeping with the ethical standards I've tried to maintain my entire life," he said. "Whether I deserve it or not, I guess I became a symbol of what the average worker would like corporate America to be in a time when the American dream has been pretty badly injured."

It's a sad and infuriating fact that most CEOs would never do what Feuerstein did. That's why he, like Johnson & Johnson's Jim Burke, is an icon. In a post-Enron world, it's good to remember that even in the world of business, there are heroes.

A WORD ABOUT JOURNALISM

Used-car salesmen used to be the ones who got the rap for slimy behavior. Now it's politicians, lawyers, and journalists. But for every talking head offering slanted or partial coverage on television, for every reporter who may fudge a dateline or invent a quotation, there are many more who present the facts accurately and in depth.

Some journalists even risk their lives to get the story. Virtually all the reporters who went to Afghanistan and Iraq to cover the wars of 2002 and 2003 compromised their safety to get the story, and a few made the ultimate sacrifice. As Father Malloy pointed out, there are many journalists every year who "have been murdered or put in prison for speaking the truth to power."

To take those kinds of risks, a journalist doesn't have to be embedded in a military convoy in the midst of battle. In places where freedom of speech is not a given, even editors often put their lives on the line.

Father Malloy cited two heroic examples: Pedro Joaquin Chamorro Cardenal, once the editor of Nicaragua's *La Prensa,* and his wife, Violeta Barrios de Chamorro, whom Father Malloy got to know when she came to Notre Dame to accept an award and, later, when he visited her in Nicaragua.

Many of the heroes I've written about in this book are quiet heroes, subtle heroes, heroes of the inward journey. The Chamorros are the kind of old-fashioned heroes they used to make movies about—brave, principled, and committed, even in the face of death.

PEDRO AND VIOLETA CHAMORRO
Nicaraguan Heroes

Pedro Joaquin Chamorro Cardenal, born in 1924 to a distinguished Nicaraguan family, spent his life in the world of politics and journalism. Like his father before him, he became the editor of *La Prensa,* the most influential newspaper in Nicaragua. And like his father, he was an outspoken critic of General Anastasio Somoza Garcia, the former head of the national guard, who took over the government in 1934 and arranged the assassination of rebel leader Augusto Sandino. Chamorro was to suffer the same fate.

His struggles with the Somoza regime began in 1944, when he denounced the dictator in a speech and was imprisoned. Soon after, the Somozas shut down *La Prensa* and the Chamorro family moved to Mexico. Chamorro, formerly a law student, decided to enter journalism. In 1948, his family returned to Nicaragua and his father once again began to edit the paper.

Two years later, Chamorro married Violeta Barrios, the daughter of a wealthy cattle rancher. And two years after that, his father died and he took over the paper. He continued to oppose the repressive, corrupt Somoza regime. And he continued to reap the consequences. Over the years, Chamorro was jailed, tortured, and repeatedly brought to trial.

When Somoza was assassinated in 1956, Chamorro was accused of complicity and driven into exile in Costa Rica with his family. They returned in 1959. Chamorro and a few of his compatriots devised a plan to overthrow Somoza's son, Luis Somoza Debayle, who had taken over after the assassination. The insurrection failed. Chamorro was accused of treason and jailed for nine years. Undeterred, he returned to *La Prensa* upon his release in 1969. As before, he campaigned vigorously for democracy and human rights, and he actively opposed the Somozas, despite daily censorship. When the Somozas suspended constitutional rights in 1975, Chamorro became head of an opposition party.

Did Chamorro understand the danger he was in? He did. In a letter to Somoza's son Anastasio Somoza Debayle, who had taken over from his brother, Luis, he wrote, "I am waiting, with a clear conscience, and a soul at peace, for the blow you are to deliver."

That blow came on January 10, 1978, when Pedro Chamorro Cardenal was gunned down on the streets of Managua.

"During his whole life," Violeta recalled twenty years later, "Pedro Joaquin was a tireless fighter for democracy in Nicaragua and against the dictatorship of Somoza. This cost him incarceration, torture, exile and finally death. He was warned many times that plans existed to assassinate him, yet no threat derailed him from fulfilling his mission to impart the truth and preach democracy."

His assassination rocked the country. Riots broke out and there was a general strike. In death, Pedro Chamorro accomplished what he had not been able to do in life: He sparked a revolution.

Enter Violeta. Now a widow with four children, she took over at the newspaper, speaking out forcefully against the Somozas and quickly proving to be as heroic as her husband. Six months after Chamorro's death, the dictatorship was toppled and the Sandinistas took over. It was a great moment in the history of Nicaragua. But the need for heroism had not passed, as Violeta soon discovered.

Initially a supporter of the Sandinistas, she was invited to become a member of a five-person governing junta. She accepted but soon grew disillusioned and resigned. Increasingly critical of the new government, she found that the onerous censorship she had struggled against under the Somozas continued to be a problem with the San- dinistas. There were even several attempts to bomb the newspaper. She persevered in her opposition to the regime and in her commit- ment to getting the news out.

As the 1980s progressed, the Socialist dream of the Sandinistas disintegrated. With high unemployment, an economy in tatters, and the country wracked with political unrest, the Sandinistas accused *La Prensa* of being backed by the CIA and repeatedly closed it down. Violeta Chamorro fought to keep publishing. It probably didn't help her emotional state of mind to know that the editor-in-chief of the competing Sandinista paper, *La Barricada,* was none other than her son Carlos.

By 1990, dissatisfaction was so widespread in Nicaragua that the Sandinistas agreed to hold free elections. Their candidate for presi- dent was Daniel Ortega. His principal opponent, running under the banner of the Opposition Union Party (UNO), was Violeta Barrios de Chamorro.

To the astonishment of many, she won handily. During her seven years as president of Nicaragua, she revitalized the economy, reduced the size of the army, and instituted many reforms. She tried to broker a settlement between the Sandinistas and the opposition parties. Most of all, she presided over her country's transition to democracy. In 1997, when her term was up, she retired from politics.

What's heroic about her? Let me put it this way: What isn't? Not that she doesn't have her critics; every politician does. The fact remains that, in a time of terror, Violeta Chamorro fought tirelessly for freedom of the press, stood up for democracy, and did her best to bring peace to a troubled land.

On the Front Line

It doesn't diminish the heroism of the Chamorros to say that they lived in an exceptionally explosive time and place. Nor does it lessen their contribution to point out that, due to their involvement with *La*

Prensa, they had the means to act heroically. Heroism arises most dramatically when the need for it is strongest.

Our times are also deeply troubled, albeit in a different way. We are facing terrorism, war, economic debacle, environmental disaster—you name it. In 2000, we even suffered through a bitterly contested presidential election—and not for the first time either: Think of "Rutherfraud" B. Hayes in 1876. Or think of the sharp divisions between red states and blue states in 2004. Our system is deeply flawed. As Winston Churchill remarked, "Democracy is the worst form of government, except for all the others."

Nonetheless, we have periodic elections in which we regularly throw the rascals out—a grand American tradition. But in times as perilous as these, relying on elected officials isn't enough. We all need to be involved. More needs to be done—much more.

With the stakes as high as they are today, we have a greater need for heroes than ever before. I asked Father Malloy what he thought:

MM:I think there's always a strong need for heroism, just as there's always a strong need for prophecy or for good leadership. In any crisis, there are many roles that people can play. Some are sought out and some are thrust upon us by the force of events. I've read nine or ten books about 9/11 and the various ways people responded to the crisis. Those are reminders that most of us live our lives according to certain routines. We try to do the best we can within our limitations. But sometimes we're called upon to do things at the next level. When that happens we just hope that we have been prepared.

RD: Is there a way to prepare oneself?

MM:I'm a big believer in character. That elusive quality is hard to define. It is a product of the many choices we have made in life. Making the right choices, even when they're difficult, can become easier over the course of a lifetime. If we practice, it becomes instinctive. It's often easier to do that later in life. People can develop the capacity to make the right choice.

Is he right? Can people grow their moral capacity? I am heartened by the idea that people can increase the capacity for heroism by practicing. But what, exactly, should we do? The answer is anything but clear, especially for those of us who may not feel particularly courageous.

Fortunately, as George Bernard Shaw said, "You cannot be a hero without being a coward." To be a hero, all you have to do is decide to make the world a better place, starting wherever you are. Doesn't matter if your efforts fail. The point is to do something . . . but what?

Turn to chapter 18 for a few suggestions.

CHAPTER 11

A Conversation With
MEL MANISHEN
On Phil Holland and Others

W illiam Safire, unreconstructed Nixonian, writes a weekly column for the *New York Times'* Sunday magazine in which he delves into the origin and history of popular words and phrases. I've been waiting for a long time for him to dissect the phrase "giving back," an expression so often invoked by athletes, movie stars, and CEOs trying to polish their reputations that I had hoped to avoid it in this book.

But "giving back" is ubiquitous for a reason. It allows us to avoid two words that make us squirm: "charity," which hints at luckless poor people in desperate need of soup kitchen assistance; and "philanthropy," which suggests well-heeled, well-clad givers who dispense financial favors to worthy organizations that had the forethought to put them on their boards. The perceptions of those words being what they are, it is difficult to imagine a philanthropist actually meeting a recipient of charity.

"Giving back," on the other hand, doesn't sound patronizing. It lacks the aura of superiority. Instead, it suggests involvement, even parity. More than a synonym for being philanthropic or making a charitable contribution (and taking it off your taxes), it combines an acknowledgement of one's own good fortune with a commitment to addressing the needs of the broader community, possibly in a hands-on way. It is precisely the attitude that more of us need to take.

Mel Manishen is the person who brought the concept up to me as an element of heroism. "I admire people who are passionate about what they do and they give something back," he said. "It's the giving back."

A man of vast enthusiasms, Manishen recently retired as president of Rockwell Modular Automation, Inc., and Empire Sheet Metal Manufacturing Company of Winnipeg, Canada. His pioneering use of robotics in manufacturing and machine building, along with his vision and marketing skills, made him a highly successful, albeit small, industrialist.

He is also a contented parent, something you don't have to ask him about twice. Or even once. When I asked him to tell me about himself, here's what he said: "I was in the sheet metal business for over 50 years and I have three sons. One is 53; one is 51; one is 43. The 43-year-old is a doctor, the one who's 51 is a criminal lawyer, and the one who's 53 is a music critic for the local paper. And that's about all I can tell you about me." Which tells you something about Mel Manishen.

One of his heroes is his friend Israel Asper, a billionaire media mogul who labored ceaselessly to establish the Canadian Museum of Human Rights in Winnipeg but died before achieving that vision. "At the end of the day, you have to have mattered," Asper said. "You have to ask yourself: Did you make the world a better place than it was when you entered it, or did you just take up space?"

Another hero Manishen admires came from the opposite end of the economic spectrum: José Antonio Gutierrez, a twenty-two-year-old who became the second U.S. casualty in Iraq. Once an orphaned street kid in Guatemala, he headed north via freight train; spent a few years in Mexico; knocked around in California's foster care system for a while; and eventually found a loving family and a true home in the United States. Then he joined the Marine Corps. Why? He wanted to give back. He was made a U.S. citizen after his death.

Finally, Manishen praised Phil Holland, a quintessential example of a man who gave back—and in kind.

PHIL HOLLAND
Your Own Businessman

You never know what influences a person to do something heroic. Sad to say, tragedy is often a motivator.

Phil Holland was always entrepreneurial. In his twenties, he found a job in New York working for a major corporation. A couple of years later, he quit in order to go back to California and start his own business. "People told me I was nuts," he said, "because I was on the ladder to corporate heaven and now I didn't even know what kind of business I wanted to start." He forged ahead anyway. Over a period of years, he became involved in a variety of businesses.

One was a small company, later sold to Pillsbury, that manufactured donut-making machinery. Then there was a company that designed and built apartment houses in Los Angeles. Finally, he invested in a chain of Mexican restaurants, a venture that misfired completely.

"After that failure, which I might add included a personal bankruptcy, I was in the bottom of a pit," Holland told me. "It was 1970. I borrowed five thousand dollars from a friend and I started the first of what became Yum Yum Donut Shops in California." The donuts sold well and the stores proliferated.

Sorrow and Success

His personal life was not so sunny. His son, Jamie, was diagnosed with leukemia. Holland began to spend a lot of time at Children's Hospital in Los Angeles. While there, he got to know his son's roommate, a teenager with "a burning itch to become an entrepreneur." When that young man, who was recuperating from a long illness, learned that his roommate's father owned Yum Yum Donuts, he began to pump him for information. Holland was delighted to give it.

Somewhere along the line, it occurred to Holland that his lessons consisted largely of telling his eager student what to avoid. "Creating your own business is like walking into a minefield blindfolded," he said. There are plenty of caveats, plenty of mistakes waiting to trip up the eager entrepreneur. Holland felt that he was in a good position to know. "I viewed myself as the world's number one authority on how to make mistakes in your own business, because I have made them all," he said.

After the death of his son, Holland sought some distraction by writing. He took those lessons and turned them into a book. *The Entrepreneur's Guide* was published in 1984 by G.P. Putnam's Sons.

In 1989, Holland sold his interest in Yum Yum Donuts to his partner. By then, there were 138 Yum Yum Donut shops, making it the largest privately owned donut shop chain in the country. Rather than retire, he got into the shopping center business. He also wrote another book: *How to Start a Business without Quitting Your Job: The Moonlight Entrepreneur's Guide.* It was published by Ten Speed Press in February 1992.

Chaos and Courses

Two months later, tragedy struck again, only this time it was a civic tragedy, not a personal one. Four white LAPD police officers were acquitted of assaulting Rodney King, and riots broke out. From his home high on a hill, Holland could see fires burning all over Los Angeles. Fifty-two people died in those riots and 2,383 were injured. There was over a billion dollars worth of property damage.

A group called Rebuild LA arose to deal with the problems, but Holland wasn't impressed. "I thought that organization was bureaucratic and clumsy and inefficient. It wasn't the way I would go about it. As the champion of entrepreneurs, I decided to let the entrepreneurial lone wolf come out and do it my way."

With the help of his wife, Peggy, a former teacher and principal, he turned the information in his books into a curriculum of ten lessons. Then he went to Compton, an economically depressed area of the city, and distributed advertising flyers emblazoned with the words "Free Course. How to Start a Business." His friends told him he was crazy. But people signed up in droves. "And the more I did the more they came," he said.

One of his students was a member of the Hispanic Chamber of Commerce in Compton. He arranged to have the course translated into Spanish and he convinced the organization to put a three-line announcement for the class in *La Opinion,* the local Spanish-language paper. "It drew so much attention that the Mexican consul general in Los Angeles got wind of it and all the politicians in Compton got wind of it, and they all turned out for the graduation ceremony," Holland said. He put together a board of directors and started a nonprofit.

Because he hoped to expand beyond the class he was teaching twice a week in Compton, he had to find a way to distribute the course. Originally, Holland thought it would be possible to offer it through the Rotary Clubs. After all, there are eighteen thousand of them throughout the world, and they're dedicated to good causes. But things just didn't work out. "It was an example of something that happens in business all the time: A concept that appears to be wonderful does not turn out to be wonderful in reality." Fortunately, it was 1999, and there was another way to go: the Internet.

Today, anyone in the world can take that course by logging onto www.myownbusiness.org. Or go to the website of the Small Business Administration (SBA.gov), and you'll find a link.

Why is this heroic? It's giving back in the most effective, hands-on way. Holland is returning to the community his most valuable possession: knowledge.

Using the information in this course, thousands of people have created small businesses. Phil Holland believes that these entrepreneurs can make a huge difference in their own lives, in the life of their community, and even on a global level. "The best way to make the world a better place is to nurture economic vitality," he says. "And the best way to do that is to encourage new businesses."

Holland finds his mission satisfying and fun. "It's more fun giving money away than it ever was making it," he says. He quotes Albert Schweitzer: "Anyone who would find true happiness must find a way to help people."

But if that makes you imagine that Albert Schweitzer is his hero, think again. I fell into that trap and was quickly corrected. His hero is Warren Buffet—a man who, many will say, embodies the entrepreneurial spirit at its best.

CHAPTER 12

A Conversation With

BRIGADIER GENERAL ROBERT F. MCDERMOTT

On David Robinson, Charles Lindbergh, and Others

The phrase "a great American" has become a cliché. Brigadier General Robert F. McDermott is the real thing. He has served his country in war and in peace—as a pilot in the air force, as an educator, as a businessman, and as a philanthropist. He's a hero by anybody's measure.

He grew up in Boston during the Depression. His father, Alphonsus, a veteran of World War I, played trombone in symphony orchestras; in a brass quartet that entertained shoppers in Filenes and other department stores; and in the pit orchestras of two local theatres, the Metropolitan and the RKO. An Irish tenor, he also sang at weddings, funerals, and masses—two every Sunday, in two different towns.

But his best gig, to his little boy, was as a member of the band at athletic events. "I went to Red Sox or Braves baseball games and I watched the Boston Redskins play football because my father played music at those games," he remembers. "At the Boston Braves games, I would sit right behind the batter's box with my father. I never could have afforded to see baseball and hockey and football, but my father took me along."

General McDermott developed a love of both sports and music (he plays jazz trombone) along with an interest of his own: aviation. "My father had a car, and so every Sunday we drove somewhere. One of our tricks was to stop by the airport and watch the airplanes land.

That was because of my interest in flying." That interest ultimately led McD, as he likes to be known, to his first career. (The nickname came from Alice McDermott, whom he met at West Point and married when he graduated.)

A Military Man

After attending Boston Latin School, he went to Norwich University, transferred to West Point, and graduated as a pilot in 1943. A P-38 pilot in the European theater of operations, he flew sixty-one combat missions, returning home with a chest full of ribbons and medals. He worked on General Dwight D. Eisenhower's staff after the war and then on the Air Staff. In 1948, he was sent to Harvard for his MBA.

In 1950, he returned to West Point to teach economics. By 1954, he was itching to get back to flying. He even lined up an assignment on an aircraft carrier. But to his disappointment, he was assigned to the newly created U.S. Air Force Academy in Colorado. That was where General McDermott made his mark.

The education then offered through military institutions was strong on military subjects and athletics but academically narrow. In 1957, a year after President Eisenhower appointed him dean of the faculty, General McDermott introduced a series of reforms which ultimately revolutionized military education, not only at the Air Force Academy but also at Annapolis and West Point.

"In those days," he told me, "if you went to West Point, you were going to be a civil engineer; if you went to Annapolis, you were going to be a marine engineer; and if you went to the Air Force Academy you were supposed to be an aeronautical engineer. Well, why should everyone be an engineer? We're not all going to build fortifications or weapons. We're going to do a lot of things."

General McDermott transformed the place. He instituted an admissions system that gave weight to character and leadership as well as to athletic ability and good grades. He broadened the curriculum, added twenty-eight majors, upgraded the faculty, expanded the library, and established cooperative graduate programs with leading universities.

He even introduced a course in fine arts. That topic might not have arisen in our conversation had it not been for the fact that shortly before we spoke, terrible reports came out of Iraq about the looting of museums and the failure of our troops to defend them. Why did that happen? "Somebody didn't have the appreciation that comes with education," he said. And he went on . . .

McD: I'm going to tell you a story about General [Curtis] LeMay, the old "nuke 'em" guy. When I came to the Air Force Academy, he had heard that I was too liberal in my ideas and that I even offered a fine arts course. The reason I introduced it was that, after the war in Europe, I visited Rome and Greece, and I got to see these wonderful masterpieces that man had created over the centuries. And I realized that I knew something about music because of my father, but I'd never had any education in the fine arts. I decided to introduce an elective course in fine arts into the Air Force Academy.

RD: How did LeMay react?

McD: He didn't go for it. He said, "I don't like this 'softcore' stuff that you're teaching." I said, "Well, come look around with me." We walked around—I'm a walk-around man—and I saw a self-portrait of the football quarterback Terry Isaacson. I didn't plan it. But there it was, in the studio. So I said to LeMay, "Do you recognize Terry Isaacson's self-portrait on the easel?" He did. And it changed his attitude.

When I worked for Eisenhower, he often spent his time in the evening sitting down and painting. It was the same with Winston Churchill. He spent his recreational time painting. The good Lord didn't endow me with any artistic talents, but I wanted to know about it and I figured maybe others would, too. So I put in this course.

In 1959, McDermott became a brigadier general and was appointed the first permanent dean of the Air Force Academy. He retired in 1968. He has been hailed as "the father of modern military education." In 2003, the Air Force Academy named the Robert F. McDermott Library in his honor.

Career #2

During the four years he spent teaching economics at West Point, McDermott wrote two books, one on personal finance and another on insurance. After he retired from the military in 1968, he moved to San Antonio, Texas, and took a job with the United Services Automobile Association (USAA), the company that offers insurance to members of the military.

Here's what he found: a sea of paper so extensive that the company had to hire dozens of college students to work at night just to track down missing files; a system so cumbersome that the basic task of issuing a new insurance policy involved fifty-five separate steps at fifty-five desks; and a workforce so dispirited that the annual turnover rate was 43 percent.

When he retired twenty-five years later, in 1993, he left behind a changed organization. He diversified it, computerized it, increased its assets, and improved its rating so that it was consistently named one of the top companies in the nation. He also added employee benefits that included campuslike headquarters spread out over 286 acres, a physical fitness center, a health clinic, increased employee training, full tuition reimbursement for college courses, and a four-day work week. The annual turnover rate fell to 7 percent.

Career #3

While working at USAA, General McDermott was also active in the community. He became the chairman of the chamber of commerce in 1974; he founded the San Antonio Economic Development Foundation; he founded the Texas Research and Technology Center and helped bring biotech to San Antonio; he founded a world affairs council and a free-trade alliance to promote global outreach and opportunities; and for thirteen years, he chaired Riverwalk Jazz. His impact on his community has been enormous.

With help from people such as President George H. W. Bush, comedian Bob Hope, golfer Byron Nelson, and country singer George Strait, he mobilized a team to save the PGA Golf Tournament for San Antonio. Then in 1993, he organized a group of local investors to buy and keep the Spurs NBA basketball team in San Antonio.

General McDermott says that he is most proud of his education initiatives in San Antonio. Those include extensive mentoring in needy school districts, creation of magnet and charter schools, Junior Achievement, Education Partnerships (with business), and graduate degree programs in public and private institutions in science, technology, and engineering.

On Heroism

"In your life, you will find many heroes around you and may become one yourself," General McDermott told me. "It's important to consider every personal relationship as an opportunity to learn or to teach, to recognize a hero or to be one yourself. If you do, you're going to find many, many heroes."

When we spoke, he named athletes, aviators, astronauts, educators, military leaders, even a musician or two. What makes them heroic? In his view, heroes have two qualities in common: They work to develop their talents and they treat other people according to the Golden Rule. Here's how he put it:

McD: A hero is a person of character. He lives by the Golden Rule; he has a moral compass; he does the right thing for the right reasons. Those are the characteristics I see in all the heroes I think about.

There's a quote I think of when I speak of leadership to young people. It's from Luke 12:48: "From those to whom much is given, much shall be required." I used that to tell them that we're all given endowments from the good Lord and it's our moral responsibility to use those talents. Why? So that we can love our neighbor— the purpose of the Golden Rule. Heroes are people who develop self-discipline, discover and develop their talents, and give selfless service. That's what the Golden Rule is all about. You do it not for yourself, not for your glory, not to get a plaque, but for the good of humanity and your fellow man. That's what makes a hero.

Who are his heroes? One of them is the basketball player David Robinson of the San Antonio Spurs.

On Sports Heroes

I love sports as much as anybody—probably more than most— but I have been increasingly distressed by what I see there. Only last week, the sports sections were featuring two stories: one about a professional athlete accused of sexual assault and one about a college athlete accused of murder.

But that was a week ago, and those stories are old news. As I write, the lead article in today's sports section is about Mike Tyson and how he managed to squander a fortune. To me, sports has become a sorry exercise in greed, celebrity, undeserved privilege, and out-of-control behavior.

And yet, people will always see athletes as heroes because sports really do mirror our lives, just as athletes really do reflect our fallibilities and our dreams. Their skills are astonishing. Their successes are admirable and enviable. And yet, no matter how gifted they are, athletes never stay at the pinnacle of their sports. They age; they injure themselves; they miss easy putts; they strike out. Most of the time, most baseball players don't even get on base. And those who do make it to first don't necessarily score. Even hitting a home run doesn't guarantee that a team will win the game. Athletes make mistakes. Umpires make bad calls. A game can get rained out. And it's a melancholy fact that often the opposing team is just plain superior.

Yet even the unspectacular athlete sometimes makes an amazing play, and the most luckless team on earth occasionally triumphs. Who can forget the Miracle Mets? Or the redoubtable Red Sox, who won the World Series in 1918—and then again in 2004? No matter how unlikely, victory is always possible.

Athletes are heroes because we see them fail, every one of them. (Think of Michael Jordan's baseball career.) And then we see them triumph. It holds out hope for the rest of us. And if their off-season behavior fails to live up to their prowess on the field, well, so be it. Heroes are flawed, just like the rest of us.

Of course, some have flaws that are worse than others.

The press focuses on athletes who fall down on the job. Yet as General McDermott explained, there is something stirring and beneficial about the game that transcends the problems of individual players. And it's not just metaphorical.

McD: I feel very strongly that professional teams do more to unify a city than almost any other activity and certainly more than any other form of entertainment. Movies or TV or music divide people into groups. Some like classical music; some like—what do they call it?—hip-hop. But sports bring a city together, especially one that's multi-ethnic like San Antonio. When I came here in 1968, racial relations were tense. Today, there's much less racial bias. I attribute a lot of this to having a professional sports team and to David Robinson in particular. Everybody who comes to a game is paying attention to one thing, and that is the athletic experience. The African Americans are there, the Hispanics are there, the Caucasians are there, the Asians, the Muslims, the Catholics, the Jews, the Protestants, they're all there—fat

> people, thin people, old people, young people—it's amazing what a cross section of society you get. It pulls a city together. Sports can do wonderful things.

Unlike most sports figures, San Antonio Spurs basketball star David Robinson has extended his beneficence beyond the team to the city. *Sports Illustrated* calls him "an all-around tremendous human being." The *San Antonio Business Journal* called him a "godsend" and a "hero." Here's why "the Admiral," as he is known, reaps such praise.

DAVID ROBINSON

Born in Key West, Florida in 1965, David Robinson played one year of high school basketball before entering the Naval Academy in Annapolis, Maryland, in 1983. Over the next four years, he majored in mathematics, was named College Player of the Year (1985–1986), and grew seven inches. Upon his graduation in 1987, the San Antonio Spurs chose him as their number one NBA draft pick.

But Robinson had to fulfill his military obligations first, so he postponed his professional career for two years while he served as a commissioned officer in the U.S. Navy. During that time, he was starting center on the 1988 U.S. Olympic basketball team—the last such team to use amateur athletes exclusively.

Then in November, 1989, his military service completed, the seven foot one center played his first game as a professional with the San Antonio Spurs. He scored twenty-three points for an eight-point victory over the Los Angeles Lakers.

Thirteen years later, the Admiral retired after setting many records, playing on ten All-Star teams, and winning just about every honor you can imagine from NBA's Rookie of the Year (1990) and NBA's Most Valuable Player (1995), to one of the NBA's 50 Greatest Players of All Times (1996). He also played on two Olympic teams, each of which captured a gold medal.

But being an exceptional athlete doesn't make him a hero (except in the eyes of his fans and teammates). What makes him a hero is something else: The Carver Academy, a private school for inner city children located on a grassy, newly created campus on San Antonio's economically blighted east side. The school, which will ultimately serve three hundred kids from pre-kindergarten to eighth grade, features small classes and a strong curriculum offering, among other courses, German, Japanese, and Spanish.

Robinson and his wife, Valerie, started it in 1997 with a $5 million donation. Since then, they have donated an additional $4 million for a total of $9 million, thought to be the largest philanthropic donation ever made by a professional athlete. In addition, Robinson has involved himself directly with the school and with the kids—not just symbolically. He has an office at the school and knows most of the kids by name. His commitment is more than financial.

> McD: David Robinson has recognized and developed the many gifts that God gave him, and he uses them to love his neighbor, to please his neighbor, to serve his neighbor as he'd like to be served. Nobody can match David's record as a basketball player. He's also an accomplished musician. He is doing something with his mind all the time. Plus, you couldn't meet a more genuine, gracious person. There's not a bit of arrogance in the man. Among my heroes, he ranks right up there.

OTHER HEROES

Who else? McD's answer was quick and to the point. He named golfer Byron Nelson, ballplayer Roger Staubach, Dwight D. Eisenhower, and astronaut David Scott. He added Bob Hope "for his patriotism and for basing his family comedy on only one four-letter word: 'quip'"; George and Barbara Bush "for living family values"; and "Charles Lindbergh, in particular."

In particular? "Yes. Charles Lindbergh. I met him when I was a little boy, and I got to know him personally when I was at the Air Force Academy. I know that he has serious flaws. His behavior during the period leading up to World War II was unconscionable. But as an aviator myself, I can never forget his early accomplishments."

I was glad that the general mentioned Lindbergh. Because if ever there was a hero, it was Charles Lindbergh, whose solo flight across the Atlantic in 1927 galvanized the world. Tall, handsome, laconic, and indubitably brave, he was the ideal hero. But if ever a hero fell from grace, it was Charles Lindbergh, who repeatedly visited Germany in the late 1930s, made anti-Semitic speeches (and diary entries), tried to keep the United States out of World War II, and was reviled as a traitor and a Nazi. Here's his story—including his encounters with General McD.

CHARLES LINDBERGH

Born in 1902, Charles Lindbergh was the painfully shy son of a Minnesota congressman and a schoolteacher. The pivotal event of his life took place in 1912, when his parents took him to an air show. It inspired him to fly. He went to the University of Wisconsin in Madison for two years and enjoyed his experiences in the ROTC but was otherwise unmotivated. Then, in 1922, he moved to Lincoln, Nebraska, and went to flight school. Soon he was barnstorming around the country, wing-walking and parachuting out of airplanes and establishing a reputation as a daredevil. It occurred to him that "if I could fly for ten years before I was killed in a crash, it would be a worthwhile trade for an ordinary lifetime."

The next year, with the help of his father, he bought his first plane. Not long after, he signed up for a U.S. Army flight school and became an airmail pilot, a job widely considered the most dangerous in the country. Despite the excitement of that job, he grew bored. He began to fantasize about better planes and more exotic destinations.

One journey was especially alluring: the trip from New York to Paris. In 1919, a French immigrant had offered a $25,000 prize to the first person to fly non-stop between those two cities. In 1926, with the prize still unclaimed, Lindbergh decided to try. A heavily equipped biplane piloted by a French aviator had recently crashed and gone up in flames before it lifted off the ground, killing two crew members. Lindbergh resolved to keep his plane light by flying solo and by eliminating everything he considered extraneous, including an extra engine, a parachute, a gas gauge, and a radio. After gathering financial support, he found a manufacturer to build the plane he wanted and applied for the prize.

Less than two weeks before Lindbergh's flight, two French aviators took off from Paris. Lindbergh feared that he had lost his chance. But the Frenchmen disappeared forever somewhere over the Atlantic. The way for Lindbergh was clear.

On May 10, 1927, Lindbergh flew his new plane, *The Spirit of St. Louis,* from San Diego to New York, breaking the record for transcontinental speed. Momentum was building. Lindbergh was attracting publicity. A few days before the scheduled flight, he posed for pictures with his mother. When a photographer asked her to kiss him good-bye, she demurred. "I wouldn't mind if we were used to that," she explained, "but we come of an undemonstrative Nordic race."

Triumph

Six days later, on a drizzly May morning, he took off. The trip was a perilous one. He fought darkness, fog, ice, and overwhelming fatigue—and, while he did, the world held its collective breath. When he landed in Paris, thirty-three-and-a-half hours later, he was greeted by 150,000 wildly cheering French people. From there, his celebrity exploded. In New York, between 3 million and 4.5 million people lined the streets for a ticker-tape parade—more than had shown up for the parade that ended World War I.

It's hard to overemphasize the extent to which Lindbergh was adored. Within a few weeks, he had become a hero for the ages. He was even called "the new Christ," unlikely as that may sound today. "We measure heroes as we do ships, by their displacement. Colonel

Lindbergh has displaced everything," said Charles Evans Hughes, later chief justice of the Supreme Court. "America is fortunate in her heroes; her soul feeds upon their deeds; her imagination revels in their achievements. There are those who would rob them of something of their lustre, but no one can debunk Lindbergh, for there is no bunk about him."

That's certainly how he struck seven-year-old Robert McDermott, who watched a parade in Boston from atop his Uncle Charlie's shoulders. "That evening, my father played at a reception for Lindbergh," he told me. "I went along as sort of a mascot. I met Lindbergh and I got a Lindbergh coin. To a little boy, Lindbergh was a real hero. He was someone that I wanted to be."

Tragedy

In February, 1932, Lindbergh's year-old baby Charles was kidnapped and murdered. Colonel H. Norman Schwarzkopf (father of Stormin' Norman of Gulf War fame) headed the investigation. A suspect wasn't found until September 1934, when a German carpenter named Bruno Hauptmann was charged with the crime. In what was dubbed the "trial of the century," he was found guilty and sentenced to death.

Afterward, Lindbergh and his wife, Anne Morrow Lindbergh, who became famous as an author in her own right, left the country. They lived in England and then in France. While there, Lindbergh, who had once considered becoming a doctor, spent a lot of time with Nobel Prize–winning scientist Dr. Alexis Carrel. Together, they researched the possibility of keeping organs alive outside the body by using a pump of Lindbergh's invention. Their book, *The Culture of Organs,* was published in 1938. Carrel, according to Lindbergh's biographer A. Scott Berg, was Lindbergh's hero.

And that was exactly the problem. Because in addition to being a brilliant scientist, Carrel was a believer in selective breeding or eugenics and in the idea that criminals and weaker members of society ought to be weeded out. "There is no escaping the fact that men were definitely not created equal," Carrel said. Lindbergh agreed.

More Tribulations

While living in France, Lindbergh was asked to investigate Germany's strength in aviation. Lindbergh was treated royally. He visited airfields and even accepted a swastika-encrusted medal from Hermann Goering. He was impressed. Germany could not be defeated, he thought. He recommended that the United States avoid going to war.

The Lindberghs also found Germany such a stimulating place that they decided to move there. But in November 1939, only a few days after they located a house in a Berlin suburb, hundreds of Jewish homes, shops, and synagogues were destroyed in a night of violence known as Kristallnacht. The Lindberghs changed their mind about living in the Third Reich, though Lindbergh still counseled isolationism.

Lindbergh's image was becoming tarnished. Then, on September 11, 1941, he made a speech which sealed the deal. The United States was being pushed into war, he said, by three main groups: "the British, the Jewish and the Roosevelt administration." Public reaction was immediate. Although isolationist sentiment in those pre–Pearl Harbor days was strong, Lindbergh was still denounced for his bigotry. And although he later supported the war, even flying over fifty combat missions in the Pacific, his sympathy with the Nazis was not forgotten. Despite what Charles Evans Hughes had said in 1927, there seemed to be plenty of bunk about him.

After the war, Lindbergh worked as a consultant to Pan Am, the United States Air Force, and other organizations. He also became interested in environmental causes. By the time he died, in 1974, much of the rancor over his World War II statements had diminished. But he never regained the heroic stature that surrounded him in his youth like a halo. As F. Scott Fitzgerald wrote, "Show me a hero and I will write you a tragedy."

A Hero, Nonetheless?

Still, to some people—and perhaps to aviators in particular—he will always be a hero. One of those is General McDermott, who encountered Lindbergh for the second time in the 1950s:

McD: I got to know him personally in 1954. President Eisenhower appointed him to the board to select the site of
the Air Force Academy. When that board visited West
Point, I was designated to be liaison to Lindbergh. He
was a very quiet man, not flamboyant in any way. But he
told me he would like to know what a cadet is all about,
and could I arrange for him to meet one of them. I
picked a top cadet named David R. Scott who went on to
become an astronaut. Lindbergh was interested in what
he had to say.

My relationship with Lindbergh continued from that
point on. Lindbergh's son came to Colorado to go to
college, so Lindbergh would come out to visit. He
always came to the Air Force Academy unannounced.
There was zero publicity. He would just show up at my
office. We would talk to cadets and he would want to
visit classes. He would not let me introduce him. When
the instructor called the class to attention, I would say
"At ease gentlemen. I have a visitor with me. We just
want to sit in with you." And we'd sit in the back of the
room and he would ask questions afterwards and make
appropriate comments.

RD: Did anyone ever recognize him?

McD: Nobody recognized him.

RD: That surprises me. He was both famous and handsome.

McD: Yes. He had unusual physical characteristics and his blue
eyes were unbelievably bright. I don't know why they
didn't recognize him. Maybe it was just as well. Later
on, not many years after I left the academy, he died. I visited his grave site in Hawaii. To me, he'll always be a
hero, despite his flaws.

RD: And yet, as you know, he was soft on Hitler, especially
during the 1930s. How do you put his less admirable
traits into perspective?

McD: It's true that he got off-base with Hitler. His instincts were just plain wrong. He didn't comprehend what was going on. That doesn't justify it. But Lindbergh eventually came into World War II and voluntarily flew missions in the Far East. I think Lindbergh was obsessively focused on aviation. Hitler was advancing aviation faster than we were. And that was his interest. That's why he was interested in the Air Force Academy. And that is why he voluntarily flew missions in the P-38. He taught us a lot about the airplane; about how to get more mileage out of it; how to lean back on the fuel; how to stay up longer hours, and so on. He was a true aviator and what he wanted to do was to help all aviators and to help our country.

I was too young in the 1930s to understand Lindbergh's support of the America First isolationist movement, but not too young to empathize with Lindbergh's tragic loss of his son. Perhaps his World War II volunteer P-38 combat missions served as a public penance for his prewar shortcomings.

RD: Knowing the troubled trajectory of his life, how would you evaluate him as a hero?

McD: Maybe I can summarize it this way. The Lord endows potential leaders in varying degrees with a special dimension, a yearning to explore and to stimulate others to do the same. Early in the twentieth century, Lindbergh electrified that yearning among young people. Despite his failings, he deserves heroic credit for that accomplishment.

Yet Another Slip from the Pedestal

Not long after General McDermott and I talked, "Lucky Lindy" was in the news again. Seems that for seventeen years starting in 1957, he had a secret affair with a milliner in Germany, who had three children with him. Growing up, the children did not know his real name, but they had over a hundred letters that seem to back up their story—which became even juicier a few days later when it turned out that Lindbergh also allegedly had two children with the milliner's sister. Are these stories credible? I can't say. The children, now grown up, have promised to take DNA tests. So we shall see.

And if he is guilty as charged? Does it matter? Lindbergh was lionized not only because he was brave and had initiative but also because his values seemed to be in the right place. We now have two examples of unacceptable, disgraceful behavior—one in the public sphere and one in his private life, both taking place over a period of years. Can we recognize Lindbergh's achievement while acknowledging his flaws? Can we agree, with General McDermott, that the young Lindbergh might legitimately be considered a hero of aviation?

I think we can. But only if we acknowledge that hero worship can be a dangerous thing. Best not to invest too much in any one hero. Instead, like General McDermott, we need to fill our hearts with the images of "many, many heroes."

Finding a Hero

Must a hero be a person whose accomplishments are worthy of admiration? Or can a hero be a concept, an ideal to live up to? General McDermott told me a story that made me redefine my notions of heroism. See what you think . . .

McD: When I was five years old, I had two sisters and heaven-on-earth came to me: A baby brother was born. Every morning after my mother nursed the baby, she would come and get me. I would lie in bed with the baby and tickle his toes and his ears and it was just wonderful. I had a brother.

Three months later, that brother was dead. He was born with a floating kidney and in those days, they didn't know how to handle that. All of a sudden he got sick and he died.

That just about killed me. But as a result, my father got closer to me. And because he didn't have an eight-to-five job he had to go to every day, he would take me to a concert or to the beach or we would go to a Bruins hockey game. He kept me with him whenever he could—whenever I didn't have school to attend.

My parents did have another baby, but it turned out to be a girl. I was their only son. My father told me that all babies under seven go right to heaven when they die because God wanted them up there. He also told me, you can go ahead and talk to your brother and he will be with you; he will be your guardian angel.

I lost my brother. But I still had him. I've felt that way all of my life, that I do have my brother, David, with me. He was my hero.

That idea became a part of my conscience. It made me want to do the right thing because my brother would want it that way. If you're the older brother, you've got to set the example.

RD: So he was your hero, and you tried to be his hero.

McD: That's right. It's had it an interesting impact on my life and the way I think about things. My brother's name was David. When I had a son, I named him David and he became a doctor. He told me that no baby with that condition today would die.

So my brother's namesake, my son, became a doctor—and that doctor's son is right here in San Antonio and he's studying to be a doctor, too, and his name is David. And my daughter's son, her one and only son, is also named David and he is in his second year of medical school at Stanford. I've got three Davids in the family and all three will be doctors. I had nothing to do with that.

I doubt that anyone would agree with the general about that. The proliferation of Davids, each serving humanity as a doctor or a soon-to-be-doctor, is part of his legacy—the legacy of heroism.

CHAPTER 13

A Conversation With

MARILYN CARLSON NELSON

On Ruby Bridges, Sarah and Mary Katherine Goddard, Lydia E. Pinkham, Amelia Earhart, and Others

"My heroes tend to be pioneers, people who had the courage to step into unknown territory," Marilyn Carlson Nelson told me. Perhaps the most powerful woman in the business world today, she is the CEO of Carlson Companies, which operates travel agencies, hotels, restaurants, cruise lines, and marketing services. Employing about 188,000 people systemwide, it is one of the largest family-owned companies in the world.

And while it's true that Marilyn is the founder's daughter, it's also true that she is an extraordinary leader. Labeled one of the top twenty-five executives by *Business Week,* she chairs the National Women's Business Council, is a member of the World Economic Forum, and serves on the boards of Exxon-Mobil, the Mayo Clinic, and the Singapore Tourism Bureau. She is also the recipient of scores of honors and awards. Among them is the Royal Order of the North Star, bestowed upon her by King Carl XVI Gustaf of Sweden, where her great-grandfather was born.

Her great-grandfather, one of her heroes, left Sweden in 1864 to escape from hunger and from the ancient custom of primogeniture, according to which the oldest son inherited everything while the others were forced to rely on themselves. He decided to do just that. As Marilyn told me, "He wanted to go to the promised land and he was willing to bet on himself."

Like many Scandinavians, he and his family made their way to Minnesota. "They thought that personal freedom, free enterprise, and freedom to worship were worth taking a risk for, worth losing everything and sacrificing for," Nelson said.

Another hero with the pioneering spirit was her father, Curtis L. Carlson. In 1938, with the Depression lingering and the winds of war beginning to blow, he decided to quit his job at Proctor & Gamble, where he had been named salesman of the year. Using fifty-five dollars he borrowed from his landlord, he took off on his own. "My mother was scared to death. But he had decided to start a company," Marilyn told me. "That's the company I run today."

A graduate of Smith College with a major in international economics and a minor in theatre, Nelson did not immediately enter the family business. She worked for a couple of years as a securities analyst—and was asked to sign her name "M. C. Nelson" so that as few people as possible would know the terrible truth about her gender. In 1965, she took a job with one of the subsidiaries of Carlson Companies and began slowly working her way up the corporate ladder. At the same time, she and her husband were raising four children. In 1998, she succeeded her father as chairman and CEO of Carlson Companies.

To celebrate the occasion, she went up in an F-16 fighter plane and boldly piloted it through a roll and a 9G maneuver. I'm not exactly sure what a 9G maneuver is, but it involves multiplying the force of gravity by nine and is not something I would ever consider doing.

Outside of her family, Nelson has a long list of heroes who are as intrepid as she is. One of them is a little girl whose image may be more famous than her name.

RUBY BRIDGES
Civil Rights Pioneer

In the autumn of 1960, the momentous decade really began. In September, Emily Post, symbol of a more repressed era, died. On November 8, John F. Kennedy was elected president. And on November 14, Ruby

Nell Bridges went to first grade accompanied by four armed federal marshals and a crowd of screaming, out-of-control white people.

That moment had been coming for six years, ever since *Brown vs. Board of Education*, the landmark Supreme Court decision that mandated integrated schools. In the spring, African American kindergarten students in New Orleans were given a test to determine which ones would be sent to white schools. Because the test was purposely difficult, few were expected to pass. But five did, including Ruby. Three of those children were assigned to the McDonogh School. One dropped out of the program. Ruby was assigned to the all-white William Frantz Public School.

Her parents, the children of sharecroppers, argued about the wisdom of letting their small daughter participate in this historic undertaking. Ruby's mother thought it was the right thing to do, that there was a larger principle involved. Her father thought they were asking for trouble.

They were both right. That morning, as she put on a white dress and white hair ribbons for her first day in the new school, six-year-old Ruby knew nothing about the fierce racism that both necessitated and threatened the plan to desegregate the schools. Ruby and her mother were picked up by the federal marshals and driven five blocks to the elementary school. When they got there, the mob was so big that Ruby thought it must be Mardi Gras.

That day, Ruby and her mother never got out of the principal's office.

The second day, she and her mother walked the same gauntlet, past the woman who threatened to poison her; past the middle-aged "cheerleaders," as they were chillingly called, who screamed obscenities at her; past the teenagers chanting, "Two, four, six, eight, we don't want to integrate." She met her teacher, a white woman from Boston named Mrs. Henry, and was escorted to her new classroom. She was the only student there because every other child in the class had been taken out of the school.

The third day, her mother had to go to work so Ruby went to school accompanied only by the federal marshals. That scene—two federal marshals in front, two behind, and Ruby in the middle—

inspired Norman Rockwell to create an iconic American image in a painting called *The Problem We All Live With.*

For an entire year, Ruby remained the only student in Mrs. Henry's class. During that time, her father was fired from his job at a gas station; her grandparents were kicked off the land where they had lived and worked for twenty-five years; the owner of the local grocery refused to sell to them; and Ruby picked up a Boston accent. She also got to know the Harvard-based child psychiatrist Dr. Robert Coles, who interviewed her at her home throughout the year (and wrote about her in, among other volumes, *Children of Crisis* and a children's book called *The Story of Ruby Bridges*). When she went to second grade the next year, she had a new teacher (who made fun of her accent) and a room full of classmates, several of whom were African American. She had integrated the school.

In the years that followed, Ruby graduated from an integrated high school and entered Marilyn Carlson Nelson's industry, travel and tourism. For fifteen years, she worked as a travel agent. She married and raised four children. Then, in 1993, her youngest brother was killed in a drug-related shooting and she returned to William Frantz Public School, this time as a volunteer.

Since then, Ruby Bridges Hall has become well-known, thanks to Dr. Coles, a Disney television movie, and a children's book of her own (*Through My Eyes*). She has also reconnected with Mrs. Henry. Today she devotes her time to the Ruby Bridges Educational Foundation and visits schools throughout the country to make sure that her story and the history behind it are not forgotten.

That brave little girl from not-so-long-ago made a big impression on Marilyn Nelson. Part of the reason, she told me, had to do with the church she attended growing up:

MCN: Growing up in the 1950s, we went to a large urban church in downtown Minneapolis. At the time there was enormous prejudice. An African American A.M.E. Church in the heart of the city was closing because the highway was going to go through it and they didn't have enough money to build a new church. Our minister was heroic in that he began to encourage our elitist, elegant downtown church to take in this African American congregation from a different side of town. There were factions and high emotions. He provided leadership by teaching that it was consistent with our faith to be inclusive.

I was in high school and right around that time I read *Cry, the Beloved Country* by Alan Paton. I remember putting it all together and realizing that what he said was extremely important. It wasn't too long after that that Ruby Bridges had the courage to be the first black girl to go to an all-white school. I remember the pictures of that little girl walking through the jeering crowds. I was overwhelmed with how brave she and her mother were. And I thought she had a mission in her life—something that was more important and bigger than she was—to stand and fight for. That little girl became a real hero for me.

I don't expect to be a hero, but if a little girl can take on such an enormous pioneering roles, then I have to ask myself what can I do in my life to push back boundaries and make positive change.

Pushing Back the Boundaries of Business

In a lifetime of having heroes, Marilyn Nelson has often looked to women who were pioneers in one way or another. They include . . .

SARAH AND MARY KATHERINE GODDARD
Colonial Entrepreneurs

Despite serious constraints on what women could do and own early in our nation's history, a group of entrepreneurial women who lived during colonial times made a remarkable impact. Sarah Goddard, a doctor's wife born in the first decade of the eighteenth century, was one of them. Her daughter Mary Katharine Goddard, born in 1738, was another.

Their business career began in 1762, the year Sarah's husband died. She and her son, William, set up a print shop in Providence, Rhode Island, and Mary Katherine joined them. In addition to their print work, the Goddards also published the *Providence Gazette and Country Journal,* that city's first weekly newspaper. After three years, with financial difficulties piling up, William grew restless and left. Sarah and Mary Katherine took over and formed a new enterprise, the highly successful Sarah Goddard and Co., Publishers.

After Sarah died in 1770, Mary Katherine joined her ambitious brother in Philadelphia, where he had opened another shop and was publishing another paper. Mary Katherine managed the business. In 1773, William moved to Baltimore where he also opened a print shop and established Maryland's first newspaper, the *Maryland Journal & Baltimore Advertizer.* Once again, soon after she joined him, he left town. Although he continued to be intermittently involved with the paper, she acted as sole publisher and editor until 1784, when the two siblings quarreled and he took over. Fortunately, she had another position. In 1775, she had been appointed first postmaster of Baltimore, a post she maintained for fourteen years.

The high point of her career came in 1777, when the Continental Congress asked her to print the first signed copy of the Declaration of Independence. The low point came in 1789, when she was dismissed from the post office because she was a woman, the powers that be having decided that the job required more travel than a woman could handle. She objected strenuously. Two hundred local businessmen signed a petition on her behalf and she even appealed to George Washington. When her efforts proved futile, she turned her attention to a bookstore connected to the printing business. She ran that store successfully for another twenty years.

LYDIA E. PINKHAM
"Savior of Her Sex"

Since interviewing Marilyn Carlson Nelson, I've mentioned Lydia E. Pinkham (1819–1883) to a number of people. Her name invariably rings a bell, but no one has been able to identify her. That's because hardly anyone takes Lydia E. Pinkham's Vegetable Compound any more. But once upon a time, women relied upon it, even if what they were really relying on was the placebo effect . . . or the black cohosh . . . or the alcohol, which was "used solely as a solvent and preservative."

It's easy to mock the Vegetable Compound. And it's true, Lydia Pinkham is not considered a towering figure in the annals of pharmacology. But let's put her in context. In the nineteenth century, the issue of whether doctors ought to wash their hands was controversial; becoming a doctor took less than a year of training and involved no hospital time; and bleeding, leeching, blistering and purging were common practices. These remedies were so extreme that Dr. Benjamin Rush, a Philadelphia physician who signed the Declaration of Independence, described them as "heroic," which was not a good thing.* Common medications in the 1840s and 1850s included strychnine, opium, and calomel, which consisted in large measure of metallic mercury. As a result of its widespread use, mercury poisoning—a truly horrific affliction—was commonplace.

As for gynecology, it was an excessively surgical enterprise, too awful to contemplate in those days before anesthesia and basic antiseptic measures.

Home remedies, then, weren't necessarily worse. And Lydia Pinkham, mother of five, was interested in the topic. The product of a lively Quaker home in Lynn, Massachusetts, she knew Frederick Douglas and William Lloyd Garrison, both of whom were friends of the family. An active supporter of abolition and women's rights, she

---

* Only in medicine does the word "heroic" carry negative connotations. Think of living wills. People sign them for one reason: They'd rather be allowed to die than be subjected to "heroic measures" to sustain life.

joined the Lynn Female Anti-Slavery Society when she was only six-teen, but the political issues of the day were far from her only inter-ests. Phrenology and spiritualism also intrigued her, as did the Eclectic Movement, a school of healing that recommended diet and herbal remedies as the first line of defense. She pored over *The American Dispensatory* by Dr. John King, a book that analyzed the com-ponents of plants. One of them was an herb called *Aletris farinosa* or True Unicorn, which was said to prevent miscarriage and to bene-fit the female reproductive system.

Combining that with other herbs recommended by Dr. King (plus fenugreek, her own contribution), Mrs. Pinkham made up an infusion and offered it to women in the neighborhood as a remedy for monthly distress and other female ailments. Soon strangers were coming from miles around. She would give a bottle to anyone who asked, and if a woman happened to bring along a child, she was generous with the horehound candy.

That's how things stood until the Panic of 1873, when her hus-band, a would-be real estate magnate, went bankrupt. The family moved into more humble quarters, and their grown children pitched in to help. By 1875, things still looked bad. One day, they held a fam-ily meeting. While they were gathered around the table, a group of women from nearby Salem knocked on the door in search of the veg-etable compound. Mrs. Pinkham sold them six bottles for five dollars.

Her son Daniel saw the commercial possibilities and persuaded the family to go into business. They branded the potion Lydia E. Pinkham's Vegetable Compound and came up with a marketing cam-paign. There were handbills ("Only another woman can understand a woman's ills") and pamphlets and newspaper advertisements. But none of them were particularly effective. Something wasn't working.

Then they put the gray-haired Mrs. Pinkham's picture on the label, and sales took off. Over the next several decades, her name and face became so ubiquitous they inspired songs and jokes ("Oh, I've smashed my bottle of Lydia Pinkham's!" "Aha! A compound fracture!").

Mrs. Pinkham's picture wasn't just an image, for she stood behind her product in a profoundly personal way. With every ad exhorting the customer to "write to Mrs. Pinkham at Lynn, Mass., and she will advise you," letters came pouring in. She answered every one until the flood of correspondence became overwhelming. When she was unable to respond to each letter herself, she devised a series of form letters and employed a cadre of young women known as "typewriters" to send them out over her name.

Mrs. Pinkham recommended cleanliness, fresh air (*"Ventilate! Ventilate! Ventilate!"*), exercise, whole grain cereals and bran, fresh fruits and vegetables, herbal remedies, and therapies such as magnetic healing. She kept up with the medical literature, and if she was occasionally wrong (cream of tartar does not cure smallpox), she often prescribed correctly, and she recognized a case of hypochondria when she heard it.

She also sought to educate the public. Appalled by the ignorance in the letters, she explained the facts of life to her customers in a free booklet. Addressed to "married women and those about to be," it discussed everything concerning the female body including puberty, conception, childbirth, and menopause. Written in a straightforward style using scientific terms, it had a circulation literally in the millions.

In the 1880s, tragedy struck. Her sons Daniel and Will contracted tuberculosis and died within months of each other. Shortly thereafter, Mrs. Pinkham had a stroke. She died in May 1883.

The business continued to be wildly successful. With orders rolling in, no one thought it necessary to change the advertising. The advice department continued to operate. Over the next couple of decades, sales continued to grow. Trouble struck in 1905 when the *Ladies' Home Journal*—a muckraking periodical back then—published a picture of Mrs. Pinkham's tombstone, thus revealing that she was dead and hence could not be dispensing all that wisdom. This was a public relations disaster for the company. As a PR professional, I can tell you that it's always best in such circumstances to come clean. But like Richard Nixon and Bill Clinton, the Pinkhams obfuscated. They didn't mean to suggest that the Mrs. Pinkham who answered all those letters was Lydia, they said. It was a different Mrs. Pinkham: Jennie, her daughter-in-law.

But as reporters soon learned, Jennie had nothing to do with anything. The correspondence was actually answered by a roomful of women equipped with form letters.

The next year, the Pure Food and Drug Act was passed, forcing the company to reveal the high alcoholic content of the medication and to scale back its more outrageous claims ("For the cure of kidney complaints of either sex, this compound is unsurpassed."). Yet sales continued for decades. Even today, Lydia Pinkham Herbal Tablets are available. You can get them from Walgreens.com.

Was Lydia E. Pinkham's Vegetable Compound an effective medication? Or was it snake oil? I can't say. I do know that one of the ingredients—black cohosh—is touted today by women in search of relief. It may well have helped. Certainly, the women who wrote letters to her extolling the compound's virtues believed that it did.

Beyond that, Lydia Pinkham was a remarkable businesswoman. Was she a hero? "She was customer-focused," Nelson told me. "She was one of the first who believed that women held the key to their own health. She was ahead of her time in thinking that women were not inherently weak and that they could manage their own health care—with diet and exercise and probably a few shots of the famous Lydia E. Pinkham's Vegetable Compound."

"Weakness is Never the Source of Power." —Lydia E. Pinkham

AMELIA EARHART
Goddess of Flight

If you're looking for pioneering women, you can't do much better than Amelia Earhart. Her adventurous spirit made her a feminist heroine (and it didn't hurt that she looked like Katharine Hepburn). But in recent years, accusations of carelessness and overconfidence have dimmed her aura. Truth is, she was a hero because she operated on the edge—which sometimes means falling off.

She was six years old when the Wright Brothers got off the ground at Kitty Hawk; ten when she saw her first airplane ("a thing of rusty wire and wood . . . not at all interesting,"); and twenty when she caught the bug. She was working with wounded soldiers as a nurse's aide in Toronto, Canada, and occasionally she visited a nearby airfield. The pilots were young, she remembered. "But the planes were mature. They were full-sized birds that slid on the hard-packed snow and rose into the air with an extra roar . . . I remember that when the snow blown back by the propellers stung my face, I felt a first urge to fly." Since she couldn't get permission to go up, her first flight had to wait.

After the Armistice ending World War I, she had to have a minor operation on her sinuses. Inspired by the experience, she enrolled in the pre-med course at Columbia University in New York. After a year, she decided that medicine wasn't for her, and she went to California to visit her parents. That was where she had her first airplane ride. "As soon as we left the ground, I knew I myself had to fly," she wrote. "'I think I'd like to learn to fly,' I told the family casually that evening, knowing full well I'd die if I didn't. 'Not a bad idea,' said my father just as casually. 'When do you start?'"

Within the week, she took her first flying lesson from a woman named Neta Snook. Later that year, she purchased her first plane, a bright yellow Kinner Airster. She set her first record in 1922 by flying to fourteen thousand feet and in 1923 she got her pilot's license. But when her parents split up in 1924, she drove to Boston with her mother and became a social worker.

20 Hrs. 40 Min.

She came to public notice in 1928 when a book publisher, George P. Putnam, was searching for a woman to accompany two men, a pilot and a co-pilot/mechanic, on a trip from Newfoundland to Wales. There were several candidates, but for one reason or another they couldn't go. At last, someone told him about a young social worker in Boston, a member of the National Aeronautics Association, who occasionally took to the air. The minute he saw her, he knew she was right for the job. He offered her the position and she accepted it.

On June 17, 1928, a little over a year after Lindbergh's historic flight, the Fokker F-7 *Friendship* took off from Trepassy Harbor, Newfoundland. It landed in Wales twenty hours and forty minutes later. Thus Amelia Earhart became the first woman to fly across the Atlantic.

Adulation followed. The fact that she had crossed the ocean as a passenger didn't seem to matter. She starred in a ticker-tape parade and was invited to the White House to meet President Coolidge. The public was enthralled by the tall, slender young woman who bore such a strong physical resemblance to Lindbergh that she became known as "Lady Lindy," a sobriquet she despised. "It is hard to describe to later generations what it was like to live in a world dominated by two such shining youthful deities," wrote Gore Vidal in 1985. He called them "the god and goddess of flight."

Unlike Lindbergh, she worked at her fame by constantly setting new records and lecturing about them. And although she never achieved the lofty heights of his lifelong celebrity, her renown was also worldwide.

After the flight, with George Putnam's encouragement, she wrote *20 Hrs. 40 Min.,* which described the transatlantic flight. In 1931, she married him in a secret ceremony. The decision to marry was not an easy one for her. She was so ambivalent that, while they were waiting for the judge, she handed him a letter in which she wrote, "I must extract a cruel promise, and that is you will let me go in a year if we find no happiness together." She also wrote that she would absolve him from "any medieval code of faithfulness to me, nor shall I consider myself bound to you similarly." She even kept her last name, a decision with which he concurred (though she answered to Mrs. Putnam and he joked about being Mr. Earhart). On his side, he made sure she was constantly in the news and, as a result, has been accused of exploiting her. Yet they had a deep connection. She even wrote love poems to him.

One More Good Flight

In 1932, on the fifth anniversary of Lindbergh's famous flight, she cemented her place in aviation history by becoming the first woman to fly solo across the Atlantic. Seven women had died in pursuit of that record. Other flights followed and other records. She was the first person to fly solo from Honolulu to Oakland, from Los Angeles to Mexico City, and from Mexico City to Newark. (The first woman to fly coast to coast as a passenger was Lydia E. Pinkham's granddaughter, Lydia Gove, who chartered a plane for the purpose in 1926.)

In 1937, Amelia Earhart decided to fly around the world, a feat that had yet to be achieved by a woman. "I have a feeling that there is just about one more good flight left in my system and I hope this trip is it," she wrote. She teamed up with a navigator named Fred Noonan. After one false start, they took off from Miami on June 1, 1937, heading to Puerto Rico and then east around the world. By June 29 they had made their way to New Guinea. The next leg of the trip was to take them 2,556 miles to tiny Howland Island, a trip of almost twenty-one hours.

Somehow, they got off course. Radio contact was made, but the signals were weak. And as she said in one of her final transmissions, the gas was running low. The plane disappeared.

Despite a massive search, neither Earhart nor Noonan were ever found.

Since then, many theories have evolved to explain Earhart's disappearance. Was she involved in military operations, perhaps as a spy? Did the Japanese force her down and capture her? Did she take on a new identity, move to Long Island, and marry a man whose name was an anagram of a group of islands in the Pacific? Probably not. Most likely she died at sea.

Amelia Earhart was not the first female aviator, and she was not necessarily the best, although she was first on a number of important occasions. Still, had she not disappeared in such a mysterious way, it is doubtful that her name would have such a powerful hold on the imagination. Nothing becomes a hero like a dramatic death.

But there's more to Amelia Earhart than that. She was not just a pioneer of aviation, she was a pioneer for women. She spoke out for equality and simultaneously represented it. Well after she became famous, she worked as a career counselor for women at Purdue University. She supported the Roosevelt administration and promised to give flying lessons to her friend Eleanor, who went ahead and got a student permit (though nothing ever came of it). She supported the Equal Rights Amendment (and nothing ever came of that either). She even designed her own line of clothes, meant for the active woman. She was aware of the larger societal issues and she did what she could to further them. As Mrs. Roosevelt said, "She helped the cause of women, by giving them a feeling there was nothing they could not do."

Marilyn Carlson Nelson put it this way:

MCN: Heroism doesn't mean testing yourself to see what you can do. And it doesn't mean being a role model. It's bigger than that. It means forgetting yourself in the spirit of service or accomplishing something that's going to impact others. There's a selfless quality to it. Amelia Earhart is an example. She did test herself. But beyond that, she opened the skies to women and encouraged them to pursue independent careers.

"Courage is the price that life exacts for granting peace."
—AMELIA EARHART

OTHER HEROES

Mary Katharine Goddard, Lydia E. Pinkham, and Amelia Earhart were not the only heroines Marilyn Carlson Nelson talked about with me. She admires Sophia Smith, who started Smith College. She looks up to Jennie Grossinger, who came to this country as a child from Austria and went on to found Grossingers, the famous resort in the Catskill Mountains. But those historical heroes are dwarfed by a few of the 188,000 people who work for her.

One of them is Christopher Knabel. In 2001, he was manager of the Regent Wall Street Hotel, located only blocks from the World Trade Center in New York City. On September 11, with the air thick with smoke and debris, the hotel lost all power. Instead of heading home to his family, he located a generator to power the hotel, borrowing it from the HBO show *Sex and the City,* which had been on location in the area. He also convinced his employees to stay on and cook. Under his direction, they turned the magnificent ballroom at the Regent into a relief station for police and other Ground Zero workers. They stayed open twenty-four hours a day. "He didn't just stand by and watch what was happening," Marilyn said. "He stepped forward and became part of the solution."

Or consider another act of heroism. José Racasa came to Hawaii from the Philippines and waited on tables for twenty-two years. One of his customers at the Radisson Waikiki Hotel was a man who came in every Wednesday to eat lunch before his Rotary Club meeting. One week he wasn't there. When he reappeared at his regular table and Mr. Racasa asked where he'd been, the customer explained that his kidney had failed. He was a candidate for a kidney donation, he said, but it might be five or six years before he could get one with the right blood type.

Out of the blue, Mr. Racasa offered one of his own kidneys. He explained that he was type O, the universal donor. The guest refused the offer. But the waiter persisted. He went to the hospital, met with psychologists, and ultimately underwent the operation to give his kidney to the man he'd been serving all those years. According to Nelson, "Everybody who knows this man says that he's a very together, positive, grateful, extraordinarily giving person." I'm not surprised.

RD: What ties these people together? What is heroism?
MCN: What comes to mind is selflessness. Heroes are willing to give of themselves for someone else. Or they have a vision that drives them to accomplish something that benefits others.

Who benefits? In the case of the altruistic waiter, a single individual benefited. In the case of Ruby Bridges, a nation benefited. Either way, whether the benefits are large or small, heroes don't hesitate. When an opportunity to act heroically presents itself, they step forward.

And when the opportunity to act heroically needs to be created, when someone needs to push a door open for the very first time, they do that, too.

CHAPTER 14

A Conversation With
MONSIGNOR JOHN O'KEEFE

On Arthur Ashe and Cardinal Joseph Bernardin

Once upon a time, firefighters were thought of as municipal employees, admired but not necessarily revered. But that was before September 11, 2001. Since that fateful day, firefighters have become heroes of the first order—which is only fair, for unlike people in other lines of work, they agree to risk their lives, and all too often, they meet death on the job.

Monsignor John O'Keefe knows something about that. A native Manhattanite, he was president of Archbishop Stepinac High School in New York's Westchester County for eleven years and is now at St. Margaret's Church in nearby Rockland County. He is also the son of a firefighter who died on the job in 1966, leaving behind a wife and five children.

"My father gave his life for the people of New York at a very young age," Father O'Keefe said. "He was always a great man in the eyes of his family and friends, especially dying the way he did. We still, after all these years, honor his memory."

The idea that it is heroic to die while trying to serve others is not new. But let us not forget: Dying can be an act of heroism in and of itself.

Take, for instance, two of Father O'Keefe's heroes: the tennis player Arthur Ashe and the theologian Cardinal Joseph Bernardin. Both led remarkable lives. And both died in ways that were courageous, public, and ultimately heroic. Here are their stories:

ARTHUR ASHE
Sailing into the Wind

Arthur Ashe (1943–1993) was a man of true grit and bad luck in approximately equal measure. A skinny child who loved to read, he grew up in Richmond, Virginia, in a wood-frame house located in a park that included four tennis courts. When he was seven years old, his twenty-seven-year-old mother died suddenly. He was devastated. Shortly thereafter, a man named Ron Charity, the best African American tennis player in Richmond, noticed the small boy hanging around the courts and offered to teach him to play.

Five years later, Ashe was ranked as the best twelve-year-old player in the nation. But this was the segregated South, and boys like Ashe were expected to sit in the back of the bus and to attend all-black schools. Despite his obvious talent, Ashe was offered few opportunities to play. As a high school junior in Richmond, he was barred from municipal competitions and not allowed to play on most public courts. As a senior in St. Louis, he found that things were not much better. The white players he knew practiced their serves at private clubs that he wasn't allowed to join. Once, he was even chased off a public court.

Despite those obstacles, he was still in high school when he won his first national championship—the U.S. Lawn Tennis Association's National Junior Indoors competition—and was offered a tennis scholarship to UCLA.

In his sophomore year, 1963, he was invited to join the team representing the United States in the Davis Cup tournament. He was the first African American to achieve that honor. It was the first of many. Even when he had to take time out for military service after graduation in 1966, he continued to win tournaments. In 1968, still an amateur, he won the U.S. Open (which brought him $280 in expense money). From then until 1979, he won a total of fifty-one competitions, including the Australian Open and his greatest athletic triumph, Wimbledon, which he won in 1975 against Jimmy Connors. That year he was rated the number one player in the world.

Choose Your Battles

But it wasn't his skill as a tennis player that distinguished Arthur Ashe, though his skill was phenomenal. Nor was it his race: After all, he wasn't the first African American tennis champion in this country. That honor belongs to Althea Gibson.

It was the quiet way he dealt with the racial and political issues of the day.

He knew, for instance, that not every battle is worth fighting. When a local country club barred him from an "exclusive" weekend tournament as a student at UCLA, his coach asked if wanted to press the issue. Ashe chose not to. But later on, when he became famous and the club changed its mind, he declined their invitations. The Balboa Bay Club wasn't worth bothering with.

South Africa, on the other hand, was. He denounced that country's racist policies and campaigned to have South Africa thrown out of the International Lawn Tennis Association and excluded from the Davis Cup matches. He applied three times for a visa to play there. When he finally received one, his very presence drew attention to the cause.

He marched on the United Nations to protest apartheid and in 1985 was arrested for demonstrating in front of the South African embassy in Washington, D.C. He also banded together with other activists and helped found several organizations, including Artists and Athletes Against Apartheid, which he cochaired with Harry Belafonte.

Two months before Martin Luther King, Jr., was assassinated, the civil rights leader wrote Ashe to thank him for his support. Yet Ashe was seen as a reluctant activist and was often criticized for not speaking out aggressively enough on racial issues. He objected to the pressure. "For the first seventeen years of my life, white people in Virginia had told me what I could do, where I could go to church, in which taxi I could ride, where I had to sit on the bus, in which stores I could try on a coat," he wrote in his memoir *Days of Grace*. "Then, in my second seventeen years, militant black people were trying to tell me, once again, exactly what to think and do. I rebelled."

His understated approach—he admired Thoreau, Gandhi, King— cost him not only friends but peace of mind. "There were times, in fact, when I felt a burning sense of shame that I was not with other blacks—and whites—standing up to the fire hoses and the police dogs, the truncheons, bullets, and bombs ...," he wrote. "As my fame increased, so did my anguish. I knew that many blacks were proud of my accomplishments on the tennis court. But I also knew that some others, especially many of my own age or younger, did not bother to hide their indifference to me and my trophies, or even their disdain and contempt for me."

Bad News

Ashe's tennis career came to an abrupt halt in 1979 when, at age thirty-six, he had to undergo quadruple coronary bypass surgery. "The doctors say I will live to be a hundred," he joked. "But they won't put it in writing." Four years later, he needed a second bypass operation. Forced to give up tennis, he turned to more intellectual pursuits and was offered a job at Yale University.

He opted instead to teach at Florida Memorial College, a historically black institution. His course was entitled "The Black Athlete in Contemporary Society." He described his experiences there as "one of the more discouraging seasons of my life." Shocked by the poor performance of his students, he insisted on the importance of maintaining high academic standards for athletes—an issue that is still with us today. With Ashe's backing, the NCAA did raise its standards. But Ashe, who broke so many racial barriers in what was once a whites-only sport, was accused of racism.

His teaching experience at FMC alerted him to another problem, one which he was able to redress. In preparing his syllabus, he discovered that little had been written on the history of African Americans in sports. To make up for the absence of scholarship, he hired researchers and spent three years (and $300,000) writing. The result: a three-volume work entitled *A Hard Road to Glory: A History of the African American Athlete.* Nelson Mandela read it in prison.

... *And More Bad News*

In 1988, shortly after finishing his book, Ashe's hand went limp. A CAT scan revealed a mysterious splotch on his brain. It would require surgery. And there was more bad news: A routine blood test showed him to be HIV-positive, a result of a transfusion he had received five years earlier during his second bypass. When he finally had brain surgery, the suspicious area turned out to be not cancer but toxoplasmosis, an opportunistic infection associated with immune deficiency diseases. Arthur Ashe had AIDS.

A Heroic Death

For four years, he kept that information private but in 1992, with the media hot on the story, he was forced to reveal the news. He was flooded with requests to speak. He did so often, addressing, among other groups, the United Nations General Assembly and the graduating class of Harvard Medical School. (He volunteered to speak there when he heard that Magic Johnson had backed out at the last moment.) He also collaborated with writer Arnold Rampersad on a memoir, *Days of Grace,* and created the Arthur Ashe Foundation for the Defeat of AIDS. In short, he was tremendously busy helping others.

He was well aware of what was happening to him personally. "No doubt science will one day come up with a vaccine, or even a way to reverse the effects of AIDS on the human body. But that will be a cure for other people, too late for me," he wrote. "Meanwhile, I keep sailing on in this middle passage. I am sailing into the wind and the dark. But I am doing my best to keep my boat steady and my sails full."

Ten months after he made his announcement, Arthur Ashe died of AIDS.

The Challenge of Dying

How does a person who knows he is dying go about completing his life? Many people, I imagine, focus on themselves. Often they have to. Medical procedures and diminishing energy give them little choice.

Other people flounder in fear and denial.

But a few people venture forth resolutely in the other direction. Arthur Ashe was one. Roman Catholic Cardinal Joseph Bernardin was another. His way of death was so extraordinary that some people used the word saintly.

CARDINAL JOSEPH BERNARDIN
Facing Your Fears

Born in South Carolina, Joseph Bernardin (1928–1996) was the child of two Italian immigrants: a stonecutter, Giuseppe, who died when his son was six years old, and a seamstress, Maria, who wanted her boy to become a doctor. Instead, he became a priest and was ordained in South Carolina in 1952. Fourteen years later, at age thirty-eight, he was sent to Atlanta, where he became the youngest bishop in the country. His mother was at the installation ceremony. "Walk straight," she advised. "And don't look too pleased."

People occasionally accused Cardinal Bernardin of harboring secret ambitions. If so, he must have been delighted, for he moved steadily up the ladder, becoming archbishop of Cincinnati in 1972 and president of the National Conference of Catholic Bishops in 1974. In 1982, he was transferred to Chicago. A year later, Pope John Paul II appointed him cardinal.

Needless to say, he had his critics. He infuriated many with his efforts to reorganize the finances of his troubled archdiocese. Some people grumbled that he worked too slowly and was too ready to compromise. Women seeking a greater role in church activities complained that he was receptive to their cause but not active in pursuing it. And not everyone appreciated the fact that his thinking was shaped by the liberalizing influence of Vatican II and Pope John XXIII. But people were impressed by his ability to listen and his efforts to seek consensus. For instance, he met with the Israelis and the Palestinians and even tried to unite the liberal and conservative branches of the church. He was talked about as a possible American pope.

Another impressive aspect of Cardinal Bernardin was his willingness to grapple with the most contentious issues of the day. He spoke out against the war in Vietnam; challenged the policy of nuclear deterrence; worked for world peace and social justice; created an AIDS task force; and set up a series of dialogues with other religions. He was particularly lauded for addressing the troubled relationship between Christians and Jews. In a speech at Hebrew University in Jerusalem, he admitted forthrightly that "Anti-Semitism has deep roots in Christian history." He insisted that before reconciliation between those two groups could take place, the true history of their relationship had to be known.

He was also adamant in his call for a "consistent ethic of life," which meant opposing not only abortion but capital punishment, nuclear war, and all forms of violence. His support of progressive social policies that addressed poverty was part of what he considered a "seamless garment" of ethics. Did he stir up controversy? Sure. That didn't bother him.

In fact, he stated clearly that he was afraid of only three things: false accusation, cancer, and death.

False Accusation

In the 1990s, he was ambushed by misfortune. His trials began in 1993 when a former seminarian whom he had known in the 1970s charged him with sodomy. Today, such accusations against members of the clergy have become so distressingly commonplace that we forget: Sometimes the accused is innocent. In the midst of a storm of publicity, Cardinal Bernardin faced the television cameras and maintained his innocence. "The allegations are totally false," he said. "I am 65 years old, and I can tell you that all my life I have lived a chaste and celibate life."

A few months later, his accuser withdrew his statement, claiming that he had been a victim not of sexual abuse but of hypnosis-induced false memory. Cardinal Bernardin was completely forgiving. He prayed with the young man, who had AIDS, and even celebrated mass with him. Later, when he became ill himself, he commiserated with his accuser about the difficulties of disease. He even acknowledged the other man's empathy. "He had some idea of the suffering I was experiencing," Cardinal Bernardin reported.

Cancer

In June 1995, Cardinal Bernardin learned that he had pancreatic cancer. The experience transformed his life. He delegated most of his usual tasks to other people and announced that he intended "to spend time with the sick and the troubled." He did just that, speaking with hundreds of afflicted people and even giving his home telephone number to patients he met in the hospital. He made himself so available that when mourners at a wake handed him slips of paper with the names and numbers of cancer sufferers, he called them too. It's fair to say that he transcended his own troubles and made profound contact with others.

Death

In August, 1996, Cardinal Bernardin announced that the cancer had spread to his liver and was inoperable. Other people might seek privacy in such circumstances. He had the opposite impulse. Informed that he had a year to live, he spoke publicly and with dignity about dying, his fear of death, and his belief in the afterlife. He didn't hide his suffering. He even admitted that he often wept at night. Yet he seemed calm.

When asked how he could be so serene, he said, "First of all, you have to put yourself totally in the hands of the Lord. Secondly, you have to begin seeing death not so much as an enemy but as a friend. And thirdly, you have to begin letting go. And if you can do those three things, then you experience peace."

He continued to be productive. During his last few months, he met with the pope in Italy; visited a death row prisoner; finished a book (*The Gift of Peace*); wrote to the Supreme Court about physician-assisted suicide (he opposed it); accepted the Presidential Medal of Freedom from President Clinton at a White House ceremony; and, almost to the end, visited his mother daily at her nursing home.

He died in November 1996, widely hailed for the manner of his death.

And On Another Topic...

Facing death is seldom a concern for the young. So I asked Father O'Keefe to talk about the teenagers he works with and the people they admire:

JO: Admiration is one thing. Seeing someone as a role model is another. Young people are impressed by individuals they know who rise to the occasion and do what needs to be done, especially if the circumstances are difficult. If you ask kids in high school to name a hero, they will hardly ever write about a famous person. They will write about a person they know—a coach, a parent, maybe a brother or sister who might be fighting a disease. They look to personal heroes.

RD: Is there anyone in the public arena who stimulates admiration?

JO: Sure. They admire and even emulate professional athletes and rock stars. But they don't see them as heroes in the sense of individuals who stand for moral values or have overcome a challenge in their lives. I do know that the Stepinac students identified with [New York Giants running back] Tiki Barber when he visited the school. He talked about growing up without a father and being raised in a poor neighborhood solely by his mother. She had five jobs. The kids identified with Tiki because a lot of them are also being raised in single-parent families or have had to face other serious issues in their lives.

RD: Do they admire someone like Michael Jordan?

JO: The kids admire his athletic skill, his success, his riches. Whether he is a person to inspire a teenager to become an individual who knows what is right and has the courage to do it—that's a different issue. Most kids know the difference between success and heroism.

RD: That's good to hear.

JO: Ever since September 11, the word "hero" has been identified in New York culture with the firefighters who gave their lives at the World Trade Center. Those people are heroes. And as I said, kids can appreciate heroism. They understand that it requires great personal sacrifice. Hard work and determination are necessary, and there is often some form of suffering. The kids know this. That's why they admire firefighters. What has happened is that heroism is now associated, as it always should have been, with service to other people.

RD: How do they feel about someone like Martin Luther King, Jr.?

JO: Well, they admire what he stood for. They admire what he was about. Martin Luther King is a true hero. But history is history. He died in 1968. That's twenty years before these children were born. It's our job to keep the spirit of the man alive—and that can only be done by the adults who surround them. Young people today look for individuals in their own lives who are able to triumph over adversity, even when the going is tough. Their real heroes are people they personally know.

RD: How do you inculcate values in young people?

JO: Adolescents are taught by example. I tell all the teachers, they'll love your subject if they see that you do. If you're passionate, they will become passionate. Adolescent education is about character and moral development. You are teaching them how to live a good life. You can talk about courtesy, kindness, justice, and concern for others. You can talk about service. But the kids must see these values in action. In the end, it's the moral example of those who have influence in their lives that matters most.

CHAPTER 15

A Conversation With
GLENN SCHAEFFER

On Wole Soyinka, Muhammad Ali, and Tadao Ando

I met Glenn Schaeffer years ago, when he was an ambitious young stockbroker looking for a career change and I was the CEO at the public relations firm, Hill & Knowlton, that hired him. He became the account executive for a Las Vegas casino and eventually the president and chief financial officer of Mandalay Resort Group, which operates sixteen casinos nationwide. He is proud to say that he helped make the Las Vegas Strip the world's leading travel destination.

But if you're imagining that this chapter is going to be about the unexpectedly heroic aspects of Dean Martin or Liberace, think again. This chapter is about—among other topics—the role of literature in the fight against tyranny and the importance of architecture. It is also about what it means to be somebody like Glenn Schaeffer, whose financial successes failed to bring him the fulfillment he was seeking.

But then it was never his intention as a young man to become a businessman. He wanted to write literary fiction. Born and raised in Los Angeles, he studied comparative literature at the University of California at Irvine and subsequently attended the University of Iowa's famed Writer's Workshop, where he made an important discovery: "I discovered that I didn't have the burning ambition of some of my classmates," he told me. "I was more geared toward worldly success than critical esteem."

He achieved that success at the cost of his literary ambitions. Fortunately, he also maintained several friendships from the Writer's Workshop. "It happens that a couple of my classmates from Iowa—

Richard Wiley and Douglas Unger—are professors here at the University of Nevada in Las Vegas," he told me. "Every so often we would get together for lunch. One day about three years ago, Richard brought up the idea that somehow I return to the literary fold. He said, 'There must be something you would like to do.'"

Schaeffer responded by saying, "Well it certainly wouldn't be sitting in a room by myself staring at a wall trying to write a book. I can make money on the Las Vegas Strip a lot faster."

When Wiley said, "Maybe there's a way to become a literary executive," Schaeffer was intrigued. What would a literary executive do? The answer became clear: create an organization. In 2000, Schaeffer founded the International Institute of Modern Letters, which aims to be the premier force in literary philanthropy by supporting emerging and established writers around the world and providing assistance to writers who have been politically persecuted.

With that in mind, Schaeffer got in touch with the International Parliament of Writers (IPW). Founded in 1993 after the assassination of the Algerian writer Tahar Djaout, it was best known for its City of Asylum program, which offered refuge to writers who were being censored, tortured, or otherwise persecuted in their native countries. Although there were over two dozen such cities in Europe, there was not a single City of Asylum in the United States.

"And so over the course of more lunches we determined that Las Vegas would become the first host city in North America for that program," Schaeffer said. Its first writer-in-residence was the African poet Syl Cheney-Coker, who had been forced to flee his native Sierra Leone. (He returned following a regime change.) Its second is the Chinese artist and writer Er Tai Gao, who published an essay that the authorities didn't like and as a result was repeatedly imprisoned and sentenced to hard labor in China. In 1992, he escaped to the United States. His account of the systematic censorship and destruction of literary life in China during the Cultural Revolution and up to the present is forthcoming.

I asked Schaeffer why he has devoted himself to this cause. Here's what he said . . .

> GS: Literature is a change agent and the books that change us are tipping points. There is not a single example of a sustainable growth economy or liberal democracy without a free, independent, literary press. And so if the question is, why would a businessman of literary academic training be so enamored of fine literature as to become a philanthropist of this small part of the world economy, the answer is that it doesn't take too many good books to change what people believe and to make society a better place.
>
> RD: Has this involvement been fulfilling?
>
> GS: Yes. We're still in start-up. We can't do everything, we can't be everywhere. But for something like one million dollars a year of programmatic dollars we can serve a pretty important function.
>
> RD: What specific challenges do you see?
>
> GS: Today, 80 percent of the world's imprisoned writers are in Islamic regimes. But anywhere you find suppression of literary voices, that is the first act of tyranny. The first thing Hitler did before he burned the Reichstag was to burn the books.

Schaeffer has provided opportunities and fellowships for writers and translators at the University of Nevada and at the University of California at Irvine. He also created a major literary prize for emerging writers from New Zealand and endowed a chair in Creative Writing at the University of Nevada. The first holder of that chair, and the first person Schaeffer named as a hero, is the Nigerian writer Wole Soyinka. "Not only is he an accomplished writer and one of the more important playwrights in the world today, he is a reformer for peace," Schaeffer said. "He is an activist who takes brave stands, often at physical peril, in places where most people won't go."

WOLE SOYINKA
Years of Protest

There's something about prison literature that never fails to fascinate. Wole Soyinka's contributions to the genre, a group of poems and a memoir entitled *The Man Died: Prison Notes of Wole Soyinka,* were written in the late 1960s during the twenty-two months he spent as a political prisoner in solitary confinement. Permitted no writing materials, he made his own ink and wrote on toilet paper, cigarette packages, and between the lines of print in books that had been smuggled in to him. By then, he was already a writer with an international audience—which didn't stop the military dictatorship in Nigeria from imprisoning him. It wasn't the first time he'd come up against the forces of tyranny, and it wouldn't be the last.

Born on July 13, 1934, Akinwande Oluwole Soyinka grew up in a small town in southwestern Nigeria. His father was an Anglican canon and the headmaster of the mission school. His mother, whom he called "Wild Christian," was a fervent believer. But the myths and customs of the Yoruban people were all around him, and he grew up fully immersed in both cultures. His memoir *Aké: The Years of Childhood* is considered a masterpiece. It ends when he was eleven years old.

The next year, he left Aké and went to nearby Ibadan to attend school. At eighteen, he began studying drama at the university there. He completed his studies at the University of Leeds in England. Afterward, he spent a short time working in theatre in London followed by an even briefer spell singing and playing the guitar in Paris. He returned to Nigeria in 1960 with a Rockefeller grant to study African drama. He also formed his own theatre company. Nigeria had just become independent. It was, he said, his intention to help build a new nation.

But Soyinka was not impressed with the new leaders. "I knew we were in serious trouble: they were ostentatious, exhibitionist, profligate; they couldn't wait to step into the shoes of their departing colonial masters. We realized the struggle had to begin at our own doors—with the enemy within." Soyinka's plays rattled the ruling class, but he also spurned the Négritude movement, which advocated rejection of European influences. He was interested in the blending of cultures, and his work reflects it.

He also advocated human rights and social justice. In 1965, he protested a rigged election by holding up the Nigerian Broadcasting Company's studios and demanding that they broadcast a tape criticizing the election as fraudulent. He was charged with illegal broadcasting and imprisoned for three months.

The next year, the army seized power and civil war broke out. When Soyinka wrote an article advocating a cease-fire, he was accused of supporting the Biafran rebels and imprisoned. Other writers, Lillian Hellman among them, campaigned for his release. Nonetheless, he spent almost two years in solitary confinement, "deprived of books, deprived of any means of writing, deprived of human companionship."

He scribbled in secret, writing poems and taking notes in whatever way he could. In his isolation, he found himself mulling over algebraic equations, an obsession that disappeared once he got out. When he was released, he discovered that adjusting to freedom and enjoying human companionship, the very things he had longed for, weren't easy.

He ended up staying by himself at a friend's farm in southern France, completing his prison memoir, and writing *The Bacchae of Euripides,* a play that imagines the ancient story from an African perspective and draws upon similarities between the Greek gods and the Yoruban orishas.

He didn't return to Nigeria until 1975 when Yakubu Gowon, the military general who had become head of state almost a decade earlier, was overthrown in a bloodless coup. Soyinka became a professor of English at a Nigerian university. In 1986, he was named the first African to win the Nobel Prize in Literature.

For the next seven years, as one coup followed another, Soyinka continually decried dictatorship, speaking out against the Nigerian despots who had subjected that country to so many troubles. He also continued to teach at universities around the world including Cornell, Yale, Harvard, the University of Nevada at Las Vegas, and Emory.

In 1993, presidential elections were canceled and General Sani Abacha, the armed forces chief of staff, grabbed the reins of power. The next year, Soyinka's Nigerian passport was seized. Charged with treason and sentenced to death in absentia, he went into exile. The danger was real: In 1995, a dissident writer named Ken Saro-Wiwa was executed along with eight other activists. Only when Abacha died in 1998 and his successor dropped the charges against him did Soyinka return.

"The man dies in all who keep silent in the face of tyranny," Wole Soyinka said. He continues to write, to teach, to speak out against brutality, and to consider the implications of cultural identity, power, and what it means to be a nation.

Although Soyinka has been acclaimed as Africa's finest writer, he is not universally loved. Critics have accused him of being strident, complex, grandiloquent, obscure, self-conscious, antifeminist, and impenetrable. He has even been accused of "logorrhea." But that kind of criticism goes with the territory.

Is he a hero? If a lifetime spent speaking out against dictatorship and brutality in a climate where you can end up in jail is not heroism, I don't know what is. But when I asked Schaeffer why Soyinka is a hero, he did not limit himself to his political bravery.

> GS: He has endurance, imagination, and grace under pressure, to quote Hemingway. He continues to improve as a writer—which is rare, by the way. To say that Wole Soyinka lives a peripatetic life is an understatement. But he has continued to mature as an important literary voice in multiple genres, which is another thing you almost never see. I hold him in high esteem.

A CHAMPION

Another man Schaefter holds in high esteem is the boxer Muhammad Ali.

RD: You also mentioned "the Greatest," Muhammad Ali. Why is he a hero?

GS: Several reasons. He stood up. People forget what it meant to be a black champion who was outspoken about American racism 35 years ago. He never backed down whether it was in the ring or in society. I particularly admire the work he does in charity today, given his disabilities. I don't think there's a match in the history of American athletics for the inner fortitude and bravery of this man.

RD: I would agree. Most athletes avoid anything that smacks of politics. Ali jumped right in. He is extraordinary.

MUHAMMAD ALI
The Louisville Lip

If you're anywhere close to my age, you remember Muhammad Ali when he was still known as Cassius Clay. Using that name—his slave name, as he called it—he first came to public attention in 1960, when he won a gold medal at the Olympics. He was Cassius Clay in 1964, when he challenged Sonny Liston for the heavyweight championship and won, confounding virtually everyone including the sportswriters in attendance, 93 percent of whom had predicted a Liston victory. From the ring, giddy with victory, he pointed down at the journalists and repeated, "Eat your words! Eat your words!"

By then, he was world-famous not just as an athlete, but as a personality. His style in the ring—"float like a butterfly, sting like a bee"—was unlike anything the world had ever seen: quick and graceful, with dancing feet and his hands held low. His doggerel was equally deft. And his ability to promote himself was without precedent. As he himself said many times, "I am the greatest."

But his athletic ability was only part of the story. The day after he beat Liston, he announced at a press conference that he had become a Muslim. He knew it wouldn't be a popular decision. "I believe in Allah and in peace . . . ," he stated at a press conference. "I know where I'm going and I know the truth, and I don't have to be what you want me to be. I'm free to be what I want." One of the expectations he was countering was the notion that he would be a hero like the beloved Joe Louis, who was a killer in the ring but humble and deferential outside. Years later, Ali explained it this way to the writer and editor David Remnick: "I had to prove you could be a new kind of black man. I had to show that to the world."

A Rose by Any Other Name . . .

And prove it he did. A few weeks after the Liston fight, he legally changed his name to Muhammad Ali. It's hard to remember now how complicated and derisive the reaction to all this was. Islam mystified people, and to many people, black and white, the words "Black Muslim" were terrifying. Even his father, Cassius Marcellus Clay, Sr., wasn't happy about his decision. But as Ali said, "Black Muslim is a press word. It's not a legitimate name. The real name is 'Islam.' That means peace."

Although his new name made many people uncomfortable, it was eventually accepted. As he told Thomas Hauser (whose excellent oral history *Muhammad Ali: His Life and Times* has provided most of the quotes included here), "I'm the only man in history to become famous under two different names."

For the record, it's worth noting that Ali was initially a follower of Elijah Muhammad, who believed that white people are devils and decisively rejected Malcolm X before his assassination in February 1965. After Elijah died, Ali aligned himself with Elijah's son, Wallace. "He learned from his studies that his father wasn't teaching true Islam, and Wallace taught us the true meaning of the Qu'ran," Ali remembered. "He showed that color didn't matter. He taught that we're responsible for our own lives and it's no good to blame our problems on other people." In the 1980s, Ali also spoke out against Louis Farrakhan, explicitly stating, "What he teaches is not at all what we believe in."

The Draft

Then there was the matter of the war in Vietnam. Classified 1-A, Ali was called up in 1964. However, he failed the written test—twice. "I said I was the greatest, not the smartest," he explained. He was reclassified 1-Y—not qualified—and that was that. Or so he thought.

Then in 1966, standards for military service were lowered. To his distress, Ali was reclassified and called up again.

He refused to serve. It wasn't that he was unpatriotic. In 1960, after he won his Olympic gold medal, a Russian reporter asked how he felt about representing a country where he couldn't even get served at all the restaurants. "Tell your readers we got qualified people working on that problem, and I'm not worried about the outcome," he replied. "To me, the USA is the best country in the world, including yours."

But when he was called up for induction, he said, "I ain't got no quarrel with them Viet-cong," and claimed to be exempt as a minister of Islam. Public reaction was swift. "Cassius makes himself as sorry a spectacle as those unwashed punks who picket and demonstrate against the war," said the sportswriter Red Smith, refusing to acknowledge the fighter's chosen name. Ali was stripped of his title and the boxing commissions revoked his boxing license. The federal government revoked his passport. He was called a traitor.

But the philosopher Bertrand Russell wrote to him expressing solidarity. And Ali, who toured college campuses around the country, gained enormous support for opposing an increasingly unpopular war. For refusing to serve, he received a $10,000 fine and a five-year sentence. He appealed and was eventually vindicated by the Supreme Court, which voted eight to nothing in his favor in 1971.

But for more than three years at the peak of his career, he was not allowed to fight.

Back in the Game

When he returned to the ring, he went head-to-head with Joe Frazier, the new heavyweight champion, in a contest billed as the "fight of the century." He lost decisively. In a rematch two years later, he won. But by then, Frazier was no longer champion: George Foreman was. So in 1974, Ali challenged Foreman in a fight in Zaire (Congo) which he dubbed the "rumble in the jungle." He won in the eighth round. The next year, he went to the Philippines to fight Frazier for the third time—this was the "thrilla in Manila"—and once again he triumphed.

After that, it was downhill. In 1978, Ali fought two times against the irritating Leon Spinks. He lost the first fight and won the second, regaining the championship for the third time. He soon retired, which was a smart idea. Later, he returned to boxing, which was not so smart, and suffered a humiliating defeat at the hands of Larry Holmes. In 1981 he retired from the ring for good.

Since then, he has distinguished himself. Like many fighters, he suffered enormous physical damage, and today he has Parkinson's disease. He can barely speak and visibly trembles, as everyone could see in 1996 when he opened the Olympics by holding aloft a torch. Nonetheless, he has testified before Congress on the subject, visited many third world countries on behalf of various good causes, and worked on behalf of many charitable organizations. His religious devotion is as strong as ever. He has no bitterness.

A gentle person, he inspires people everywhere in the world for all the right reasons. A man of principle, he has always stood up for what he believed, whether it was a popular position or not, and he has always accepted the consequences.

He also created himself in a way that few can claim. He was an uneducated young man with nothing but talent and determination. His childhood boxing mentor maintained that he had never seen a boy work as hard.

Finally, he defied the expectations of virtually everyone and became successful on his own terms. His achievements were especially meaningful for African Americans. As Andrew Young said, "Muhammad was probably the first black man in America to successfully break with the white establishment and survive. He set his own course religiously, politically, and culturally. And in that sense, he was very important because he established a new concept of equality."

But his appeal is universal because the vitality of his personality—to call it charisma understates it—was intoxicating. He went his own way and suffered the consequences. Yet he radiated joy—and still managed to become champion of the world, not once but three times.

HEROES OF ARCHITECTURE

Fighters make good heroes because their enemies are so tangible. Artists are a tougher call. Oftentimes, their enemy is simply stodgy thinking. It is their challenge to change that.

Of those, the most influential are architects, because they change the environment for everyone. I can't think of a great architectural project that has not had a profound effect on the people around it. St. Paul's Cathedral in London has had a vast impact on that city. The same is true of the Hermitage in St. Petersburg, Russia; the Ginza in Tokyo; and even New York's Lincoln Center, which, for all its flaws, acoustical and otherwise, created a new neighborhood and elevated the importance of classical music in that city. Or look at Frank Gehry's Guggenheim Museum in Bilbao, Spain. It has literally revitalized an entire city. These remarkable places changed the lives of everybody for the better.

I believe that on some level, people know what is good—but they have to be led to it. Over the years, bad architecture gets eliminated. Good structures endure because they uplift the human spirit. Anyone can see that with parks. Ever see a barren lot become a park? I've seen this happen in my own community, Darien, Connecticut, where the owner of a sporting goods store took a plot of land in front of his retail store and made it into a small park with a fountain. Was this a smart business decision? Very. The store makes a different impact now. It's no longer just a retail establishment; it's a place to go. And people do go there. There was a method to his madness.

Great architecture changes the way we live and the way we see. In the middle of the last century, people like Frank Lloyd Wright and

Philip Johnson and I. M. Pei were on the cutting edge. We think of them now as modern masters. At the time, they often met with resistance.

Pei, for example, was asked to develop a new design for a subterranean entrance to the Louvre. He came up with the glass pyramids. But that design, which enlivened the whole area, was so radical, such a scandalous addition to a revered cobblestoned plaza, that it almost didn't get made. I was there in the Elysée Palace when Pei showed the plans to the French president François Mitterand, who had commissioned this as a cornerstone of his legacy.

Mitterand looked at it and said, "I can't possibly endorse this."

Pei said, "Why not?"

Mitterand said, "Because the French will complain that it is not in keeping with the wonderful belle époque nature of the Louvre and they will rebel."

And this is why Pei is heroic. He said, "They should rebel. They should react. That's exactly what you want from a good piece of art. That reaction moves taste to a higher level. If it's bad taste, we'll know that. But if it's good taste, we'll know over time as it is accepted."

Mitterand said, "Should I stake my career on this?"

And Pei said, "It will actually enhance your career. It will make your legacy a positive one." And he was right.

Pei is one of my heroes. I wouldn't have thought to name Tadao Ando as a hero, but Glenn Schaeffer did. He considers him an aesthetic genius. Why is he a hero? "Heroes are people of new ideas who move a field of endeavor forward," Schaeffer said. "Ando has done exactly that by developing a fresh vocabulary of architecture in a way that has not been seen since Frank Lloyd Wright."

TADAO ANDO
Prince of Light

Born and raised in Japan, the architect Tadao Ando is that rare thing: a self-educated professional, who succeeds in pushing the boundaries of his field. As a child, he spent many hours across the street in a carpenter's shop, making wooden models and studying carpentry. At eighteen, after dabbling in boxing as a career, he began apprenticing himself to designers, city planners, and other professionals. Architects were not among them. "I did not apprentice to another architect because every time I tried, I was fired for my stubbornness and temper."

Around the same age, he also began a lifelong habit of visiting great buildings and analyzing them in detailed sketchbooks. For seven years, he wandered around the world visiting traditional teahouses, shrines, and temples in Japan as well as structures in the United States, Europe, and Africa. He also read books, including one he found in a used bookstore about Le Corbusier. When he finally saved up enough money to buy it, "I traced the drawings of his early period so many times that all the pages turned black." What he did not do was enroll in architecture school.

In 1969, the twenty-eight-year-old Ando set up his first office in Osaka, Japan. His first commission was to redesign a tenement, which later became his office. In addition to individual residences, he went on to design row houses, a school (in Italy), shrines, temples, churches, factories, apartment complexes, a conference hall, a theatre, a shopping complex, and several museums, including the Modern Art Museum in Fort Worth, Texas, and the Pulitzer Foundation for the Arts in St. Louis, Missouri. Using glass, steel, and smooth concrete, he creates buildings characterized by serenity, simple geometry, and a remarkable use of light. A prime example is his Church of Light in Osaka, a simple concrete building in which a wall is divided by two long slits, one horizontal and one vertical, that create a large glowing cross composed entirely of light. "I do not believe architecture should speak too much," he has said. "It should remain silent and let nature, in the guise of sunlight and wind, speak."

Despite his outsider beginnings, Ando has won all the major architecture prizes, including the Pritzker Prize in 1995 and the AIA Gold Medal in 2002. Why is he heroic? Because he has a unique vision that transcends easy categories and operates apart from fads and movements. Because his work, which has been described as poetic and introspective, creates tranquil spaces even within chaotic urban environments—and yet is so solidly constructed that when a major earthquake struck the Hanshin region in Japan, all his buildings survived. Because he believes that "the role of architectural space as a spiritual shelter is crucial." And because he has stated that "for me the most exciting thing is when architecture can do something to make people's lives better, to inspire them."

So what makes a hero? When I asked Glenn Schaeffer to address that issue one more time, he said, "Heroes are people who answer to an inner voice and are motivated by improvement for others beside themselves."

I can go along with that.

CHAPTER 16

A Conversation With
RABBI ARTHUR SCHNEIER

On Carl Lutz, Andrei Sakharov, and Others

All the people I interviewed for this book are personal heroes of mine. But some of them are especially inspiring, and not just to me. An example is Rabbi Arthur Schneier.

Born in Vienna in 1930, he lost his father when he was six years old. His life changed again on September 1, 1939, when Germany invaded Poland and World War II began. That same day, he and his mother fled Vienna and went to Budapest to join his grandparents. They had a six-month tourist visa. When it expired, he and his mother had to hide in different places to evade detection. For several years, he had to be one step ahead of the Gestapo.

Fortunately, Rabbi Schneier had a protector as well as a personal hero: his grandfather, a prominent Hungarian rabbi. His grandfather was everything a boy might admire. "First of all, he had a great personality," Rabbi Schneier remembers. "He was six foot two, with great presence, a man of vision and wisdom, a very warm, compassionate human being."

He was also a man of courage. He could have been smuggled out of the Jewish ghetto. He could have saved himself. Instead, he remained with his community. In 1944, he was deported to Auschwitz and gassed.

Rabbi Schneier escaped the same fate, thanks to the consul general of Switzerland, the International Red Cross, and a number of heroic families, people whose names he cannot recall, who allowed him to stay illegally in their homes at great personal risk.

In 1947, he came to this country. He began his studies for the rabbinate, received his ordination and a doctor of divinity degree from Yeshiva University, and in 1962, became the spiritual leader of New York City's Park East Synagogue.

Three years later, he founded the Appeal of Conscience Foundation. Under the auspices of that organization, Rabbi Schneier has met with political and religious leaders from around the world. He has engaged in conflict resolution and fought on behalf of human rights and religious freedom in Kosovo, Bosnia-Herzegovina, India, Argentina, and elsewhere; led interfaith delegations to China eight times since 1981; been to the former Soviet Union fifty-eight times on various missions, including observing presidential elections there in 1996; brought humanitarian aid to earthquake and flood victims in Turkey, Armenia, and Romania; and negotiated bilateral agreements with the Czech Republic and Slovakia, Hungary, Romania, Slovenia, and Ukraine.

He is, in short, a thoroughly admirable human being. And although he has been recognized by four presidents, been granted the Presidential Citizen Medal and many other awards, and received many honorary degrees, he also has his detractors. Anyone in the public eye does. He ignores them, because at the end of the day, the result is worth the slings and arrows.

In addition to his public work, the rabbi has an extraordinary ability to listen to people and to help them. I have seen him reach out to people who are in distress. I have seen him sit with them in the synagogue. I don't know what he says to them. I do know that he has reintroduced people to society, hooked up the unemployed with business opportunities, given those who are unfulfilled a chance to do something with youth or with underprivileged people. He offers more than kind words. He opens doors for people. His most outstanding trait is his empathy. He applies it to the major trouble spots of the world, and he applies it with equal attention to individuals in need. To my mind, the man is clearly a hero.

But not to his mind.

RABBI SCHNEIER ON HEROISM

What makes a hero? In my view, empathy, good works, and the courage to take a risk for a higher purpose (such as peace and human rights). Arthur Schneier's standard is a higher one. Here's part of our conversation on the subject:

RD: What qualities would you say describe a hero?

AS: I think being a hero means staking your life. When I think of heroes, it's more in the military sense.

RD: It's interesting you would say that. Emerson defines heroism as "a military attitude of the soul."

AS: I have not read the passage, but I like the connotation. To me being a hero implies a battle. My litmus test is this: Have you placed your life in jeopardy? That's the criteria for heroism. Otherwise, you're dealing with role models. You're dealing with people who inspire by virtue of their achievements or their humanity. I was very much involved with conflict resolution in Yugoslavia during the war. Even in that conflict there were some who showed their compassion, who showed a sense of humanity and took a stand. Well, I would say that's courage. I would say they could *become* heroes.

RD: What gives some people the fortitude to take a stand when it could mean putting themselves in grave danger?

AS: It's a question of inner strength anchored in faith—not necessarily in terms of a theological definition, but in terms of having strong convictions, believing in the rightness of a cause, being motivated by a sense of justice. There must be conscience and conviction and faith. You cannot perform heroic acts unless you have faith.

RD: Is it possible for someone to be, let's say, an artistic hero?

AS: No. Absolutely not. There are people with remarkable achievements and qualities who have emerged in spite of

> adversity. But I wouldn't call them heroes. I would call
> them men and women of courage, men and women of
> strength, but not heroes. There are surgeons and medical
> doctors who have performed miraculously in terms of
> saving patients, but again it's not heroism.
>
> RD: Because their lives aren't at risk?
> AS: Correct.

Rabbi Schneier's definition of heroism is not for wimps. Although he admires many people, including George W. Bush, Tony Blair, Ronald Reagan, Pope John Paul, Natan Sharansky, and David Ben-Gurion, only a few qualify as heroes.

One who does qualify is the Swiss diplomat Carl Lutz, a "Righteous Gentile" who saved the lives of thousands of Hungarian Jews during the Holocaust—but whose heroism remains in the shadow of a more dashing figure with a more sensational tale.

Heroes of the Holocaust

That more celebrated Holocaust hero is Raoul Wallenberg, the legendary Swedish diplomat who saved many thousands of Hungarian Jews. Wallenberg's story is an exciting one. A driven man who possessed an extraordinary strength of spirit as well as what one compatriot called "an irresistible personal radiation," he acted not just bravely but dramatically during the Holocaust. After the war, he disappeared under mysterious circumstances in a Soviet prison camp. Although rumors of his existence circulated for decades, he was never heard from again.

The story of Carl Lutz is less sensational. He was not just a quiet hero, he was a bureaucrat. And rather than disappearing into the Gulag, he died a frail old man in 1975. His name does not appear in the *Encyclopedia Judaica,* and although he is revered in Israel and Hungary, he is not widely known in the United States. Yet Lutz's story is arguably even more heroic than Wallenberg's.

Carl Lutz

Born in Switzerland in 1895, Lutz emigrated to the United States in 1913. In 1920, he took a summer job at the Swiss legation in Washington, D.C. From that moment on, his path was set. Over the next fifteen years, he worked for the Swiss in Washington, Philadelphia, and St. Louis.

In 1935, he was transferred to Tel Aviv as head of the Swiss consulate. Among other duties, he lobbied to improve the living conditions of twenty-five hundred Germans who were in danger of being deported by the British. In his next assignment, that effort turned out to yield unexpected benefits.

In 1942, he was transferred to Budapest, Hungary, and given a crucially significant assignment: He was put in charge of visas. That enabled him to help several hundred Jewish children escape, with their chaperones, to Palestine. He helped as many Jews as he could to be officially declared American citizens. He also distributed thousands of protective certificates, issued by the government of El Salvador, which certified their owners as Salvadoran nationals. Using a lot of paper, he spirited a lot of grateful people out of danger.

When Hitler invaded Hungary in March 1944, and deportations to Auschwitz began, Lutz intensified his efforts using the weapons at hand, which were the weapons of bureaucracy. When he received permission to issue about eight thousand letters of protection to Jews putting them under the protection of the Swiss government and allowing them to emigrate to Palestine, he multiplied that number several times over by interpreting it as eight thousand family units rather than eight thousand individuals.

The Nazis, in his debt for his efforts on behalf of their prisoners (and, in addition, hesitant to offend the Swiss, who were officially neutral), left him alone.

Working with the International Red Cross, the Zionist Youth Movement, and various representatives from the world Jewish community, he issued safety passes, false identification papers, and other protective documents. He freed scores of prisoners by claiming that they worked for the Swiss embassy.

He also established seventy-six Swiss safe houses. One of them was the school that young Arthur Schneier attended. "My high school building became a haven for eight hundred of us under International Red Cross and Swiss supervision," Rabbi Schneier recalls.

At a time when such actions could easily have gotten him executed, Lutz confronted high-level Nazis (including Eichmann) face-to-face. He protested mightily against broken Hungarian government promises and repeatedly stood up to the Nazis.

And when he was ordered to leave before the Russians swept into Budapest in 1945, Lutz—unlike the head of the Swiss delegation—stayed behind with the Jews.

By the time the war ended, most of Hungary's 742,800 Jews were dead. In Budapest, 124,000 remained. Approximately 50,000 of them owed their lives to Carl Lutz.

During the war, Lutz talked strategy with Raoul Wallenberg, who arrived in Budapest in July 1944. One difference between them was that, while the Swedish government supported Wallenberg's efforts to save Jews, the Swiss refused to help. Lutz was on his own.

As his daughter, Agnes, told a reporter from the *Jewish Bulletin News of Northern California,* "The Swiss government was adamant that its employees remain neutral. But my father was a very spiritual man. He was raised as a strict Methodist, and taught Sunday school. He saw the atrocities being committed and felt he had to do something."

After the war, Lutz continued to work for the Swiss, who were made so uncomfortable by his report about his wartime activities that they waited until 1958 to acknowledge it. Eventually, recognition trickled his way. Before his death in 1975, he was even nominated for the Nobel Peace Prize.

What made him do it? "In Budapest, I knew no fear," he wrote. "The humanist in me held sway. I acted in accordance with my convictions, without asking Bern or getting support from there."

At the risk of his life, he did the right thing, and he did it in the face of a totalitarian nightmare, making him a true hero, even by Rabbi Schneier's exacting standards.

ANDREI SAKHAROV

Another hero who defied a totalitarian regime was Andrei Sakharov, a brilliant scientist whose staunch defense of human rights earned him a Nobel Prize—and many years in exile.

Born in 1921, Sakharov studied physics at Moscow University and graduated with honors in 1942. During the war, he was assigned to an arms factory as an engineer. Afterward, he returned to graduate school and studied under a physicist named Igor Tamm. It was a fateful contact. In 1948, Tamm invited him to join a group of scientists who were working on an momentous undertaking: the Soviet Union's nuclear weapons program. "I spent the next 20 years continuously working in conditions of extraordinary tension and secrecy," Sakharov wrote. His contributions to this project were so essential that he became known as the father of the Soviet hydrogen bomb.

A Change of Heart

But his doubts and worries multiplied and eventually he could no longer keep quiet about them. In 1957, he wrote an article about the dangers of radiation. He also began to speak out on other issues, including the bogus doctrines—discredited in the West—of the biologist Trofim Lysenko, whose opposition to genetic theory hobbled Soviet science for decades (and caused many reputable scientists to be accused of treason).

In 1961, he was publicly denounced for the first time. At a banquet, he slipped Khrushchev a note explaining why he was against nuclear testing, which Khrushchev wanted to resume after a halt of two-and-a-half years. A few minutes later, Khrushchev stood up and raised a glass of wine as if to give a toast. Instead, he berated Sakharov. "Sakharov, don't try to tell us what to do or how to behave," the Communist leader jeered. "I'd be a jellyfish and not Chairman of the Council of Ministers if I listened to people like Sakharov!"

Sakharov continued to lobby against atomic testing. His efforts were successful in 1963 when the global nuclear powers signed a test ban treaty.

As the years went by, Sakharov spoke out repeatedly, excoriating the Soviets for human rights abuses and opposing the rehabilitation of Stalin.

The Final Straw

Despite their displeasure, the Soviets didn't go after Sakharov until 1968, when he wrote an article that was translated into English and published in the *New York Times*. "Thoughts on Progress, Peaceful Coexistence, and Intellectual Freedom" advocated an end to the Cold War, insisted on the importance of human rights (though he did not use that phrase), and condemned the Soviet system.

In the article, Sakharov recalled, "I wrote about the crimes of Stalinism and the need to expose them fully (unlike the Soviet press, I pulled no punches) and about the vital importance of freedom and opinion and democracy. I stressed the value of progress, but warned of the need for substantive changes in foreign policy."

The Soviets struck back. Sakharov was fired and no longer permitted to do secret, high-security work. He was also, in his own words, "excommunicated from many privileges of the Soviet establishment." Less than a year later, his wife, Klavdia, died of cancer.

He continued to denounce human rights abuses and to call for the release of prisoners of conscience. In 1970, he formed the Moscow Human Rights Commission in conjunction with two other Soviet dissidents. As the symbolic leader of the Soviet dissidents, his efforts on behalf of human rights gained worldwide respect. When he won the 1975 Nobel Peace Prize, the citation referred to him as "the conscience of mankind."

When the Soviets refused to allow him to travel to Oslo to accept the prize, his second wife, Elena Bonner, a human rights activist in her own right, spoke in his place.

Exile

In 1979, Sakharov protested the Soviet invasion of Afghanistan. KGB agents grabbed him off the street and informed him that he had been banished to Gorky, some 250 miles from Moscow.

He spent seven years in Gorky "virtually isolated and watched day and night by a policeman at my door," he wrote. He was shadowed everywhere he went. His apartment was bugged and robbed. He wasn't allowed to have a telephone, and only his wife, his children, and three residents of Gorky were allowed to see him. Others who tried to visit were punished with "psychiatric confinement."

He continued to publish statements on key issues, but he was repeatedly denounced. An article in *Izvestia* even accused him of advocating a nuclear war against his own country. In addition, his manuscripts were repeatedly stolen; he had to rewrite his *Memoirs* three times.

Sakharov's family also suffered. When the authorities refused to let his daughter-in-law, Liza, join her husband in America, Sakharov and Elena Bonner went on a hunger strike. He was forcibly hospitalized and fed, but at last the authorities gave in. Liza was permitted to join her husband. Sakharov called the hunger strike "our finest hour, a proof of our mutual love and commitment."

In addition, Bonner was put on trial for "slandering the Soviet system" and denied essential medical treatment after she had a massive heart attack.

But, the tide turned. In 1985, Bonner was allowed to travel to the United States for a heart bypass. And in 1986, Mikhail Gorbachev had a phone installed in Sakharaov's apartment and called to welcome him back to society. The years of exile were over.

Sakharov died on December 14, 1989, a month after the fall of the Berlin Wall. At his funeral, which fifty thousand people attended, he was compared to Gandhi, who shared his belief in nonviolence, and to Buddha who, like him, rejected a life of privilege in order to help others.

His scientific achievements are still being assessed. His fight on behalf of human rights and his willingness to suffer for his principles have made him a hero. "I knew Sakharov," Rabbi Schneier told me. "I greeted him a few days after he came out of Gorky in Moscow. He risked his life. He could have ended up in Siberia. He is definitely a hero."

A Prayer for America

A few days after September 11, Rabbi Schneier led a prayer at a mourning service held in Yankee Stadium. "O Lord, remember the victims of the September 11 barbarism whose lives were snuffed out by terrorist evil," he said. "And remember the heroic rescuers from the police, fire and emergency services who lost their lives while trying to save the lives of others."

There was more. But right there, the Rabbi expressed his view of heroism. It means risking your life for others—even in the face of organized atrocity. And sometimes, it means dying.

CHAPTER 17

A Conversation With
JIM WIEGHART

On I. F. Stone and a Host of Heroes

I f you had to choose a dozen heroes who have lived during your
own lifetime, could you do it? Or would you flounder around and
conclude that the contemporary world just doesn't produce heroes
any more?

Most people, I have noticed, fall into the latter category. One
who does not is my colleague Jim Wieghart, who graduated from the
University of Wisconsin in 1958 and has been involved in journalism
and public affairs ever since.

He has been a prize-winning investigative reporter for the *Mil-
waukee Journal-Sentinel,* press secretary for Senator William Prox-
mire of Wisconsin, editor and Washington bureau chief of the *New
York Daily News,* and chairperson of the Department of Journalism
at Central Michigan University. He has covered numerous presidential campaigns, traveled overseas with several presidents, been on the
scene in Vietnam, during Watergate, and throughout the Iran-Contra
hearings as director of public information for the Office of the Independent Counsel. Since 1993, he has worked with The Dilenschneider Group as a senior consultant. Jim Wieghart has seen heroes and
would-be heroes up close.

Here's part of our discussion about heroism:

RD: I've heard you talk about two kinds of heroism. The first
kind, you said, is exemplified by such typical American
heroes as Audie Murphy and the firemen at the World
Trade Center.

JW: Yes. I think in contemporary American culture the word "hero" has a different meaning than it has had historically. We label as heroic those who at an instant in time have confronted difficult, even death-defying issues and either succeeded or not succeeded, but risked their lives to do it. That's the typical American view of what a hero is.

RD: What's the other kind of heroism?

JW: A more traditional definition of the hero is of an individual, a man or a woman, who has accomplished outstanding achievements, shown great courage, and made a great contribution. That's a broader definition of it.

RD: And a better one. Using that definition, whom do you consider worthy of being called a hero?

Wieghart's Heroes

Once I asked that question, Jim talked about one hero after another. His list included the actor Christopher Reeve, the athlete Lance Armstrong, and the following, every one of them a major player in the events of our lives:

JIM AND SARAH BRADY

On March 30, 1981, John Hinckley, a would-be assassin trying to impress the actress Jodie Foster, fired a stream of bullets at President Ronald Reagan, his press secretary James S. Brady, and two officers. Reagan was shot in the chest but recovered fully.

Jim Brady was hit in the head with an exploding bullet. He underwent hours of brain surgery and was still under the knife when all three major television networks reported his death. The announcement, as Brady has said, was premature.

But his injuries were grievous. He required many operations, underwent years of painful rehabilitation with therapists he referred to as "physical terrorists," and to this day struggles with partial paralysis and speech problems.

Still, life went on for the Bradys. Then one day in 1985, their six-year-old son climbed into a pickup truck at a relative's house and found a loaded handgun.

At that moment, an activist was born. Sarah, who once wanted nothing more than to become a modern-day June Cleaver, decided to do something about the plague of gun violence that has afflicted this country.

JW: Jim Brady and his wife, Sarah, were very popular in the Reagan White House. He was the press secretary and all of us who covered Washington at the time were very taken with him, even though we didn't necessarily agree with the Reagan administration. But he was very honest and when he was so devastatingly wounded, you would think that would have been the end of the chapter. It was only the beginning.

Since then, Jim and Sarah have waged a consistent and vigorous battle on gun control—and they're still at it.

The Brady Bill, signed by President Clinton in 1993, mandates a five-day waiting period and a background check on everyone trying to purchase a handgun from a licensed dealer. The Brady Center to Prevent Gun Violence is still working to reform the gun industry and to reduce the toll.

WILLIAM E. COLBY

William E. Colby (1920–1996) was a spy. A Princeton graduate, he joined the Office of Strategic Services (OSS), the forerunner of the CIA, in 1943, and parachuted into German-occupied France and Norway to work with resistance groups behind enemy lines. After the war, he got a law degree. In 1949, he joined the newly formed CIA and was posted to Stockholm, to Rome (where he ran a secret program designed to keep Communists from winning elections), and to Saigon. In 1973, Nixon appointed Colby director of the CIA.

Throughout his career, he was involved with one covert operation after another. The most notorious was the Phoenix Program. During the war in Vietnam, it targeted suspected Vietcong who had infiltrated various government agencies and eliminated—that is, killed—them.

> JW: The Phoenix Program was immoral. But as Colby saw it, he was trying to protect the South Vietnamese people who were trying to cooperate with their government and with the United States government in running a republic. Guerillas would come into their villages and assassinate people and then hide among them. People were afraid to point them out because they would be killed. So as Colby saw it, it wasn't immoral.

Estimates of the number killed range from a low of 20,587—Colby's count—to a high of 60,000.

What was heroic about this guy? Simply this: He told the truth.

Soon after Colby took his oath of office in September 1973, the CIA became the focus of some seriously bad publicity. On September 11 of that year, Chile's democratically elected president, Salvador Allende, was overthrown by a military coup in what was widely thought to be an operation funded by the CIA. A little over a year later, an article in the *New York Times* revealed the clandestine activities of the CIA's Operation Chaos, an illegal domestic program that tracked antiwar activists and other dissidents during the Nixon administration. People were outraged.

In the frenzy that followed, the CIA was called a "rogue elephant" and committees sprouted up all over Congress to look into the misconduct.

> JW: To head them off, President Ford appointed Vice President Nelson Rockefeller to head a commission to look into CIA abuses. He made it clear to Colby that this would be a

whitewash, a "once-over-lightly." But when Frank Church, who was chairman of the Senate committee that was doing the investigation, called Colby in, Colby laid it all out. He told the truth.

Once he started talking, conservatives and liberals both attacked him, for different reasons. It was even suggested that he might be working for the KGB. In 1976, President Gerald Ford fired him and appointed George H. W. Bush in his place.

JW: After that, people like [Henry] Kissinger and all the influence peddlers in Washington shunned him. Of course, Kissinger, who is still a famous and influential person, was an unashamed liar. As was Dick Helms, who was Colby's predecessor at the CIA. Both of them lied about us having a role in Chile. I don't think there's any evidence that we actually participated in the assassination of Allende, but we certainly enabled it. Kissinger lied about it. Helms lied about it. After Helms pleaded guilty to lying and got nothing, they threw a big party for him. They toasted him as a hero. Kissinger was one of the leading toasters. But they didn't have a party for Colby.

After he left the CIA, Colby practiced law and worked as a consultant. He died in 1996 in a canoeing accident.

Or was it an accident? When his body was not found for eight days, suspicion arose. The autopsy showed that he had died from drowning and hypothermia. But it also revealed that he suffered from hardening of the arteries. Might he have had a heart attack or stroke? Or were nefarious forces involved? We shall never know.

JW: Colby led a remarkable life and was a true believer in American values and the American system. He felt— and we talked about it afterwards—that Congress has

> constitutional responsibilities. We work for the govern-
> ment and swear to uphold the Constitution. If someone
> asks you a question, you tell them the truth. And that's
> what he did. Most of the things we now know about
> the abuses of the CIA are on the record because of his
> testimony.

Ironically, not long before he died, Colby did collaborate with the KGB's former chief of foreign counter-intelligence, who now lives in Washington, D.C. Their mission? A CD-ROM game entitled Spycraft.

ALBERT EINSTEIN

A friend recently asked me whether Albert Einstein (1879–1955) was a hero because he discovered the secrets of the universe or a vil-lain because he unleashed the atomic bomb on unsuspecting humanity.

When Wieghart, who maintains a lively interest in physics and astronomy, listed Einstein as one of his heroes, I asked him the same question. "Einstein was a great hero in my judgment," he said. "He created and discovered the science of the 20th century and now the 21st century."

Yet he has also been blamed for the bomb, in part because his the-oretical work laid the groundwork for it, and in part because he wrote a letter to President Franklin D. Roosevelt warning that the Germans might be on the verge of constructing an atomic bomb. In response, Roosevelt appointed a committee and in 1941 inaugurated the Man-hattan Project, which produced the bomb.

Einstein had nothing to do with that program but he regretted the letter. "Had I known that the Germans would not succeed in produc-ing an atomic bomb," he declared, "I would not have lifted a finger."

Nonetheless, the perception that he was somehow responsible for the bomb was widespread. In July 1946, less than a year after the attacks on Hiroshima and Nagasaki, *Time* magazine published Ein-stein's picture on the cover. Behind him: a mushroom cloud.

"I do not know who invented the myth that Einstein's equation $E = mc^2$ made the atomic bomb possible," writes Abraham Pais, a theoretical physicist and biographer of Einstein. "It is true that this equation plays an important role in nuclear physics, but to say that this made possible the construction of weapons is like saying that the invention of the alphabet caused the Bible to be written."

To this day, many people unfairly associate him with the bomb. The truth is, until another scientist mentioned the idea of fission to him, he had not thought of it—which doesn't mean that his work didn't point squarely in that direction.

> JW: The whole theory of nuclear fission, the chain reaction that the scientists in the Manhattan Project worked with, came out of relativity physics. In that respect they were using Einstein's work—and Einstein knew this. The funny thing is, it was such a secret project, but almost every theoretical physicist in the 1930s was aware of the potential. Ideas are immutable and you can't control them. There are no secrets in that respect.

In addition to his scientific accomplishments, Einstein was a humanitarian, a pacifist (until Hitler convinced him that sometimes you have to fight), an advocate of universal disarmament, a Zionist (who declined the presidency of Israel when it was offered to him), an opponent of McCarthyism, and a concerned citizen who declared racism "the worst disease from which the society of our nation suffers." He was called "the conscience of the world."

But above all, he was a scientist who developed his most profound ideas simply by thinking long and hard about them. And he did it without a computer.

JOHN F. KENNEDY

For many years, I have vacillated on the question of whether JFK is a hero. Recently, I've been leaning in his direction. Then I spoke with Wieghart and he convinced me.

JW: John F. Kennedy won a Distinguished Service Cross for heroism in World War II, but he suffered a great back injury that caused him pain and misery throughout his life. At the same time, he became a leader and accomplished a great deal.

I was just coming of age when Kennedy was elected president. Like many people of my generation, I had the desire to go to Washington, to accomplish great things, to strive for excellence, to improve the country. A whole generation of Americans did that in one way or another, some by going into government service, some into journalism, some into other endeavors. That is one of the marks of a hero: to inspire others to do something of public value.

No politician of our time has lit that torch like John F. Kennedy.

TED KENNEDY

Then there's Ted Kennedy. Seldom considered heroic, even by those who share his politics, Teddy Kennedy's reputation will be forever marred by Chappaquiddick.

Yet his impact has been enormous. Jack Kennedy was president for a thousand days; Teddy has been in the Senate for four decades. Wieghart makes the case:

JW: I worked for a year for Ted Kennedy. A lot of people would not classify him as a hero and maybe they shouldn't; I don't know. But the fact of the matter is that Kennedy has had a very difficult life. His three older brothers were all killed. One was a war hero, one was assassinated as president, one was assassinated as a candidate for the presidency. Bobby's assassination in particular was an extraordinary blow to him. They were very close.

> He has persevered. He's been in the Senate since 1962. He had a terrible back injury in an airplane crash with Birch Bayh in 1964, and he still suffers from it. But he soldiers on and has a tremendous record.
>
> The year I worked for him happened to be the year when the Congress passed and President Reagan vetoed the bill to apply sanctions to South Africa until it got rid of apartheid. Everyone just threw up their hands, but Kennedy said, "We're going to override that veto." He led the fight. There were some other leaders, but he was the spark plug. And by God, it's the one veto of Reagan's that Congress overrode. Sanctions were put in place and not long after that things began to happen in South Africa that led to the release of Nelson Mandela and the end of apartheid.
>
> That's the kind of leadership we need.

Of course, leadership is not the same as heroism, although the two may coexist. Kennedy is a leader because he stands up for and articulates certain essential American ideals—and also because he is a savvy politician who knows how to make things happen on the ground. I don't know if he counts as a hero. If he weren't a Kennedy, maybe he would just be an elder statesman, revered by some, disparaged by others. But he is a Kennedy and as such has lived under the threat of assassination for most of his life. And he hasn't let it stop him from fighting for civil rights, social causes, health care, and other issues that matter to us all.

MARTIN LUTHER KING, JR.

Once upon a time, George Washington was first in the hearts of his countrymen—unchallenged. No more. Today, the person who is mentioned most frequently as a hero (at least to me) is the great civil rights leader.

JW: My idea of a great hero in contemporary times is Martin Luther King. He fits a broad definition of heroism, having surmounted great difficulties, confronted the widespread and difficult problem of racial discrimination, and accomplished a great deal toward combating it, all the while knowing he was in peril because the issue was so divisive and politicized. He accomplished a lot, even though he was only thirty-eight years old when he gave his life for the cause. I would put him at the top of a list of heroes who meet the historical demands of the word.

NELSON MANDELA

Nelson Mandela won the Nobel Peace Prize in 1993 after a lifetime spent resisting South Africa's apartheid policies and then reshaping that government.

JW: Nelson Mandela is an outstanding example of a person whose life is dedicated to an important mission. Despite great obstacles, great pain and suffering, and twenty-seven years in prison, he maintained his beliefs. And when he was finally released and became a great political leader, he didn't strike back at the people who inflicted that pain and suffering on him. He turned the other cheek and worked with them to achieve reconciliation and solve the country's many problems.

ON JOURNALISM

Jim Wieghart has been a journalist for longer than Ted Kennedy has been a senator. Plenty of his heroes are people who report for a living, whether in broadcast or in print media.

They include Peter Lisagor, John Chancellor, and Walter Cronkite, all of whom were print journalists before they became television fixtures; Joseph Kraft, a political columnist; and broadcast journalist Edward R. Murrow, an icon of World War II. Those people, Wieghart says, were inspirational. I asked him about the journalists he admires today.

JW: There aren't many. There are a few like Tom Brokaw and Peter Jennings who have been around a long time, but you look behind that group and you don't see a hell of a lot.

As far as writing is concerned, it's pretty bad. But there are some young journalists coming on, many of whom work overseas. I'm a member of the Overseas Press Club. We have an awards dinner every year and it's unbelievable. These young people go into difficult areas where they're risking their lives to write the truth. Daniel Pearl is an example. Somehow they persevere and most of them survive, and those are the people who are honored by the Overseas Press Club.

Then you go to Washington to the White House Correspondents Dinner or to the Broadcast Dinner, and the president is there. The awards they give seem so paltry and puny to me because very little effort, very little talent, very little challenge goes into what these men and women are doing. Maybe it's not their fault, maybe it's the fault of the country; I don't know. It's a whole different scene there.

When I think of a hero in this business, I think of a guy like Izzy Stone. He was a legend. He ground away sixty years of his life reading congressional reports and testimony and digging out truth that was vital to know. He was not a flashy guy. He never worked for the *New York Times.* But he was an inspiration to a lot of us who cared about the business and I always read what he wrote and I always appreciated being a friend. I would count him as a hero.

I. F. STONE

If ever a human being deserved to be called an independent journalist, that person was the incorruptible, iconoclastic, fiery commen-
tator I. F. Stone (1907–1989). The son of Russian Jewish immigrants, he
plunged into journalism at age fourteen with his own newspaper,
which he wrote, published, and delivered by bicycle. In those early
efforts, his future was clear. He came out in favor of the League of
Nations, in favor of Gandhi, and against the yellow journalism of William
Randolph Hearst. Even then, he was a political radical through and
through. "What you are, you're born," he told his biographer Robert C.
Cottrell. "Your political attitudes are pretty much born with you."

But after three issues, his father called the project to a halt due to
bad grades. *The Progress* folded. Izzy, as he was called, never looked
back.

Throughout high school, he worked as a part-time reporter. He
also nurtured a fantasy of becoming a professor, but those bad grades
worked against him. "I wanted to go to Harvard," he recalled in 1969,
"but I couldn't because I graduated 49th in a class of 52 from a small-
town high school." Instead, he went to the University of Pennsylvania, which was required to accept graduates of local high schools. He
dropped out his junior year and entered journalism full-time, working
at the *Camden Courier-Post,* followed by a host of other publications.
Among them were the *New York Post,* the *Washington Star,* and the
Philadelphia Record, where, at twenty-three, he became the nation's
youngest editorial writer on a major urban daily. In 1939, he became
associate editor of *The Nation.*

In 1946, concerned about the plight of Jewish refugees who were
being denied entrance to Palestine, he accepted a freelance assignment from the radical journal *PM* and illegally sailed with the Jewish
underground organization Haganah past the British blockade into
Palestine. When his editor at *The Nation* learned about his exploits,
she promptly fired him, although she continued to publish his articles. Over the next few years, he wrote for *PM, The Nation,* and the
Daily Compass, among others.

During the Red Scare of the early 1950s, Stone denounced McCarthy and was accused of being a Communist, although he was not called to testify. "Everybody assumed I was Karl Marx's baby brother, in the oversimplified atmosphere of Washington," he told the journalist Andrew Patner. "And they were looking for big game. They were looking for guys on big papers that would really be a sensation. It wouldn't be much of a sensation to prove I was a Marxist-Leninist."

At the same time, his compatriots on the left denounced him for supporting Adlai Stevenson rather than the candidate of the Progressive Party. He felt like a pariah. And with many of the radical newspapers he wrote for shutting down, he needed a job. When he called *The Nation* in hopes of getting back his old position, he was refused.

That was when he returned to his adolescent impulse and created his own paper. He borrowed $3,000 from a friend, patched together a mailing list, and sent off a letter soliciting subscriptions and promising "uninhibited commentary and let-the-chips-fall-where-they-may reporting." Fifty-three hundred people sent in $5 for a subscription. They included Eleanor Roosevelt, Bertrand Russell, and Albert Einstein, whose check he framed.

I. F. Stone's Weekly was published continuously from January 1953 until December 1971. During that time, the number of subscribers grew to seventy thousand but the price never changed, and he never took advertising. In its pages, he spoke out in his elegant, witty way against McCarthyism, Cold War politics, racial discrimination, government lies, J. Edgar Hoover, and the war in Vietnam.

Always a man of the Left, he maintained his sense of outrage but was never doctrinaire. When he visited the Soviet Union in the 1950s and pronounced it "a hermetically sealed prison, stifling in its atmosphere of complete, rigid and low-level thought control," he lost hundreds of subscribers—which didn't stop two congressmen from denouncing him as a Communist a few years later.

I. F. Stone did more than express his opinions in a provocative style. "You can't be a prisoner of your preconceptions," he said. He didn't rely on received opinion. He did his homework in a profound, productive, and heroic way.

He didn't spend his time schmoozing. He didn't have friends in high places. He had terrible vision (and the coke-bottle glasses to prove it) and equally bad hearing, but he also had a prodigious memory. He ploughed through the documents—all the documents. He pored over committee reports, white papers, the *Congressional Record.* He read half a dozen newspapers from beginning to end. As he often explained, "The great thing about the *New York Times* and the *Washington Post* is that you never know where you'll find a front-page story."

In the 1960s, when the protest movement began to flourish, he experienced a surge of stature and popularity. He even became a regular on the *Dick Cavett Show.* Exactly as he had once predicted to his wife, Esther, he had gone from "pariah to character . . . to national institution." In the process, he made enough money to buy a new house and to set up a retirement fund.

By 1971, angina pectoris forced him to give up the *Weekly.* After that, he was lionized in print, on television, and even at the Cannes Film Festival, where a documentary about him was screened in 1974. He continued to write articles, especially for *The New York Review of Books.*

But he wanted to make a bigger contribution. At an age when most people retire, he undertook the hero's journey. He decided to study the idea of freedom of thought. He began by reading about seventeenth-century England. That sent him back to the Protestant Reformation. But it was impossible to understand the Reformation without understanding the Middle Ages. In that manner, he ended up studying the Greeks. "When I first got back to ancient Athens, I thought in my ignorance that I would be able to do a cursory study, based on standard sources, of free thought in classical antiquity," he wrote. "But I soon found that there were no standard sources."

In college half a century earlier, he had taken a single semester of ancient Greek. Building on that experience, he learned enough additional Greek to read the Gospel according to John, *The Iliad,* and everything that Plato, Xenophon, Aristophanes, and Aristotle wrote about Socrates. His obsession with Socrates—and with democracy—led to his last book, *The Trial of Socrates,* in which he analyzes why the city known as the birthplace of democracy condemned Socrates and offers ideas about how Socrates could have been acquitted, if only he'd presented his case differently.

In his effort to find "one last scoop," he did what he had always done: He read the documents with enormous care. In a self-interview in the *New York Times,* he posed the question, "How can a newspaperman find something new to report about a trial that took place so long ago?"

"You re-examine all the source material for yourself," he wrote. "You go back to the texts in the original language, so that you can evaluate every nuance. You search out internal contradictions and curious evasions. It's not so different from digging the real truth out of a Pentagon or State Department document."

The Trial of Socrates became a best seller.

I. F. Stone seems to have been a happy man. He had a good marriage, often went dancing with his wife, and above all, loved being a journalist, as he explained to filmmaker Jerry Bruck, Jr., in 1973:

> I really have so much fun, I ought to be arrested. Sometimes I think it's wrong of me, because, you know, if you're a newspaperman, as I've been since I was fourteen years old—to have your own little paper (it may be small; as Daniel Webster said about Dartmouth, "It may be a small college, but there are those that love it")—to be able to spit in their eye, and do what you think is right, and report the news, and have enough readers to make some impact, is such a pleasure, that you forget, you forget what you're writing about. It becomes like— you're like a journalistic Nero fiddling while Rome burns, or like a small boy covering a hell of a big fire. It's just wonderful and exciting and you're a cub reporter and God has given you a big fire to cover. And you forget—that it's really burning!

I. F. Stone never forgot. In December 1969, writing about the events of that year, he wrote, "There are bitter battles ahead. We had better get ready for them."

It's still true today.

ELLIOT RICHARDSON

If you were a news junkie during the Watergate scandal, you were in hog heaven. One of the most memorable incidents during that disgraceful episode was the so-called Saturday night massacre. It happened on October 20, 1973, when the investigation into the break-in of Democratic Party headquarters in the Watergate Hotel was well underway. Archibald Cox, the special prosecutor, was trying to subpoena White House tape recordings. President Richard M. Nixon did not want that to happen. He claimed that the tapes were privileged and ordered his attorney general, Elliot Richardson, to fire Cox.

Richardson refused. Instead of caving in and following orders, he resigned. (Cox was eventually fired by Nixon's solicitor-general, Robert Bork.)

Standing on principle, even at the cost of your job, is the essence of heroism.

JW: You don't see it happening very often. During Iran-Contra, [George] Schulz, [Caspar] Weinberger, and others strongly opposed trading arms to Iran for hostages. But when President Reagan decided to do it, they didn't resign in protest, even though it was illegal. They went ahead and did it. Schulz and Weinberger are highly regarded today. But the fact of the matter is that they weren't very heroic. Richardson was.

ANWAR SADAT
AND YITZHAK RABIN

It's sad to look back on glorious moments of the past when the expectations those events aroused have long since been dashed.

One such moment occurred in March 1978, when Egyptian president Anwar Sadat, who bravely broke precedent by visiting Israel and addressing the parliament there, signed a peace treaty with Israeli prime minister Menachem Begin on the lawn of the White House. Six months later, the two politicians signed the Camp David accords.

But in March 1981, Sadat was assassinated by Islamic fundamentalists.

In 1993, another hopeful event buoyed spirits around the world. Prime Minister Yitzhak Rabin and PLO chairman Yasser Arafat unveiled a plan for Palestinian self-rule and, encouraged by President Clinton, shook hands on the White House lawn.

But in November 1995, Rabin was killed by a right-wing Jewish student.

As Wieghart said, "Anwar Sadat and Yitzhak Rabin, both of whom were assassinated, took the first important step toward trying to accomplish peace in the Middle East, which still eludes us."

Some day, I like to believe, there will be peace in the Middle East. Let's hope that by then, our heroes will no longer have to be martyrs.

LAWRENCE E. WALSH

In addition to reporting on politics, Jim Wieghart has worked on the inside, most notably for Judge Lawrence Walsh, the independent counsel looking into the Iran-Contra affair of the 1980s.

During the first three years of the Reagan administration, Congress had authorized the CIA to aid Nicaragua's Contras, whom they saw as the only alternative to the Marxist Sandinistas. But in 1984, when Congress withdrew that support, President Reagan decided to seek funding elsewhere. Through his national security advisor, Robert C. McFarlane, he went to Saudi Arabia, which quietly contributed $32 million to the project. Marine Lieutenant Oliver L. North was in charge of the secret operation.

When word of it began to leak out, several officials of the Reagan administration were hauled before Congress and questioned. They lied.

After Reagan was reelected, another secret plan was developed. Although Reagan had publicly counseled against negotiating with hostages, he agreed to sell arms to Iran in exchange for the release of seven Americans who had been taken hostage by the Islamic terrorist group Hezbollah. Naturally, no one was to know. To cover up the arms deal, the administration asked Israel for help. Israel forwarded arms to Iran, then received replacements from the United States.

The administration could see no reason to tell Congress about this.

In 1986, the two operations merged. When Reagan authorized the CIA to sell weapons to Iran, Oliver North and his compatriots saw an opportunity: Why not increase the price of the weapons and use the profits to support the Contras?

It sounds even more ominous now than it did then, doesn't it? And, of course, it didn't work. North jacked the price up 370 percent; the Iranians wouldn't pay.

Then in November 1986, the unexpected occurred. McFarlane and North went to Tehran bearing gifts—a chocolate cake and a Bible—and a Lebanese newspaper published an article about it. The scandal broke. A little over a month later, Lawrence E. Walsh was appointed independent counsel.

JW: He was in his seventies when he was appointed to that task. Everyone thought he would issue a few indictments against North and the obvious culprits and call it a day. I'm sure that's what the panel that appointed him expected. He's a lifelong Republican. But he's also a man of integrity and he went after the scandal vigorously and without any yielding to partisanship, much to the dismay of a lot of Republicans. Bob Dole, Reagan, Bush, they all castigated him. He persisted quietly and with great determination.

His whole life had been devoted to the public service. He came from a poor background. He was born in Canada and was a crime buster with Dewey when Tom Dewey was district attorney in Manhattan. Then, when Dewey became governor of New York, he went to work for him and when Dewey ran for president twice, he was in the campaign. After that, he became immensely successful in private practice, and when Eisenhower was elected president, he was one of his first judicial appointees. A couple of years later, Eisenhower asked him to resign his lifetime appointment to the bench and come to the Justice Department to handle the Little Rock school integration crisis, which he did.

And when he finished he went back into private practice and became president of the American Bar Association. He was called into public service again under Nixon and then again to be head of the Iran-Contra investigation. And he did that, too.

The investigation lasted six years and cost more than $50 million. In the conclusion to his report, Walsh wrote, "The underlying facts of Iran/Contra are that, regardless of criminality, President Reagan, the secretary of state, the secretary of defense, and the director of central intelligence and their necessary assistants committed themselves, however reluctantly, to two programs contrary to congressional policy and contrary to national policy. They skirted the law, some of them broke the law, and almost all of them tried to cover up the President's willful activities."

But by the 1990s, Reagan was showing clear signs of Alzheimer's Disease and it seemed pointless to pursue an indictment. Ultimately, fourteen participants were indicted and eleven convicted. Of those, two were overturned on technicalities and six were pardoned by President George H. W. Bush. The remainder received minor sentences of probation, community service, and token amounts of money.

Nonetheless, Walsh's report lays out the entire scheme in numbing, Constitution-flouting detail. Was he a hero? Wieghart says he was.

JW: He's a wonderful guy. I have worked for many people and covered many people, but I would rank him at the very top in terms of integrity, honesty, perseverance, intelligence, commitment to clean governance. That's what heroes are made of.

ON HEROISM

What does it finally mean to be a hero? Politics provides a stage for heroism. Yet in Wieghart's vision, and in mine as well, heroism transcends politics.

RD: Do you think that heroism is connected to ideology?

JW: I do not. I don't think heroism is a conservative or liberal idea. I think it's a commitment of some kind. There are conservatives who have been heroic like John McCain and there are liberals who have been heroic like John F. Kennedy and Martin Luther King and Walter Reuther. I think it's a fundamental belief in our system of government and the way it should work.

Over the last thirty years, we've become extraordinarily materialistic. I think the covenant that established our government wasn't an economic system. It was a way of linking the people together and forming a government to serve them. The Constitution begins with the phrase, "We the People of the United States." Well, the people have either abdicated power or it's been subsumed from them by powerful forces, or a combination of the two. But in any event, clearly, the people are not running the government and clearly the government is not serving the people.

That's why part of the definition of heroism has to include leadership and achievement and accomplishment. People will have to select leaders who are going to do the right thing and who are not going to tell them what they want to hear.

Here we are in a war against terror and we're invading countries and we're spending enormous amounts of money doing so. We're cutting taxes and running up extraordinary deficits for our children and grandchildren to pay and nobody's sacrificing except the poor miserable guys getting shot at in Iraq and Afghanistan. The people have not been asked to sacrifice. If George Bush, after 9/11, had not only summoned us to a war on terrorism but called on young Americans to perform some public service and wealthy Americans to kick in some money, he could have emerged as a great hero. But he didn't rise to that challenge.

RD: I've been reading Winston Churchill's World War II speeches. He held out a vision of the greater good, and he had the ability to make people want to sacrifice.

JW: So did Franklin D. Roosevelt. He's always been my favorite president even though I came from a first generation American family and we were very poor and he was very rich and came from an old family. We all felt that he had us in mind. That's not a feeling that you find anymore. When you ask people about their government, it doesn't evoke positive reactions.

I remember when *Grapes of Wrath* was made into a movie. It was about a dispossessed family from Oklahoma who traveled across the country, from county to county, looking for a place to settle and getting thrown out by people who said, we've got enough poor people here. Finally they come to California where they stay in one of these encampments. And this guy in a white suit arrives, and they're thinking, here comes another authority figure who's going to tell us to move on. Instead he says, I represent the United States government and I'm here to help you. I saw that movie in a theatre, and when he uttered those words, people applauded. I can't imagine that happening today.

There's a sea change in that. I don't know whether it's permanent, but I suspect it's not because I don't think values change.

RD: Heroism is a basic American value. How can we encourage it?

JW: The first thing would be for people to quit thinking, What's in it for me? We've got to start thinking, What's in it for us? especially when we confront environmental issues, health issues, education issues, and so on.

I think 9/11 brought out a desire, a longing for heroes—not phony heroes like John Wayne who dodged the draft in World War II, but real heroes, like the firemen who rushed into the building knowing full well the chance of survival was slim. And maybe we ought to start looking at heroes among ordinary people. Believe me, there are a lot of them. We don't celebrate them, but maybe we ought to. That might be a place to start.

RD: Let me ask you one more question. What qualities do you see as forming the essence of heroism?

JW: I think the essence of heroism is the love of humanity and the effort to make us better; to live in harmony and peace and prosperity and justice; and to make the world a better place.

To make the world a better place—that's what heroism is all about. There are large ways to do that and small ways, activities that require a major commitment, and things we can do right now.

One thing is sure: We urgently need heroes to emerge from every walk of life, every corner, every town. And there ought to be lessons we can learn from people who have gone before us about how to conduct our lives and how to make the world a better place.

The people I've written about in this book have lived their lives fueled by optimism and courage, not cynicism. They have a vision they're willing to sacrifice for, and they have persevered in order to achieve it. It is my hope that their stories might inspire the rest of us to act similarly.

CHAPTER 18

ON HOW TO BE A HERO

My brother, Jack, one of my heroes, is a lawyer who went down South in 1963 at the request of Bobby Kennedy to use the legal process to help end discrimination. Just recently, he told me how dangerous that adventure really was. The movie *Mississippi Burning* was just the tip of the iceberg, he said. He told me that when he returned to Ohio, he would get threatening telephone calls at two o'clock in the morning. He was called a Communist. One night, someone tossed red paint on his driveway. Those were frightening times.

But then, heroes always emerge in frightening times. Not because it's easy, but because it's essential. It's as important now as it was during the civil rights era.

How do we shrug off our complacency and encourage heroic actions in ourselves and in the people we know? Obviously, very few can match the exalted achievements of most of the heroes in this book, but we can all find individual opportunities to act heroically. Here are some practical suggestions that anyone can take up:

- Believe that you can actually make a change. There are so many things we try to do during the course of our lives, and so few of them create significant change. It's easy to get discouraged. Unless you believe that it's possible to create change, it won't happen.

- Motivate yourself by reading about heroes. Put John Grisham or Danielle Steele or James Patterson down, difficult as that can be, and start reading about the real heroes in society, some of whom are discussed in this book. Check out the biography section of a bookstore or library. Virtually every book there is about a person who conquered major obstacles to do something important. Whether you're reading about Charles Darwin or Katharine Graham, Lance Armstrong or Louis Armstrong, you will find that it's possible to extract from their lives a few lessons that can be applied to yours.

- Don't allow yourself to believe, even for a moment, that you're too young or too old or too powerless to do something significant.

- Set your personal agenda aside. Heroism isn't about you. It's about others.

- Identify an area of concern. It's easy to sit around complaining about war, famine, terrorism, fraudulent business practices, failing schools, poverty, AIDS, the obesity epidemic, a health care system in need of an overhaul, a disintegrating infrastructure, global warming, PCBs in the salmon, or communication difficulties with Islamic countries (the issue that most concerns me). The world is full of problems. Where to start? Identify areas that are of particular concern and interest to you. Then pick one.

- Express yourself through the conventional channels. Write a letter to the editor of your local newspaper or to a public official. Even if you do nothing more than articulate your concern over, say, Head Start or racial profiling or problems in our intelligence program, your message will draw attention to that issue.

  If you decide to write (or fax) a letter, remember this rule: The shorter the better. These days, everybody seems to have an attention deficit disorder. So do yourself a favor and keep it short. A letter that has a topic sentence, two or three supporting examples, and a conclusion will generally make its point better than a rambling screed or even a tightly constructed, but lengthy, explication.

As for the Internet, it is increasingly powerful as a means of expressing opinion. For a long time, I was of the opinion that Internet petitions were about as useful as chain letters. Then Democratic presidential candidate Howard Dean raised a million dollars—and thousands of volunteers—through the Internet, and I changed my mind. The Internet can be a useful grassroots tool. Don't dismiss it.

But don't delude yourself, either. Spending many happy hours signing online petitions or chatting with like-minded others or forwarding alerts of one kind or another to your entire address book may satisfy you emotionally, but it won't accomplish a thing.

- Be willing to sacrifice, at least a little, on behalf of the cause you have identified. I'm not talking about attending elegant fundraisers or even writing checks. Writing a check is the decent thing to do, and you should do it. But it doesn't make you a hero either, especially if you are well off. Being heroic means sacrificing, if nothing else, your time. It does not mean sacrificing dinner at Alain Ducasse.

- Being heroic means doing something hands-on. One way is to volunteer with an organization you support, whether it's a political party or the PTA. You don't have to join the Peace Corps, although you could. As of this writing, the Peace Corps has 6,678 volunteers in 70 countries, and some of those people are well along in years. For a few hours a week, you can mentor a child, tutor an adult in a literacy program, help address hundreds of other problems in an ongoing way. Is this heroic? Maybe not. But it means more than writing a check (which you should also do). You will energize your self and motivate your colleagues and maybe even help to eliminate the problem. Plus, by working with an actual human being, you will gain a sense of what's going on in the community that you simply cannot get from a fancy-dress ball, no matter how worthy the cause.

If you'd like to work with a particular organization, contact them directly. If you're looking for an opportunity without having anything in particular in mind, go to the Internet. Check out the USA Freedom Corps, Idealist.org, the American Red Cross, or VolunteerMatch.com. Then contact that organization directly—résumé in hand.

ORGANIZE

Or maybe volunteering isn't in the cards for you. OK. Maybe you're an organizer, not a follower. Maybe you're the kind of person who likes to call the shots. In that case, the burden is greater, but so is the opportunity to do something significant. Here's what you should do:

- Go to published sources to find out what's been done about the problem in other places. See if there's something you can learn from them.

- Next, create your own task force. Begin by contacting your network. If you can find ten people who are willing to commit themselves, even for a few hours a month, you've got it made. Banding together with others increases your power exponentially, especially if you can get a few influential people to join you. If you can't, you can't. Half a dozen neighbors sitting around the dining room table can also be an effective force.

- Gather your group and brainstorm. Create an idea bank and an action plan. Your action plan should include specific objectives, a timetable, and at least a dozen steps, most of which should be relatively easy to do.

- Utilize the strategy of ten. This technique is a great way to get the cooperation of busy people. What I do is this: I ask each of ten people to agree to perform one simple task a month. That's it. If ten people are doing something once a month, that's 120 actions a year. And that makes an impact.

  Who assigns those tasks? You do. What might those tasks be? Writing a letter, hosting a cocktail party, doing online research, calling an official, writing a press release, contacting the media, making a few calls, interviewing an expert—you get the idea. One task a month. Believe it or not, that's enough to get things rolling.

- Find public support. Without it, you're sunk. But to get it, you need to use every bit of guile and cunning you can muster. Create regular press releases, with regular events to go with them. Go to the newspapers, radio, television stations. Be prepared to talk about the problem you have identified, and have the facts and figures at your command.

  If there's a pollster who does public opinion polling in your community, see if he or she will include a question about the problem so that you can understand how people in the community feel about it.

  And don't forget that getting public support for even the most righteous causes requires good PR. My brother told me a story about that. It concerns Medgar Evers, the civil rights activist who was assassinated in 1963. (His killer was not convicted until 1994.) It seems that Medgar Evers was planning to hold a march in Knoxville, Tennessee. Everybody showed up for the march. But Evers called it off. "We can't do it today," he said.

My brother said, "We've got to do it today."

Medgar Evers was adamant. "We can't do it today,"
he said, "because the Pope is saying mass today in
Yankee Stadium and he's going to get the front page."
They postponed the march until the next day and got
the publicity they wanted. Timing is everything.

- Use pressure. That's the only way to create change.
Pressure the media, pressure the courts, pressure your
elected representatives, pressure whomever you need to
in order to get something done. Be the squeaky wheel.

    If you feel awkward applying pressure, think of
Gandhi. He was a master of pressure. By making a spectacle of the fact that he was fasting, he pressured people
into saying, we've got to stop this guy from killing himself. Not that I recommend going on a hunger strike.
On the contrary, I think it's a bad, counterproductive
idea. Remember Bobby Sands, the Irish Republican Army
activist who died on the 66th day of a hunger strike in
1981? I'm in favor of heroism, not martyrdom.

- Participate in the legislative process. You don't have
to run for city council to do this. All you need to do is
prepare a pithy statement laying out the problem you
have identified along with a possible approach to that
problem or even just a call for solutions. Then contact
your congressional representative or senator and ask to
have your statement inserted in the *Congressional
Record*. This is easy to do, especially if you are a
constituent.

    If he or she is reluctant, perhaps because the issue
you have pinpointed has powerful lobbyists aligned
against it, contact the media. A letter to the editor will
do. Picture the headlines: "Jones Unwilling to Address
Drug Problem" or "Jones Unwilling to Discuss Security

Concerns." Take my word for it, Jones will read your statement into the *Congressional Record* posthaste.

After that, you might want to think about drafting some legislation. It's not as hard as it sounds. Find a lawyer who is familiar with the process, write up a simple piece of legislation, and send it to your representative. Then you can say, what do you think? He or she owes you an answer as your elected representative. The answer may not be precisely what you want. Your proposed legislation may be dismissed for one reason or another. But your effort will be a positive thing in its own right. And it will focus attention on the problem.

And remember when dealing with politicians: Work with the staff. They know what's going on. They can ease the process for you, or they can erect obstacles. It depends on you.

BIG FIXES

As a society, we can take a few additional steps to create a public environment that's hospitable to heroes. To wit:

- The media must act more responsibly in reporting on people's lives. Right now, a number of people who would normally extend themselves publicly don't do it because they're concerned about the impact on themselves and their family.

- Let's compensate our public officials more generously. They have multiple opportunities for heroism because their actions reach so many. But we pay them a fraction of what people in the business world earn. To get serious people on the public payroll, let's make sure that they are properly rewarded.

- Let's see if we can rein in the legal profession somewhat.
  Compared to nations like Japan and even Great Britain,
  the legal process in the United States is overactive, with
  too many people filing frivolous suits that are simply
  aimed at grabbing the headlines. Let's see if we can do
  something about that.

- Finally, let's find a way to celebrate heroes in the White
  House, in the state house, in the media, in the business
  world, and anywhere they are found. By doing so, by
  recognizing heroes for what they've done, we can
  embolden others to take similar steps.

MISSED OPPORTUNITIES

The chance to perform big actions comes along seldom or never.
But opportunities to perform small heroic actions appear on a daily
basis. Keep your eyes open and you cannot fail to see them.

Stepping up to them is another story. Writing this book, I've
tracked the daily opportunities that come along. I have learned that
it's easy to be so preoccupied that you simply miss them.

Earlier today, for example, I was on 45th Street in midtown Manhattan and I saw a blind man waiting to cross the street. Now, I see this
guy from time to time. On several occasions, I have said to him, "Hey,
pal, let's cross the street together." I let him take my arm and we cross
the street. When we get to the other side, he says, "I'm fine now," and I
let him go. Today, I was in a rush. I didn't help him. I hope somebody
else did because the truck drivers barrel across 45th Street like maniacs
and anything could happen. But I was in a rush. I didn't want to lose
those few extra minutes. I felt instantly guilty about my inaction.

As Ralph Waldo Emerson pointed out, "A hero is no braver than an
ordinary man, but he is brave five minutes longer." On this particular
morning, I couldn't find two minutes.

That lapse has been weighing on my mind all afternoon. Should
I have gone back and helped the guy across the street? Of course I

should have. But I didn't. Literally or symbolically, we all sometimes fail to help the blind person cross the street, and by the time we think to remedy the situation, it's too late.

That's why it's important to create a structure for being heroic. Tutoring a child, initiating a letter-writing campaign, volunteering as a patient advocate at a local hospital—or, for that matter, spending a year with Doctors Without Borders—all stem from the same human impulse that leads one to help a blind man across the street.

Taking actions like those makes the world a better place. The least we can do is to set aside a few hours a month in which to make the effort. And while it's true that heroism is not something that can be slotted into a Tuesday-Thursday niche like so many hours of community service, it never hurts to have a schedule.

EPILOGUE

Heroes, I have said, are filled with hope. Personally, I struggle with despair. I can't help worrying that the world is teetering on the brink of disaster—and that we are facing challenges so vast and tangled that they can only be solved by genuine heroes.

Let me give you a few examples of the principal challenges I see ahead:

- A huge bridge needs to be built between the world of Islam and the worlds of Christianity and Judaism. We haven't even begun to put the first pylons in place to make that bridge a reality.

- We must deal with massive social problems. Despite all the advances that we have seen in the United States since the 1960s, despite tangible improvement in the lives of African Americans, women, gays, disabled people, and so forth, we have just scratched the surface. Racism is still with us. Sexism is still with us. Ageism is a reality. Immigration issues need to be approached forthrightly. And we must fight to maintain our constitutionally guaranteed rights and freedoms.

- The gap between the rich and the poor of this nation is yawning wider than ever. Unless that is somehow changed, we can expect serious repercussions.

- Our economy is in trouble. In the United States, we are losing manufacturing jobs at a tremendous rate. They are going to China and India and other places. Pretty soon, we may become what Adolf Hitler once described Great Britain as—"a nation of shopkeepers." In effect, we're playing in a financial casino, betting on the market every day. Something needs to be done.

- The pharmaceutical/biotechnology industry is creating drugs and making discoveries that will challenge the basic conventions of society. We need to figure out how to approach these issues now, before they get out of hand.

- The crisis in health care has yet to be resolved. It will only get bigger when the Baby Boomers retire. Meanwhile, a huge segment of the population lacks basic health insurance. On top of that, new diseases are popping up and old remedies are becoming less effective.

- Our schools are in trouble.

- Our environment is in trouble.

- Terrorism is threatening us all. (I suggest you read *Terror and Liberalism* by Paul Berman for a bracing—and disturbing—look at this problem.)

The list could go on and on.

Many people, overwhelmed by the magnitude of these problems, slip into denial or hopelessness. Heroes reject that response. They maintain a sense of possibility. Rather than turning away from these formidable challenges, they take them on. They honestly believe they can make a difference if they take action. And they do take action. That is the hero's way.

Who Are the Heroes?

They are not saints, that's for sure. Even the most exalted heroes are human beings, with everything that implies. And it is possible, I suppose, to fixate on their flaws and so find few heroes to admire.

But that would be a mistake. For recognizing a hero—warts and all—makes it possible to become a hero and to encourage others to do the same.

That's why I have filled this book with the stories of authentic heroes who have inspired real people—people I actually know—to make the world a better place. That is the goal of heroism.

When I began this book, I expected people to designate legendary heroes from every historical epoch and every field. Surely, I thought, someone will cite Christopher Columbus or Florence Nightingale; someone will name Joan of Arc; someone will mention Louis Pasteur or Alfred Nobel or even Napoleon.

It didn't happen. A few people did refer to nineteenth-century heroes, and I have written about these fascinating, largely forgotten, figures.

But I am struck by the realization that, for the most part, the heroes of the distant past fail to move us. We are excited instead by the heroes of our own epoch and, even more so, by the heroes we have met.

I am fortunate. I have personally known many heroes, including—but not limited to—the people I've interviewed for this book. Many of them are notable movers and shakers—people you might read about in the *Wall Street Journal* or the *Chronicle of Higher Education.*

Others are unknown to the general public, their heroic deeds unrecognized but far from insignificant. They include school aides, foster parents, security personnel—all kinds of people who struggle, often against daunting odds, to make life better for others.

As Victor Hugo said, "Life, misfortunes, isolation, abandonment, poverty, are battlefields which have their heroes; obscure heroes, sometimes greater than the illustrious heroes."

I believe that it behooves us all to shun passivity and to take heroic action, be it large or small. That is the way we can change the world—the only way.

Who can become a hero? Anyone! Heroes are people who have the courage and the commitment to make the world a better place.

The future depends on such people. We need to celebrate them. We need to encourage them. We need to emulate them.

Most of all, we need to become them.

SELECTED
BIBLIOGRAPHY

Ashe, Arthur and Arthur Rampersad. *Days of Grace: A Memoir.* NY: Alfred A. Knopf, 1993.

Ashe, Arthur with Neil Amdur. *Off the Court.* NY: New American Library, 1981.

Babyonyshev, Alexander. *On Sakharov.* Translated by Guy Daniels. NY: Alfred A. Knopf, 1982.

Bentley, Eric Russell. *A Century of Hero-Worship.* Philadelphia and NY: J. B. Lippincott Company, 1944.

Berg, A. Scott. *Lindbergh.* NY: G. P. Putnam's Sons, 1998.

Best, Geoffrey. *Churchill: A Study in Greatness.* London and New York: Hambledon and London, 2001.

Bingham, June. *Courage to Change: An Introduction to the Life and Thought of Reinhold Niebuhr.* NY: Charles Scribner's Sons, 1961.

Boorstin, Daniel J. *The Image: A Guide to Pseudo-Events in America.* NY: Atheneum, 1987.

Brademas, John. *Washington D.C. to Washington Square.* NY: Weidenfeld & Nicolson, 1986.

Bridges, Ruby. *Through My Eyes.* NY: Scholastic Press, 1999.

Burton, Jean. *Lydia Pinkham is Her Name.* NY: Farrar, Straus and Company, 1949.

Colby, William and Peter Forbath. *Honorable Men: My Life in the CIA.* NY: Simon & Schuster, 1978.

Coles, Robert. Lives of Moral Leadership. NY: Random House, 2000.

—. *Walker Percy: An American Search.* NY: Little, Brown and Company, 1978.

Cottrell, Robert C. *Izzy: A Biography of I. F. Stone.* New Brunswick, NJ: Rutgers University Press, 1992.

Davis, Kenneth S. *A Prophet in His Own Country: The Triumphs and Defeats of Adlai E. Stevenson.* Garden City, NY: Doubleday & Co., 1957.

—. *The Politics of Honor: A Biography of Adlai Stevenson.* NY: G. P. Putnam's Sons, 1967.

Dickenson, Mollie. *Thumbs Up: The Life and Courageous Comeback of White House Press Secretary Jim Brady.* NY: William Morrow & Co., Inc., 1987.

Dubner, Stephen J. *Confessions of a Hero-Worshipper.* NY: HarperCollins Publishers, 2003.

Earhart, Amelia. *20 Hrs. 40 Min.* NY: Arno Press, 1980 (reprint of 1928 edition).

—. *For the Fun of It.* NY: Brewer, Warren, & Putnam, 1932.

Eastman, Max. *Heroes I Have Known: Twelve Who Lived Great Lives.* NY: Simon & Schuster, 1942.

Emerson, Ralph Waldo. *Essays and Lectures.* NY: Literary Classics of the United States, Inc., 1983.

Epstein, Joseph. *With My Trousers Rolled.* NY: W. W. Norton & Co., Inc., 1995.

Forbes, Steve. *A New Birth of Freedom.* Washington, DC: Regnery Publishing, Inc., 1999.

Gibbon, Peter H. *A Call to Heroism: Renewing America's Vision of Greatness.* Foreword by Peter J. Gomes. NY: Atlantic Monthly Press, 2002.

Gilbert, Martin. *Churchill: A Life.* NY: Henry Holt and Company, Inc., 1991.

Gilmour, David. *The Transformation of Spain: From Franco to Constitutional Monarchy.* London: Quartet Books, 1985.

Glaser, Elizabeth and Laura Palmer. *In the Absence of Angels: A Hollywood Family's Courageous Story.* NY: G.P. Putnam's Sons, 1991.

Glenn, John with Nick Taylor. *John Glenn: A Memoir.* NY: Bantam Books, 1999.

Gracián, Baltasar. *A Pocket Mirror for Heroes.* Translated by Christopher Maurer. NY: Doubleday & Co., Inc., 1996.

Gutman, Israel, Editor in Chief. *Encyclopedia of the Holocaust,* Volume III. NY: MacMillan Publishing Company, 1990.

Haley, Alex. *Roots: The Saga of an American Family.* Garden City, New York: Doubleday & Co., Inc., 1976.

Hatch, Orrin. *Square Peg: Confessions of a Citizen Senator.* NY: Basic Books, 2002.

Hauser, Thomas. *Muhammad Ali: His Life and Times.* NY: Simon & Schuster, 1991.

Hesburgh,Theodore M., C.S.C. with Jerry Reedy. *God, Country, Notre Dame.* New York: Doubleday & Co., Inc., 1990.

—- *The Human Imperative:A Challenge for the Year 2000,* preface by Kingman Brewster, Jr. New Haven and London: Yale University Press, 1974.

Hook, Sidney. *Philosophy and Public Policy.* Carbondale: Southern Illinois University Press, 1980.

Kegley, Charles W., and Robert W. Bretall, eds. *Reinhold Niebuhr: His Religious, Social, and Political Thought.* The Library of Living Theology, Volume II. NY: The MacMillan Company, 1956.

Kennedy, Caroline, ed. *Profiles in Courage for Our Time.* NY: Hyperion, 2002.

Kennedy, John F. *Profiles in Courage.* Foreword by Robert F. Kennedy. New York: HarperCollins Publishers, 2000.

Lovell, Mary S. *The Sound of Wings: The Life of Amelia Earhart.* NY: St. Martin's Press, 1989.

Manchester, William. *The Last Lion: Winston Spencer Churchill: Alone: 1932-1940.* Boston: Little, Brown and Company, 1988.

—. *The Last Lion:Winston Spencer Churchill: Visions of Glory, 1874-1932.* Boston: Little, Brown and Company, 1983.

McCullough, David. *Truman.* NY: Simon & Schuster, 1992.

McKeever, Porter. *Adlai Stevenson: His Life and Legacy: a Biography.* NY: William Morrow & Co., Inc., 1989.

Miller, Lee G. *An Ernie Pyle Album: Indiana to Ie Shima.* NY: William Sloane Associates, Inc., 1946.

Miller, Merle. *Plain Speaking: An Oral Biography of Harry S. Truman.* NY: Berkley Publishing Corp., distributed by G. P. Putnam's Sons, 1973-74.

Morgan, Ted. *A Covert Life: Jay Lovestone: Communist, Anti-Communist, and Spymaster.* NY: Random House, 1999.

Nichols, David, ed. *Ernie's War: The Best of Ernie Pyle's World War II Dispatches.* With a biographical essay by David Nichols. NY: Random House, 1986.

Niebuhr, Reinhold. *The Children of Light and the Children of Darkness: A Vindication of Democracy and a Critique of Its Traditional Defense.* NY: Charles Scribner's Sons, 1972.

—. *Leaves from the Notebook of a Tamed Cynic.* San Francisco: Harper & Row, Publishers, 1980.

Niebuhr, Ursula M., ed. *Remembering Reinhold Niebuhr Letters of Reinhold and Ursula M. Niebuhr.* NY: HarperCollinsPublishers, 1991.

Paine, Albert Bigelow. *In One Man's Life: Being Chapters from the Personal and Business Career of Theodore N. Vail.* NY: Harper & Brothers, 1921.

Pais, Abraham. *Einstein Lived Here.* NY: Oxford University Press, Inc., 1994.

Patner, Andrew. *I. F. Stone: A Portrait.* NY: Doubleday, 1988.

Pearson, John. *The Private Lives of Winston Churchill.* NY: Simon & Schuster, 1991.

Percy, William Alexander. *Lanterns on the Levee: Recollections of a Planter's Son.* With an introduction by Walker Percy. Baton Rouge: Louisiana State University Press, 1941 and 1973

Poole, Edward P., ed. *As We Knew Adlai: The Stevenson Story by Twenty-Two Friends.* New York: Harper & Row, Publishers, 1966.

Pyle, Ernie. *Here Is Your War.* NY: Henry Holt and Company, 1943.

Ramsden, John. *Man of the Century: Winston Churchill and His Legend Since 1945.* London: HarperCollinsPublishers, 2002.

Remnick, David. *King of the World: Muhammad Ali and the Rise of an American Hero.* NY: Random House, 1998.

Rosenfeld, Harvey. *Raoul Wallenberg: Angel of Rescue.* Buffalo, NY: Prometheus Books, 1982.

Ross, Lillian. *Adlai Stevenson.* Philadelphia and New York: J. B. Lippincott, 1966.

Ross, Walter S. *The Last Hero: Charles A. Lindbergh.* NY: Harper & Row, Publishers, 1964, 1965, 1968.

Sakharov, Andrei. *Memoirs.* NY: Alfred A. Knopf, 1990.

Samways, Patrick, S. J. *Walker Percy: A Life.* NY: Farrar, Straus and Giroux, 1997.

Sifton, Elisabeth. *The Serenity Prayer.* NY: W. W. Norton & Co., 2003.

Stage, Sarah. *Female Complaints: Lydia Pinkham and the Business of Women's Medicine.* NY: W. W. Norton & Co., 1979.

Soyinka, Wole. *The Open Sore of a Continent: A Personal Narrative of the Nigerian Crisis.* NY, Oxford: Oxford University Press, 1996.

Stone, I. F. *The Trial of Socrates.* Boston: Little, Brown and Company, 1988.

Tobin, James. *Ernie Pyle's War: America's Eye Witness to World War II.* NY: The Free Press, 1997.

Tolson, Jay. *Pilgrim in the Ruins: A Life of Walker Percy.* NY: Simon & Schuster, 1992.

Truman, Margaret. *Harry S. Truman.* NY: William Morrow & Co., Inc., 1973.

Walsh, Lawrence E. *Firewall: The Iran-Contra Conspiracy and Cover-Up.* NY: W. W. Norton & Co., 1997.

Ware, Susan. *Amelia Earhart and the Search for Modern Feminism.* NY: W. W. Norton & Co., Inc., 1993.

Wecter, Dixon. *The Hero in America: A Chronicle of Hero-Worship.* With an introduction by Robert Penn Warren. NY: Charles Scribner's Sons, 1972.

White, Theodore H. *In Search of History: A Personal Adventure.* NY: Harper & Row, Publishers, 1978.

Whitman, Alden. *Portrait: Adlai E. Stevenson: Politician, Diplomat, Friend.* NY: Harper & Row, Publishers, 1965.

PARTICIPANTS

LAMAR ALEXANDER is the junior senator from Tennessee.

JOHN BRADEMAS is president emeritus of New York University. He represented Indiana in the House of Representatives for twenty-two years.

DOMINIC CAVELLO is the principal of St. Charles Preparatory School in Columbus, Ohio.

STEVE FORBES is president and CEO of Forbes, Inc. and editor-in-chief of *Forbes* magazine.

JOHN HAMRE is president and CEO of the Center for Strategic and International Studies (CSIS). He was the twenty-sixth U.S. Deputy Secretary of Defense.

ORRIN HATCH is the senior senator from Utah.

PHIL HOLLAND is the creator of myownbusiness.org.

JOEL KURTZMAN, an economist, is lead partner for Thought Leadership at PricewaterhouseCoopers.

THE REVEREND EDWARD MALLOY is the president of Notre Dame University.

MEL MANISHEN is the former president of Rockwell Modular Automation, Inc. and Empire Sheet Metal Manufacturing Company of Winnipeg, Canada.

BRIGADIER GENERAL ROBERT F. MCDERMOTT, the first permanent dean of the Air Force Academy, is the former chairman of the United Services Automobile Association (USAA).

MARILYN CARLSON NELSON is CEO of Carlson Companies, which operates travel agencies, hotels, restaurants, cruise lines, and marketing services.

MONSIGNOR JOHN O'KEEFE was the president of Archbishop Stepinac High School for eleven years and is now associated with St. Margaret's Church in Rockland County, New York.

GLENN SCHAEFFER is the president and chief financial officer of Mandalay Resort Group, which operates sixteen casinos nationwide.

RABBI ARTHUR SCHNEIER is the spiritual leader of New York City's Park East Synagogue and the founder of the Appeal of Conscience Foundation.

JIM WIEGHART is chairman of the Department of Journalism at Central Michigan University and a consultant with The Dilenschneider Group.